Kenya, Tanzania, Uganda

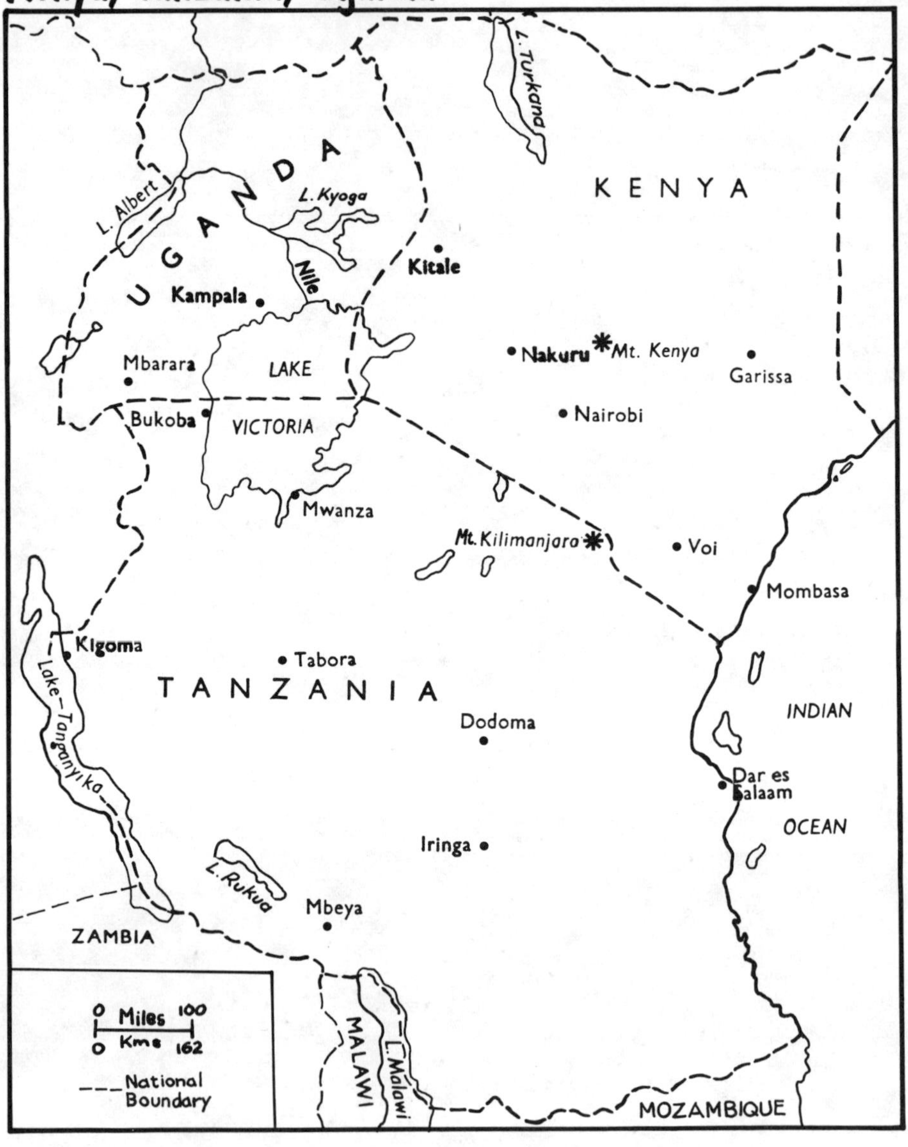

The Economies of East Africa

a bibliography: 1974-1980

A
Reference
Publication
in
African
Studies

James C. Armstrong
Editor

The Economies of East Africa

a bibliography: 1974-1980

TONY KILLICK
LAWRENCE RUPLEY
BRENDAN FINUCANE

G.K.HALL & CO.
70 LINCOLN STREET, BOSTON, MASS.

Library of Congress Cataloging in Publication Data

Killick, Tony.
The economies of East Africa, a bibliography.

Includes indexes.
1. Africa, East—Economic conditions—Bibliography.
I. Rupley, Lawrence. II. Finucane, Brendan. III. Title.
Z7165.A42K543 1984 [HC860] 016.3309676'04 83-22598
ISBN 0-8161-8583-2

This publication is printed on permanent/durable acid-free paper
MANUFACTURED IN THE UNITED STATES OF AMERICA

Contents

The Authors

Now director of the Overseas Development Institute, London, Tony Killick was Ford Foundation Visiting Professor at the University of Nairobi (1973-79), research officer, Harvard University (1972-73), economic advisor to the Government of Ghana (1969-72), senior economic advisor to the UK Ministry of Overseas Development (1967-69), tutor at Ruskin College, Oxford (1965-67), and lecturer at University of Ghana (1961-65). He has also undertaken a wide range of consultancy assignments. Most recently he has been directing a research project on the IMF and stabilization in developing countries, to be published by Heinemann Educational Books in 1983. His other works include *Development Economics in Action: A Study of Economic Policies in Ghana* (1978), *Policy Economics: A Textbook of Applied Economics on Developing Countries* (1981), and *Papers on the Kenyan Economy* (1981), and numerous journal articles.

Dr. Lawrence Rupley is tour manager for MTS Travel in Ephrata, Pennsylvania, at present. He was senior lecturer of economics at the University of Nairobi, Kenya, and also taught for a number of years in Nigeria. His articles have appeared in the *Journal of Modern African Studies* and *Bulletin For International Fiscal Documentation*, and he has made numerous contributions to *West Africa*.

Brendan P. Finucane is assistant professor of economics at Shippensburg University, Shippensburg, Pennsylvania. He has taught at the University of Nairobi and at the University of Pittsburgh, where he wrote his doctoral dissertation on Polish international trade. His principal areas of interest are developmental and international economics.

Preface

We hope that many users of this bibliography will already be familiar with Tony Killick's The Economies of East Africa (G.K. Hall, 1976), which this volume serves to update. The time frame for that earlier volume was the 1963-1974 period; for the most part, this volume takes up where the earlier one ended, although items missed in the earlier volume are included herein. It includes items published in 1980 and even a few from 1981. Like the earlier volume, this present compilation has been restricted to English-language publications relevant to the discussion of economic topics and issues in Kenya, Tanzania, and Uganda. The intended target audience for this volume is diverse, encompassing social scientists who are pursuing research on varied aspects of the East African economies. Thus, it is not intended to be useful only to economists. Given the increasingly interdisciplinary approaches to research employed by social scientists, we have purposely thrown a wide net in our coverage. The broadness of our definition of "economics" may be observed by an examination of the classification scheme and summary of entries.

We are grateful to the following University of Nairobi students for research assistance: Arthur Mukwaya, Francis M. Mwega, P.N. Njoroge, P.N. Kiguta, S.N. Maina, D.W. Makanda, F.K. Musa, D.M. Mwenze, S.M. Nzuki, C.O. Odumbe, J.O. Oketch, D.O. Okon'go, C.O. Ombok, J.A. Onyango, J.O. Orwa, and J.M. Wambugu.

For the typing of the manuscript (from many differing handwritings), we are grateful to Mrs. Grace Kamenyi and Miss Harriet Kabugi.

We wish to express our appreciation for encouragement, suggestions, and support from L.P. Mureithi, T.C.I. Ryan, K. Sharma, M. Thorne, and other colleagues of the University of Nairobi Department of Economics. We are very grateful for suggestions of items for inclusion from Beverly Gray, Joanne M. Zellers, and Ruth Thomas of the U.S. Library of Congress, Yvette Scheven of the University of Illinois Library, Daniel Britz of Northwestern University Library, David L. Easterbrook of Indiana University Library, G. Hyden of the Ford Foundation and D. Court of the Rockefeller Foundation offices in Nairobi, D.A. vanWaardenburg of the International Bureau of Fiscal Documentation in Amsterdam, and the library staff of the Overseas Development Institute in London.

Throughout the compilation we have received much cooperation and assistance from the library staff of the University of Nairobi Main Library and J.K. Ngugi and J. Kamau of the Institute for Development Studies Library.

We are very grateful for the editorial advice and suggestions of items from our editor, James Armstrong, who was most conveniently accessible to us in Nairobi.

Introduction

The Volume of Past Research

If one were to interpret the number of entries in this volume as indicative of the state of economic research in Eastern Africa, then it would be safe to conclude that, in general, a healthy, positive trend has dominated over the past decade. With some exceptions, the volume of research as evidenced by published material has increased tremendously since the early part of the 1963-1974 period. Killick stated in the forerunner of this volume (The Economies of East Africa, 1976) that he had anticipated a total of perhaps two hundred items when he began that compilation for the 1963-1974 period; he eventually included nearly one thousand entries. Similarly, for the 1974-1980 time frame we expected to obtain some one thousand entries; when we picked up the pieces of the avalanche that we discovered, the total was nearly twice as large as our expectations. Therefore, when researchers combine the two volumes (for 1963-1974 and 1974-1980), they now have ready access to some three thousand references to the regional economic literature. This portends well for the future, since publications tend to beget publications.

This present compilation has not entirely succeeded in its intention to provide comprehensive coverage of the Kenya, Tanzania, and Uganda economies. There seems to be some unavoidable geographic bias in favour of materials on the Kenya economy by virtue of the fact that the compiling was carried out in Nairobi. There is also the deliberate inclusion of a greater range of unpublished papers than in the earlier volume, and such items are more difficult to discover from a distance than when one is "on site". It would be preferable if such a compilation in the future were undertaken as a co-operative venture by the universities in East Africa. One could then expect to achieve a reasonably comprehensive and better balanced geographic coverage of the three economies. Nevertheless, researchers are now in a much better position to understand these economies and to have access to the literature that analyses them than they were ten years ago. Improvements have taken place in both the quantity and quality of the research effort. Although gaps still exist in the literature--particularly in the need to draw together the economic achievements and obstacles for the entire region--researchers have a fairly substantial base of accumulated analyses and data to build upon.

In spite of many positive aspects, two developments that have adversely affected research in East Africa are apparent in the latter half of the 1970s. First, the decline in economic research published in and about Uganda is quite noticeable. Internal political events have clearly adversely affected the climate for scholarly research both at Makerere University and the East African Institute of Social Research. Second, communication between the universities and research institutes in Tanzania and those in Kenya has suffered since the breakup of the East African Community in 1973, and the subsequent border closure and general political climate between these two countries. For example, the Institute for Development Studies at Nairobi no longer routinely receives the publications of the Economic Research Bureau at Dar-es-Salaam (and the reverse presumably is also true). It is our hope that the linkages between such institutions will soon be restored, to the advantage of researchers in all the countries. We attempted to counteract the bias in coverage by correspondence with researchers in both Dar-es-Salaam and Makerere. The U.S. Library of Congress Accessions List Eastern Africa, the bibliographies that regularly appear in the Review of African Political Economy, and Michael Sims's United States Doctoral Dissertations in Third World Studies 1869-1978 (Waltham, Mass.: Crossroads Press, 1980) were particularly helpful in extending our coverage of Tanzania and Uganda items.

On balance, much remains to be done by energetic and purposeful economists and other social scientists before the literature will be in danger of "overdevelopment". Neither should the various agencies --both governmental and private--that support research become complacent that the literature is now exhaustive and that no more needs to be sponsored. It is to be hoped that the volume of past research will rather be interpreted as evidence of the fertility of the social sciences for still further academic endeavours.

Scope of Coverage

This project primarily covers the time period from 1974 through 1980. We have not hesitated to include items published before 1974 if they did not appear in the 1976 Killick book, and have deliberately included Ph.D. dissertations back to 1970 because such items were generally excluded from the Killick 1976 compilation.

Geographically, we have defined "East Africa" to consist of Kenya, Tanzania, and Uganda. This corresponds to the coverage of the earlier volume, and arises because these three countries constituted the now-dissolved East African Community. We have continued to limit the scope to English-language materials.

Our coverage is economics, broadly defined. Our rule of thumb has therefore been that if there is genuine doubt as to whether an item primarily concerns economics, we should err by the inclusion of some doubtful items rather than risk the omission of some important ones. Close reading of the classification scheme points up some features of our bias toward breadth and inclusiveness, and is particularly visible in the categories 00--historical and biographical studies; 02--political economy, economic independence; 41--sample, locality, and farm studies; 45--land use, resettlement, and tenure; 46--agricultural extension, technologies, marketing, and price policies; 48--economic geography, natural resources, ecology, wildlife, conservation, and pollution; and 60--demographic characteristics, population growth and development, and population policies.

The major criterion for the inclusion of materials was that they be available and substantive. Thus, items that are published or that are available for circulation upon request become accessible to interested researchers if they know of such items. The major function of this bibliography is to increase such awareness among persons such as university staff members, postgraduate and undergraduate students, research institute staff members, government officials, and reference librarians. Daily newspaper items or popular magazine articles with a very short-run focus or shallow content generally have been omitted from this compilation.

In annotating items we have attempted to provide a brief descriptive summary rather than to critically evaluate each item. In addition to direct inspection of books or journals or papers, we have drawn on reviews, publishers' announcements, and abstracts provided in sources such as the Journal of Economic Literature. Although most items are annotated, unannotated items have deliberately been included on the assumption that knowledge of the existence of such items would sometimes be of considerable value even without a description. We generally have not annotated North American dissertations on the grounds that such information is accessible through Dissertations Abstracts International; references to that publication have been indicated in many cases.

Changes in Classification Scheme

While the scheme developed by Killick has proven to be very useful and instructive, certain changes have been introduced in this compilation. These alterations are outlined below to assist the efforts of one who is trying to use both Killick's The Economies of East Africa and this volume in tandem. In some cases these modifications reflect changes in the focus of the economic literature from the 1960s and early 1970s to the latter half of the 1970s. Other modifications have been made in an attempt to increase the clarity and usefulness of the classification scheme, particularly in response to comments by users of the 1976 Killick volume. Given that a classification scheme is unavoidably arbitrary to some degree, we have generally chosen to maintain continuity and consistency with the earlier volume unless there were good reasons for change.

Three new classification groups have been added in the present volume:

Group 15	Income distribution studies
Group 65	Science and technology, research and transfer of technology
Group 73	Women's studies

The present Group 34--East African cooperation and the East African Community--combines the former Groups 34 and 35. Group 42 has been divided into four sub-categories:

42a	Livestock studies and policies
42b	Crop studies and policies
42c	Range management studies and policies
42d	Fisheries

Finally, the following terms have been added to the group designations as shown:

Group 47	Harambee
Group 48	ecology, wildlife
Group 63	informal sector
Group 71	nutrition, basic needs

Analysis of Entries

Tables 1 and 2 present in summary form the changes which have occurred in the economic literature pertaining to Kenya, Tanzania, and Uganda between the 1963-1974 and the 1974-1980 periods. The tables are followed by some comments with regard to the depth of coverage on topics in the literature and some of the possible reasons for variation.

TABLE 1

GEOGRAPHICAL DISTRIBUTION OF COVERAGE

<table>
<tr><th></th><th colspan="2">Number of Entries</th><th colspan="2">Per cent of Total</th></tr>
<tr><th></th><th>1963-1974</th><th>1974-1980</th><th>1963-1974</th><th>1974-1980</th></tr>
<tr><td>Kenya</td><td>374</td><td>874</td><td>39</td><td>47</td></tr>
<tr><td>Tanzania</td><td>189</td><td>468</td><td>20</td><td>25</td></tr>
<tr><td>Uganda</td><td>113</td><td>146</td><td>12</td><td>8</td></tr>
<tr><td>East Africa</td><td rowspan="2">292</td><td>206</td><td rowspan="2">30</td><td>11</td></tr>
<tr><td>General</td><td>178</td><td>9</td></tr>
<tr><td>Total</td><td>968</td><td>1,872</td><td>100</td><td>100</td></tr>
</table>

Source: For 1963-1974 data, T. Killick, The Economies of East Africa, Boston: G.K. Hall, 1976.
Per cent columns may not add to total due to rounding.

The geographical distribution of items herein is shown in Table 1 in comparison with the 1963-1974 coverage in the Killick volume. Kenya predominates in the 1974-1980 publications with 47 per cent of the total, up from 39 per cent previously. In light of the constraints, we are pleased that the proportion of Tanzania items increased from 20 to 25 per cent of the total. Having gone to considerable pains to satisfy ourselves that the small proportion--8 per cent--of items on Ugandan economic matters is an accurate reflection of the actual volume of published research output on economic topics since 1975, we cautiously conclude that the gap is in the literature rather than in our coverage of it. The breakup of the East African Community in 1973 is the major cause of the decrease--from 30 per cent to 20 per cent--in the proportion of items in the "East Africa" and "General" categories.

TABLE 2

DISTRIBUTION OF GEOGRAPHICAL COVERAGE BY CLASSIFICATION CATEGORY, 1963-1974 AND 1974-1980

(Number of items)

Classification[a] Category	Kenya		Tanzania		Uganda	
	1963-74	1974-80	1963-74	1974-80	1963-74	1974-80
0 General	20	117	12	42	2	21
1 Development, Planning	35	84	31	49	10	13
2 Fiscal and Financial	28	38	12	14	12	11
3 International	13	35	11	21	4	5
4 Agricultural	107	237	58	162	30	41
5 Industrial	44	62	25	53	19	12
6 Population, Manpower	73	160	19	63	22	17
7 Social Economics	42	120	16	61	11	24
8 Statistics	12	21	5	3	3	2
Country Totals	374	874	189	468	113	146

[a]This classification category corresponds to the first digit of the codes in the Bibliography Summary.

Table 2 shows the coverage in various classification categories, by country. For Kenya since 1974, there is a large literature output in all the agriculture categories, the link between choice of production technique and employment, social economics, history, political economy, development administration, income distribution studies, and the role of multinational corporations.

The most numerous items for Tanzania relate to rural and community development (although the emphasis in the literature with respect to Ujamaa in recent years has focused on "why Ujamaa has failed"), crop and farm studies, development strategies and planning, political economy, population and employment, and the economics of education.

The coverage on Uganda is weak in all areas. The largest number of items occurs in agriculture, social economics, and in the general studies section. Particularly during the past half-decade, there has been next to nothing published on Ugandan international economics, development planning and administration, and fiscal and monetary policies. A major backlog of research on the Ugandan economy has certainly accumulated.

Small numbers of items for all three countries appear with respect to international trade and payments topics since the mid-1960s. This is a major gap in all three in light of the importance that international trade assumes, and is largely inexplicable to us. It is possible that such items have been incorporated in other classification categories, such as industrial or agricultural development strategies.

In response to changing realities, and hence changing research priorities, increased emphasis has been given to certain topics since 1974. The two areas that most clearly exemplify these changes are energy-related studies and research on ecological problems. The number of studies concerning peasants, women, basic needs, pastoralism, population, and income distribution has also increased. In addition, greater attention has been given to certain major crops and agricultural activities, for example, maize, coffee, cotton, tea, and the dairy industry. We regard it to be a healthy sign that the economic literature has not maintained a constant focus but has responded to the changing economic environment.

As already noted, there is a large gap in the quantity of recently published research on the Ugandan economy. While the cause of this is probably due primarily to the disruptions of political events in Uganda, it may have been aggravated by the fact that some journal and book manuscripts that had been accepted for publication by the East Africa Literature Bureau were bottled up for some years after the East African Community broke up because printing firms refused to release finished publications until the details of their payments had been sorted out. This affected items for all three countries, but may have been more noticeable in light of the small flow of items concerning Uganda. It is not clear when conditions in Uganda will permit the resumption of sustained research, nor what quantities and quality of economic data for the past decade will be available to researchers.

With reference to the relative deficiency in coverage on international trade and balance of payments topics in all three countries, it is difficult to foresee imminent changes in world-wide trade relations that would be major enough to cause a loss of interest within third world countries in issues pertaining to a new international economic order. It is probable that a greater research effort that would underpin a common stance among third world countries is necessary if meaningful change is to occur.

The breakdown of the information flow between the three East African countries is particularly unfortunate because it has made systematic comparative research difficult. There certainly are differences in economic systems, ideologies, theoretical frameworks, and the terminology of analysis, but we would hope that progress toward improvements in the quality of life for the residents of East Africa would be aided by an increase in the flow of information rather than by its constriction.

Finally, while official support for research is important, it would be regrettable in the long term if the major focus of scholars shifted completely to short-term, policy-oriented research.[1] Such a focus is often quite seductive to the researcher because of the promise of lucrative consultancy arrangements with international donor agencies or government ministries, or because of access to or participation within the government decision structure. However, the projects desired for immediate policy purposes may not always be of intrinsic interest or importance to researchers. Long-run scholarly research requires continued financial support, and a commitment to its importance by researchers themselves.

Note

1. David Court, "Scholarship and Contract Research: The Ecology of Social Science in Kenya and Tanzania," in James Coleman, Lawrence Stifel, Ralph Davidson (eds.), Strengthening Social Science in the Third World, Boston: D.C. Heath, 1981.

List of Abbreviations

Afr Rev	*African Review*
BRALUP	Bureau of Resource Assessment and Land Use Planning, University of Dar-es-Salaam
Can J Afr Studs	*Canadian Journal of African Studies*
DAI	*Dissertations Abstracts International*
EAER	*Eastern Africa Economic Review*
EAJ	*East Africa Journal*
EAJ Rural Devel	*East African Journal of Rural Development*
EA USSC	East African United Social Science Council
Econ Bull Afr	*Economic Bulletin for Africa*
Econ Dev Cult Change	*Economic Development and Cultural Change*
Econ Stat Rev	*Economic and Statistical Review*, East African Community
ERB Paper	Economic Research Bureau Paper, University of Dar-es-Salaam
FAO	United Nations Food and Agriculture Organisation
HMSO	Her/His Majesty's Stationery Office, London
IDS	Institute for Development Studies, University of Nairobi
IDS Disc P	*IDS Discussion Paper* (Nairobi)
IDS Occ P	*IDS Occasional Paper* (Nairobi)
IDS Staff P	*IDS Staff Paper* (Nairobi)
IDS Working P	*IDS Working Paper* (Nairobi)
ILO	United Nations International Labour Organisation
IMF Staff Papers	*International Monetary Fund Staff Papers*
J Admin Overseas	*Journal of Administration Overseas*
J Comm Mkt Studs	*Journal of Common Market Studies*
J Dev Areas	*Journal of Developing Areas*
J Dev Studs	*Journal of Development Studies*
J Mod Afr Studs	*Journal of Modern African Studies*
K Stat Dig	*Kenya Statistical Digest*
OECD	Organization for Economic Cooperation and Development, Paris
OIES Bull	*Oxford Bulletin of Economics and Statistics*
SID	Society for International Development
UN	United Nations Organisation

List of Abbreviations

UNESCO	UN Educational, Scientific and Cultural Organisation, Paris
WEP	International Labour Organisation World Employment Program

List of Principal Journals and Publishers

Africa Development	Council for the Development of Services and Social Research in Africa, Dakar, Senegal
African Affairs	Royal Africa Society, London
African Economic History Review	African Studies Program, University of Wisconsin, Madison
African Studies Review	African Studies Association (USA), c/o University of California, Los Angeles
Agricultural Administration	Applied Science Publishers, Ltd., Essex, England
BRALUP Research Papers	University of Dar-es-Salaam, Bureau of Resource Assessment and Land Use Planning
Canadian Journal of African Studies	Canadian Association of African Studies, Toronto
Ceres	Food and Agricultural Organization, United Nations Publications, New York
Development and Change	Institute of Social Studies, The Hague
East African Journal of Rural Development	Department of Rural Economy and Extension, Makerere University, Kampala, Uganda
East Africa Economic Review	Kenya Literature Bureau, Nairobi
Economic Bulletin for Africa	United Nations Economic Commission for Africa, UN Publications, New York
Economic Development and Cultural Change	University of Chicago Press, Chicago
ERB Papers	University of Dar-es-Salaam, Economic Research Bureau
IDS Discussion and Working Papers	University of Nairobi Institute of Development Studies

List of Principal Journals and Publishers

International Labour Review	International Labour Office, Geneva
Journal of Administration Overseas	Her Majesty's Stationery Office, London
Journal of African Studies	Heldref Publications, Washington, D.C.
Journal of Developing Areas	Western Illinois University, Macomb
Journal of Development Studies	F. Cass & Co., London
Journal of Eastern African Research and Development	Kenya Literature Bureau, Nairobi
Journal of Modern African Studies	Cambridge University Press, Cambridge
Journal of Peasant Studies	F. Cass & Co., London
Oxford Bulletin of Economics and Statistics	Basil Blackwell, Oxford
Review of African Political Economy	Merlin Press, Sheffield, England
Ufahamu	African Studies Center, University of California, Los Angeles
Utafiti	Faculty of Arts and Social Science, University of Dar-es-Salaam; Kenya Literature Bureau, Nairobi
World Development	Pergamon Press, Oxford, England
Zeitschrift für Ausländische Landwirtschaft (Quarterly Journal of International Agriculture)	Deutsche Landwirtschafts-Gesellschaft, Verlag-GmbH, Frankfurt, Germany

Classification Scheme

0--General Studies

.00 Historical and biographical studies
.01 General surveys and comparative studies
.02 Political economy and economic independence
.03 Bibliographies and research programmes

1--Economic Development, Planning, and Stabilization

.10 Growth and development: measurement and experiences
.11 General development strategies and policies
.12 Development planning and implementation
.13 Macro-economic models
.14 Public and development administration
.15 Income distribution studies
.16 Consumption and saving studies

2--Fiscal and Financial Topics

.20 Public finance and budgeting
.21 Domestic financial institutions and markets; money and credit
.22 Domestic fiscal, financial, and monetary policies

3--International Trade and Payments

.30 International trade and trade relations; terms of trade
.31 Commercial policies
.32 Balance of payments experiences and policies
.33 Foreign investment, multinational corporations, and foreign aid
.34 East African cooperation and the East African Community

4--The Agricultural Sector

.40 Structure and organization
.41 Sample, locality, and farm studies
.42(a) Livestock studies and policies
.42(b) Crop studies and policies

.42(c) Range management studies and policies
.42(d) Fisheries
.43 Agricultural development experiences
.44 Agricultural strategies and planning
.45 Land use, resettlement, and tenure
.46 Agricultural extension, technologies, and marketing and price policies
.47 Rural and community development, agricultural cooperatives, Ujamaa, Harambee
.48 Economic geography, natural resources, ecology, wildlife, conservation, and pollution

5--The Industrial and Service Sectors

.50 Industrial structure and organization
.51 Industrialization and import substitution
.52 Industry studies
.53 Entrepreneurship; business finance and administration
.54 Policies toward industry and private business
.55 Transport and communications
.56 Marketing, trading, and cooperatives
.57 Tourism
.58 Public corporations and other parastatals

6--Population, Manpower, and Technologies

.60 Demographic characteristics, population growth and development, and population policies
.61 The labour force and migration
.62 Productivity, incomes, and industrial relations
.63 Employment and unemployment; labour intensity; the choice of techniques; the informal sector
.64 Manpower and educational planning; Africanization
.65 Science and technology, research, and transfer of technology

7--Social Economics

.70 Economics of education
.71 Health, nutrition, housing, water, social policy, and basic needs
.72 Regional and urban planning and policies
.73 Women's studies

8--Economic Statistics

.80 General and macro-economic statistical publications
.81 Micro-economic statistical publications

Bibliography Summary

CLASSIFICATION CODE	TOTAL ITEMS	KENYA	TANZANIA	UGANDA	EAST AFRICA	GENERAL
00	97	57	5	5	23	7
01	27	7	11	5	3	1
02	87	46	22	9	8	2
03	29	7	4	2	8	8
Subtotal	240	117	42	21	42	18
10	23	11	8	1	2	1
11	47	13	19	6	2	7
12	28	8	11	–	3	6
13	11	9	–	1	1	–
14	35	20	4	2	5	4
15	33	20	4	1	2	6
16	12	3	3	2	1	3
Subtotal	189	84	49	13	16	27
20	29	14	2	3	3	7
21	44	21	11	6	4	2
22	9	3	1	2	1	2
Subtotal	82	38	14	11	8	11
30	21	3	7	2	6	3
31	16	8	2	1	2	3
32	9	4	3	1	–	1
33	50	20	8	1	9	12
34	32	–	1	–	29	2
Subtotal	128	35	21	5	46	21
40	19	10	5	2	1	1
41	56	30	14	6	5	1
42a	26	10	6	5	2	3
42b	44	22	19	3	–	–
42c	9	5	2	2	–	–
42d	10	3	4	1	2	–
43	20	11	3	3	2	1
44	12	5	4	–	2	1

Bibliography Summary

CLASSIFICATION CODE	TOTAL ITEMS	KENYA	TANZANIA	UGANDA	EAST AFRICA	GENERAL
45	53	31	11	5	2	4
46	97	52	21	7	12	5
47	129	40	68	5	4	12
48	38	18	5	2	10	3
Subtotal	513	237	162	41	42	31
50	9	1	4	1	2	1
51	6	2	3	–	1	–
52	40	18	13	4	4	1
53	4	4	–	–	–	–
54	18	11	5	2	–	–
55	27	9	14	1	2	1
56	11	4	2	4	1	–
57	13	7	2	–	3	1
58	18	6	10	–	2	–
Subtotal	146	62	53	12	15	4
60	59	29	13	3	6	8
61	61	27	14	5	3	12
62	52	28	14	2	–	8
63	86	61	11	2	2	10
64	31	11	7	4	7	2
65	14	4	4	1	–	5
Subtotal	303	160	63	17	18	45
70	92	37	29	15	8	3
71	61	26	20	3	4	8
72	43	27	6	3	4	3
73	45	30	6	3	1	5
Subtotal	241	120	61	24	17	19
80	6	3	1	–	–	2
81	24	18	2	2	2	–
Subtotal	30	21	3	2	2	2
GRAND TOTAL	1,872	874	468	146	206	178

The Economies of East Africa: 1974-1980

GENERAL STUDIES

00--Historical and biographical studies

00-1 ALLEN, J. DE V. "Some aspects of Swahili economic history". Department of History Staff Seminar Paper. University of Nairobi, Dec. 1976, 19pp.

Traces the stages through which the Swahilis have passed. The economic impact of a common language within the Coastal zones of Africa as well as the future of the language and its people are discussed.

00-2 ___. "The peopling of the Lamu-Southern Benaadir hinterland in the 14th-17th centuries". Department of History Staff Seminar Paper. University of Nairobi, July 1980, 22pp.

Proposes the existence of another important group of pastoralists in the region between ca. 1300 and ca. 1700 A.D. who spoke neither Oromo nor Somali. Argues that the existence of such a people would assist in unravelling the controversies surrounding the area.

00-3 ALPERS, EDWARD A. Ivory and slaves: changing pattern of international trade in East Central Africa to the later nineteenth century. University of California Press, Berkeley, 1975, 314pp.

Descriptive economic history of East Africa's involvement in international trade from the 15th to the 19th century. Argues that the current relative underdevelopment of East Africa can be traced to East Africa's participation in international trade during that period.

00-4 AMBLER, CHARLES H. "Foreign relations in central Kenya: Kitui, Mbeere and Embu in the late 19th century". Department of History Staff Seminar Paper. University of Nairobi, 1977-1978, 23 pp.

Concerned with relations among the Bantu-speaking peoples of central Kenya and particularly with the inhabitants of

GENERAL STUDIES

northern Kitui, Mbeere and Embu. Much of the evidence is from interviews conducted in these areas in 1977-1978.

00-5 ATIENO-ODHIAMBO, E.S. "The rise of the Kenya peasant". Hadith, No. 5, Historical Association of Kenya, 1972, 12pp.
Defines "peasantry" and observes the rise of the Kenyan peasant as opposed to the study of native heroes.

00-6 BARNES, CAROLYN. "The socio-economic history of coffee growing in Gusiiland, Kenya". 1974.

00-7 BEACHEY, R.W. "The African diaspora and East Africa". Makerere University Inaugural lecture, Kampala, July 1967, 15pp.
Centered on the dispersion of peoples from Africa to other parts of the world, not of their own free will but by forcible extraction from the mainland, and their transport abroad or to other parts of Africa as slaves.

00-8 ___. The slave trade of Eastern Africa. Rex Collings, London, 1976.
Covers the operation of slave trade on the East African coast in the nineteenth century. Estimates that over 2,125,000 slaves were traded on the East Africa coast in the period.

00-9 BOWLES, B.D. "Economic anti-colonialism and British reaction in Uganda, 1936-1955". Can J Afr Studs, Vol. 9, No. 1, 1975, pp. 51-59.
Argues that anti-colonialism in Uganda in the period under review was specifically related to the grievances of export-crop growers.

00-10 ___. "The peasants of Kenya during the colonial period". University of Dar es Salaam Department of History Morogoro Conference, 1975, 35pp.

00-11 BRYCESON, DEBORAH FAHY. "Changes in peasant food supply in relation to the historical development of commodity production in pre-colonial and colonial Tanganyika". The Journal of Peasant Studies, Vol. 7, No. 3, April 1980, pp. 281-311.
Explores the dynamic interaction between food production and commodity production under conditions of increasing penetration of capital and consequent erosion of precapitalist modes of production in pre-colonial Tanganyika.

00-12 BUJRA, JANET M. "Women 'entrepreneurs' of early Nairobi". Can J Afr Studs, Vol. 9, No. 2, 1975, pp. 213-234.
Describes women who were able to take advantage of a certain demographic and socio-economic situation to achieve high

incomes and acquire property during the first half of this century.

00-13 BUTTERMAN, JUDY. "The pre-colonial economy of Karachuonyo". Department of History Staff Seminar Paper, University of Nairobi, 1977, 18pp.
Describes the modes of production and exchange and the social relations governing them in precolonial Karachuonyo. Intended as an attempt to find a conceptual framework for hypotheses which are to be tested further in the field.

00-14 CLOUGH, M.B. Chiefs and politicians: local policies and social change in Kiambu 1918-36. Ph.D. dissertation, Stanford University, 1978, 330pp.
DAI, Vol. 38, p. 7499.

00-15 CONN, B.E. "Ecology in historical perspective: an East African example". Historical Association of Kenya, 1972, 16pp.
Points out that the history of an area can be learned in an ecological perspective. Takes the case of Kitui, Ukambani area, and shows how the climatology of this area has affected the oral traditions of the people.

00-16 COOPER, FREDERICK. "Slavery and the slave trade". Historical Association of Kenya, 1978, 25pp.
Discusses the impact of slavery and slave trade on the economies of East Africa in the 19th century.

00-17a ___. "The coast in the colonial economy of Kenya, 1907-1925". Department of History Staff Seminar Paper, University of Nairobi, 1978 1979, 53pp.
Examines the means by which slave owners used land and controlled labour and the way the state and the economic structures affected workers and cultivators.

00-17b CUMMINGS, ROBERT J. Aspects of human porterage with special reference to the Akamba of Kenya: towards an economic history. Ph.D. dissertation, University of California, Los Angeles, 1975.

00-18 CYPHER, J.M. "The slave trade, slavery, and English economy: 1700-1760". Working Paper, California State University, Fresno, n.d., 34pp.
Makes a quantitative evaluation of the role which the slave trade played in the development of the English economy.

GENERAL STUDIES

00-19 DUDER, C.J.D. The soldier settlement scheme in 1919 (Kenya). Ph.D. dissertation, University of Aberdeen, 1978, 1455pp. (2 Vol.)

00-20 EHRET, CHRISTOPHER. "East African words and things: agricultural aspects of economic transformation in the 19th century". Historical Association of Kenya, 1978, 27pp.
Traces the origin, direction of movement, and time of adoption of crops that originated outside East Africa, using oral and linguistic evidence.

00-21 ESMAIL, AZIZI. "Some aspects of the history of the Ismailis in East Africa". Historical Association of Kenya, 1972, 36pp.
A survey of the socio-economic history of the Ismailis in East Africa, aimed at widening the knowledge about the Asians of East Africa.

00-22 FERGUSON, D.E. "The landless and squatters in colonial Kenya". University of Dar es Salaam Department of History Morogoro Conference, 1975, 28pp.

00-23 FUREDI, FRANK. "The Kikuyu squatter in the Rift Valley 1918-1929". Hadith, No. 5, Historical Association of Kenya, 1972, 16pp.
Compares the economic life of the squatters and that of the reserve dwellers. Concludes that the squatters were living a better life than the reserve dwellers. This better life deteriorated continuously up to 1929 when the squatters protested.

00-24 GORDON, DAVID F. "Economic change and political developments in Kenya, 1945-1963". Department of History Staff Seminar Paper, University of Nairobi, 1977, 17pp.
An attempt to interpret the interplay between economic and political developments in Kenya between the end of World War II and Uhuru in 1963. Focuses on the initiatives of the colonial regime in the economic and political spheres in a context that even they conceived of as a crisis situation.

00-25 ___. "Colonial crises and administrative response: Kenya 1945-1960". Journal of African Studies, Vol. 6, No. 2, 1979, pp. 98-111.

00-26 GRAMLY, R.M. "Evidence for exchange between interior East Africa and the coast in the first millenium B.C.". Institute of African Studies Discussion Paper 57, Nairobi.
States that there is evidence which suggests that the

economy of the East African stone bowl culture was pastoral; however, there is no proof to show that trading caravans like those of the nineteenth century passed through interior East Africa in the first millenium B.C.

00-27 GREENSTEIN, L.J. "The impact of military service in world war I on Africans". J Mod Afr Studs, Vol. 16, No. 3, Sept. 1978, pp. 495-507.
Discusses social, economic, and political problems associated with the resettlement of war veterans, that is, former members of K.A.R. in the case of the Nandi of Kenya. Concludes that far from turning Africans into anti-Government radicals as some had feared, military service in the 1914-1918 campaign had little measurable effect on the politics of Kenya.

00-28 GWASSA, G.C.K. "Capital penetration and the colonial state in Kenya, 1887-1963: a theoretical consideration". Department of History Seminar Paper, University of Dar es Salaam, 1975, 21pp.

00-29 HALI, P.K. African economic initiative and response in British Tanganyika. Ph.D. dissertation, London, 1978.

00-30 HARLOW, VINCENT and CHILVER, E.M. (eds.). History of East Africa, Vol. 2. Oxford University Press, London, 1965, 768pp.
Includes Cyril Ehrlich, "The Uganda economy 1903-1945", and C.C. Wrigley, "Kenya: the patterns of economic life 1902-1945".

00-31 HARTWIG, GERALD W. The art of survival in East Africa: the Kerebe and long-distance trade. African Publishing Co., New York, 1976, 253pp.
Using mostly oral sources, considers how the Kerebe society emerged from a tumultuous century changed but still intact as a society. This was during the 19th century when the Kerebe became active participants in the international community by exchanging ivory for trade goods produced in Asia or Europe.

00-32 HAY, M.J. "Economic change at the village level: Kowe 1900-1963". Department of History Staff Seminar Paper, University of Nairobi, 1969.

00-33 ___. Economic change in Luoland, Kowe, 1890-1945. Ph.D. dissertation, University of Wisconsin, Madison, 1972.

GENERAL STUDIES

00-34 HERLEHY, THOMAS J. "Palm wine and coconuts: production, consumption and trade in a domestic precolonial economy". Department of History Staff Seminar Paper, University of Nairobi, 1980, 26pp.

An analysis of the Mijikondo coconut palm economy dominated by the Rabai during the 19th century. An assessment of the domestic precolonial economy of the Kenya coastal region, its organization, and its operation.

00-35 HOLLANDER, R.B. Out of tradition: the position of women in Kenya and Tanzania during the pre-colonial, colonial and post-independence eras. Ph.D. dissertation, American University, Washington, D.C., 1979, 399pp.

DAI, Vol. 40, No. 4240-A.

00-36 ILIFFE, J. A modern history of Tanzania. Cambridge University Press, Cambridge, 1979.

00-37 JANMOHAMED, KARIM K. "African labourers in Mombasa, 1895-1940". Hadith, No. 5, Historical Association of Kenya, 1972, 22pp.

Considers the development of wage employment in relation to changes in technology, trade, and industry in Mombasa from 1895 to 1940.

00-38 ___. "Labour protest in Mombasa". Department of History Staff Seminar Paper, University of Nairobi, 1979, 18pp.

Concerned with only one aspect of the history of African labour in Mombasa, namely, the attempts by workers to redress their grievances by protest. Grievances arose from the workers' living conditions during the period 1895-1939 when Mombasa witnessed a phenomenal urban development as the town assumed its role as the chief commercial centre of East Africa.

00-39 KAMUHANGIRE, EPHRAIN R. "Economic and social history of East Africa--with special reference to South-Western Uganda salt lakes region". Hadith, No. 5, Historical Association of Kenya, 1972, 28pp.

Looks at the penetration of foreign trade into southern Uganda and how the response of the tirbes to this trade created a social-economic stratification based on tribal lines.

00-40 KIPKORIR, B.E. "Mau Mau and Western education". Department of History Staff Seminar Paper, University of Nairobi, Nov. 1977.

Dwells on the Mau Mau emergency and the perception accorded to Western education by the pre- and post-independence Kenya Africans.

Historical and biographical studies

00-41 KJEKSHUS, HELGE. Ecology control and economic development in East African history. Heinemann, London; University of California Press, Berkeley, 1977, 215pp.
Studies the case of Tanzania in 1850-1950. Focuses on issues relating to man and his environment and on the economic basis of indigenous initiatives. Argues that 19th-century East Africans were on the offensive against a hostile ecological environment.

00-42 LEAKEY, L.S.B. Kenya: contrast and problems. Macmillan, London, 1934, 189pp.
Describes some of the problems which arose in Kenya as a result of the impact of black and white races. The author concludes that the white race has got its place, and that place can only be made safe and economically sound if the interests of the black man are studied to the full.

00-43 ___. "The economics of Kikuyu tribal life". EAER, July 1956, pp. 164-180.
Describes the economy of Kikuyu life of old, its internal system and its relations with neighbouring tribes. Shows what things are like amongst the Kikuyu today--as they were up to, and what they may well be like after, the Emergency.

00-44 LEITNER, KERSTIN. "The first general strike in Mombasa (Jan. 1947)". Hadith, No. 5, Historical Association of Kenya, 1972, 10pp.
Explains how the 1947 strike was organized and what it achieved as a first strike to be organized by African Kenyan labour in the colonial period.

00-45 LONSDALE, JOHN. "The growth and transformation of the colonial state in Kenya, 1929-52". Department of History Staff Seminar Paper, University of Nairobi, 1980, 46pp.
Traces the process whereby the state altered its strategy for promoting the interest of its dominant stratum from one dictated by categorising opposed groups as races to one governed by considerations of economic class.

00-46 MANNERS, A.J. "Economic processes and power structure: the impact of colonialism in Buganda". EA USSC Conference, Nairobi, 1972, 17pp.
Analyses the changing economic power structure in Buganda under the impact of colonialism in order to show where conflicts of interests lay.

00-47 MARTIN, E.B. "The urban development of Malindi from 1500 to 1970". Plan East Africa, Vol. 3, No. 1, Jan.-Feb. 1972,

GENERAL STUDIES

pp. 32-35.
Traces Malindi urban development from 1500-1970. Highlights on the town's economic successes and recessions at different historical periods.

00-48 MARTIN, ESMOND B., and RYAN, T.C.I. "A quantitative assessment of the Arab slave trade of East Africa, 1770-1896". Kenya Historical Review, Vol. 5, No. 1, 1977, pp. 71-91.
Shows that an estimate that about one and a quarter million slaves were traded on the coast of East Africa to coastal and northern destinations is consistent with other evidence. Provides population estimates for the main East African centres.

00-49 MARTIN, ESMOND B., and MARTIN, CHRYSSEE MACCASTER PERRY. Cargoes of the East: the ports, trade and culture of the Arabian seas and Western Indian oceans. Elm Tree Books, London, 1978.
Examines the dhow as one of the most traditional means of international transport to be found anywhere; exciting is the fact that they have resisted modernisation and the goods they carry have remained unique. Today the dhow facilitates smuggling.

00-50 MAXON, ROBERT M. John Ainsworth and the making of Kenya. University Press of America, 1980.
Biography of an early colonial administrator who confronted issues of European settlement, African rights, labour policies, etc.

00-51 MEMON, P.A. "Some geographical aspects of the history of urban growth in Kenya". Hadith, No. 5, Historical Association of Kenya, 1972.
Is concerned with the growth of urban systems using the Christaller model of the interaction between economic activity and settlement pattern. The urban system considered is that of the Kavirondo zone (Western Province and Nyanza Province).

00-52 MEMON, P.A., and MARTIN, E.B. "The Kenya coast: an anomaly in the development of an 'ideal type' colonial spatial system". Kenya Historical Review, Vol. 4, No. 2, 1976, pp. 187-206.
Explains, through a spatial-temporal analysis, the reasons why until 1940, unlike so many other areas of the Third World, the Kenya coast failed to develop through participation in the colonial economy.

Historical and biographical studies

00-53 MOTANI, N.A. "The origins of Uganda's (African) Civil Service 1912-1940". Syracuse University East Africa Series No. 29, 1978, 72pp.

00-54 MURIUKI, GODFREY. A history of the Kikuyu 1500-1900. Oxford University Press, Nairobi, 1974, 190pp.

An attempt to analyse the historical traditions of the Kikuyu. Includes a discussion of the age sets and and their provision of manpower for public duties. Concludes that the 19th century Kikuyu society was characterized by competition and egalitarianism.

00-55 NDEGE, P.O. "Colonialism and underdevelopment in Gusiiland, 1900-1939". Department of History Staff Seminar Paper, University of Nairobi, 1977, 19pp.

Uses Gusii as a case study of the impact of colonialism on African communities. Begins by an approximation of the pre-colonial modes of production in Gusiiland and then proceeds to discuss the articulation of colonial capitalism through the encouragement of petty commodity production, labour supplies, and finally commodity marketing.

00-56 OCHIENG, WILLIAM R. "Trade contacts and cultural connexions between the Gusii and the Luo in the 19th century". Hadith, No. 5, Historical Association of Kenya, 1972, 12pp.

The Luos and Gusii have contacts and cultural connections that can be explained by their respective economic histories.

00-57 OGUTU, M.A. "The 19th century staple cash crops in Africa". Department of History Staff Seminar Paper, University of Nairobi, 1978, 16pp.

An historical account of the inter-play between nations (mainly colonisers) and amongst native people of Africa in trying to get controlling shares of rubber trade in Africa.

00-58 ___. "The 19th century ivory trade in Africa". Department of History Staff Seminar Paper, University of Nairobi, May 1979.

Shows how ivory trade came into being after the rubber trade. Deals also with the sources and destinations of ivory from the African states, the use into which the ivory was put, and the general economic impact on the societies which took part in this trade.

00-59 ___. "The 19th century caravan trade routes in Africa". Department of History Staff Seminar Paper, University of Nairobi, 1979-1980, 35pp.

Discusses three types of caravan trade that had developed in Africa up to and until the 19th century. Considers the

GENERAL STUDIES

goods traded, the routes used and final destinations of the goods.

00-60 OLEWE-NYUNYA, J.D. "African peasant cooperatives; a historical model of change". Hadith, No. 5, Historical Association of Kenya, 1972, 10pp.

Traces the history of peasant cooperatives in Africa, especially why they have been adopted; secondly, discusses the issues of tradition and modernity in cooperative social change.

00-61 ONYANGO-ABUJE, J.C. "Reflections on culture changes and distribution during the neolithic period in East Africa". Historical Association of Kenya, 1974, 14pp.

Postulates that the East African neolithic cultures had a long origin. Attempts also to demonstrate that the East African neolithic populations were active and enterprising, and rejects the restriction of the East African neolithic cultures to the eastern Rift Valley alone.

00-62 OSORO, J.M. "A 'lull before the storm': a study of the African labourers in the Kericho tea estates 1939-1958". Department of History Staff Seminar Paper, University of Nairobi, 1977, 27pp.

Describes the problems and anxieties that gripped the tea community during the upheavals of the second world war and the Mau-Mau uprising. Also how some of these problems, for example, labour shortage, were solved, and how they served to make the government and employers take a positive stance on the labourers' plight.

00-63a PEACOCK, A.T., and DOSSER, D.G.M. "The national income in Tanganyika, 1952-1954". Colonial Research Studies, No. 26, HMSO, London, 1958.

00-63b PHILLIPS, RICHARD B. The agrarian settler colony and underdevelopment: a comparative case study of Kenya and Tanzania. Ph.D. dissertation, New York University, 1974.

00-64 PHILLIPSON, D.W. "The beginings of pastoralism in East Africa". Department of History Staff Seminar Paper, University of Nairobi, 1976. 20pp.

Attempts a re-evaluation of the evidence for the beginnings of food production in eastern Africa, with particular emphasis on pastoralism. The problem is viewed not as a parochial East African topic, but in the context of the later pre-history of a huge tract of territory in and to the south of the Sahara Desert.

Historical and biographical studies

00-65 PRESLEY, C.A. "Kikuyu women as wage labourers: 1919-1960". Department of History Staff Seminar Paper, University of Nairobi, 1979. 20pp.

A contribution to the growing field of literature which takes as its prime concern the delineation of the roles, activities, and unique contributions of women to the history of the African continent.

00-66 PRICE, DONALD L. "Economic change in Kisyaara location 1880-1950". Department of History Staff Seminar Paper, University of Nairobi, 1977, 9pp.

Seeks to examine the relationship of changes in Kipsigis modes of production to local economic change. The area chosen is Kisyaara which is representative of the smallholder farming areas of Kipsigis country where rapid economic change has occured.

00-67 QUIGGIN, A.H. "Trade routes, trade and currency in East Africa". Rhodes-Livingstone Museum Occasional Paper No. 5, Manchester University Press, Manchester, 1974.

00-68 RYAN, T.C.I. "A note on the economics of East African plantation slave use: an essay into cliometrics". Historical Association of Kenya, Nairobi, 1978, 7pp.

00-69 SALIM, A.I. "Land alienation: the Arab-Swahili experience 1895-1935". Hadith, No. 5, Historical Association of Kenya, 1972, 12pp.

Argues that the Swahili-Arab "tribes" of the coast had a land tenure system which was a combination of African and Muslim land tenure, characterized by inalienation. With the coming of the whites in 1895, ordinances were set which alienated land from these tribes.

00-70 SHERIFF, ABDUL H. "The development of underdevelopment; the role of international trade in the economic history of the East African coast before the 16th century". Hadith, No. 5, Historical Association of Kenya, 1972, 14pp.

That much as we should look at the benefits of international trade to the East African coast in a historical perspective, we should also look at the exploitation that the coast experienced during the same time.

00-71 ___. "Dynamics of change in pre-colonial East African societies". African Economic History Review, Vol. 1, No. 2, Fall 1974, pp. 7-14.

Discusses the validity of Boserup's model of economic and social change for conditions in pre-colonial East Africa.

GENERAL STUDIES

00-72 SIFUNA, D.N. "Conflict and cooperation in education policies: the colonial government and the Christian missionaries to 1953." Department of History Staff Seminar Paper, University of Nairobi, 1978, 33pp.

Contends that both the colonial government and the missionaries in Kenya accepted the principle of co-operation in African education, but it was the interpretation of this principle that generated some conflict. These conflicts as regards education policies form the main theme of the paper.

00-73 ___. "Training a servile class: missionary education and colonialism in Kenya". Department of History Staff Seminar Paper, University of Nairobi, 1979.

00-74 SMITH, ALAN. "The open market: the economy of Kenya's northern frontier province and the Italo-Abyssinian war". EAJ, Vol. 6, No. 11, Nov. 1969, pp. 34-42.

Argues that a free and competitive market was created in the northern frontier province by political coincidence and that it collapsed because there was not an adequate means of exchange after the Italian currency became unstable during 1936.

00-75 SORRENSON, M.P.K. Origins of European settlement in Kenya. Oxford University Press, Nairobi, 1968, 320pp.

Argues that European colonization in East Africa was more a consequence than a cause of British acquisition of territory.

00-76 SPENCER, I.R.G. "The economic development of Kenya during world war II". Social Science Research Council Report HR 6078, London, 1978, 50pp.

00-77 ___. "The economic development of Kenya 1895-1929: a reconsideration". Department of History Staff Seminar Paper, University of Nairobi, 1978, 14pp.

Argues that the influence of both land alienations and of measures to encourage Africans to leave the reserves on the growth of surplus agricultural production was not as drastic as is sometimes supposed.

00-78 STICHTER, SHARON. "Trade unionism in Kenya 1947-1952: the militant phase". In P.C.W. Gutkind, R. Cohen, J. Copans (eds.), African Labor History. SAGE, Beverly Hills, London, 1978, pp. 155-174.

Attempts to organise multiracial--Indian and African--trade unions failed during the later part of the period under study. Government efforts to discourage the growth of strong unions and to mitigate their militancy were largely successful. Much of the nationalist sentiment in Kenya at this time was directed at the political institutions rather than at employers.

00-79 ___. "African wage labour in Kenya 1903-1914". Department of History Staff Seminar Paper, University of Nairobi, 1979.
Examines the causes of African labour force participation in the years prior to 1914. Attempts to show that the positive factors of wages and consumption levels do not seem to be adequate explanations for the rate of increase in African wage-earning.

00-80 STILES, DANIEL. "An historical outline of the hunting peoples of the northern East African coast". Department of History Staff Seminar Paper, University of Nairobi, 1980, 20pp.
Discusses some of the traditional hunting communities today located on the East African coast between the Juba river in the north and Kilifi in the south. Concludes that the existence of a confusing literature referring to peoples called variously Wata, Wajanye, Alaa, or Laa occurred because previous investigators limited their research to too small an area.

00-81 SUNDSTROM, LARS. _The exchange economy of pre-colonial tropical Africa_. C. Hurst and Company, London, 1974, 284pp.
Concerned with 18th to early 20th century. Concentrates on West Africa but extends into West Central, Central, and East Africa. Emphasis on internal trade but also includes goods imported into Africa. Detailed investigation of certain commodities.

00-82 TAMBILA, ANSE. "The political economy of settlers in Kenya". University of Dar-es-Salaam Department of History Morogoro Conference, 1975, 35pp.

00-83 THORBAHN, P. _The precolonial ivory trade of East Africa: reconstruction of a human-elephant ecosystem (Kenya)_. Ph.D. dissertation, University of Massachusetts, 1979, 345pp.
DAI, Vol. 40, p. 4651-A.

00-84 TIGNOR, ROBERT L. _The colonial transformation of Kenya: the Kamba, Kikuyu and Maasai from 1900 to 1939_. Princeton University Press, Princeton, 1975, 372pp.
The author describes particular developments such as the story of missionary efforts among Maasais, the controversies over educational policy among officials, missionaries, and settlers, the circumcision controversy among the Kikuyu, etc.

GENERAL STUDIES

00-85 TURTON, R. "The changing focus of Somali economic, political and educational aspirations in Kenya: 1930-1948". Trinity College Conference, Cambridge, June 1975.

00-86 UCHENDU, VICTOR. "Polity, primacy and African economic development". EA USSC Conference, Nairobi, 1969.
Argues that polity primacy orientation helped traditional African societies to achieve social stability at the expense of sustained economic growth and development; polity primacy orientation is an input that is vital in any analysis of socio-cultural factors affecting economic development in Africa.

00-87 VAN ZWANENBERG, R.M.A., with KING, ANNE. An economic history of Kenya and Uganda, 1800-1970. Macmillan Press, London, 1975, 326pp.
Includes sections on people, production, exchange and distribution, and institutions for economic growth.

00-88 VERMOUTH, PAUL. "The beginnings of maize cash-cropping in Kamilili, 1908-1935". Department of History Staff Seminar Paper, University of Nairobi, 1978, 18pp.
Describes the pattern of life in the area around 1908. Considers the growth of external influence in the region and also examines some of the effects of the transition to maize cash-cropping.

00-89 WAMBAA, REBMANN M., and KING, KENNETH. "The political economy of the Rift Valley: a squatter perspective". Hadith, No. 5, Historical Association of Kenya, 1972, 22pp.
Looks at the factors that made Kikuyus move from Central province to Rift Valley in the colonial period. Proceeds to analyse the resistance of squatters against exploitation by settlers.

00-90 WERE, G. "Economic transformation in pre-colonial East Africa: the Bugisu case". Department of History Staff Seminar Paper, University of Nairobi, May 1977, 10pp.
Focuses on economic and social change in pre-colonial Bugisu. Is critical of Sik's contention that pre-colonial Africa had no classes and, therefore, no class conflicts, and finally demonstrates that pre-colonial African societies were not characterized by isolationism and conflicts.

00-91 WERLIN, H.H. Governing an African city: a study of Nairobi. Africana Publishing House, 1973, 108pp.
Gives an historical account of the growth of Nairobi and draws some conclusions about the city's future.

00-92 WHITE, LUISE. "Women's domestic labour in colonial Kenya: prostitution in Nairobi, 1909-1950". Working Paper in African Studies 30, Boston University, Boston, 1980.

00-93 WOOD, L.J. "Market origins and development in East Africa". Department of Geography Occasional Paper No. 57, Makerere University, 1974, 63pp.

Reviews available information relating to markets in East Africa prior to 1900 and traces the development of the contemporary rural market system in Kenya.

00-94 YLVISAKER, MARGUERITE. Lamu in the nineteenth century: land, trade, and politics. Boston University African Research Studies No. 13, Boston, 1979.

00-95 YOUE, CHRISTOPHER P. "Peasants, planters and cotton capitalists: the 'dual economy' in colonial Uganda". Can J Afr Studs, Vol. 12, No. 2, 1978, pp. 163-184.

Reevaluates the events that led to development of the cotton industry in Uganda after World War I. Examines the crisis that faced both Uganda planters and British cotton manufacturers, and also the complementary development of African and European production within the framework of the dual economy.

01--General surveys and comparative studies

01-1 BOMANI, PAUL. "Tanzania's road to development". International Development Review, Vol. 16, No. 2, 1974, pp. 2-9.

01-2 CARROLL, A. "Tanzania: special report". Commerce International, Vol. 105, No. 1424, Dec. 1974, pp. 31-37.

01-3 CERVENKA, ZDENEK. Land-locked countries in Africa. The Scandinavian Institute of African Studies, Uppsala, 1972, 369pp.

Discusses socio-economic problems facing land-locked independent African countries. Uganda is included as one of the countries.

01-4a COULSON, ANDREW (ed.). Africa socialism in practice; the Tanzanian experience. Spokesman Books, Nottingham, 1979.

Contains TANU Guidelines and "Ten years after Arusha", plus fourteen cases covering villagization, ujamaa villages, new industries, education, etc.

01-4b GERSHENBERG, IRVING. "Slouching towards socialism: Obote's Uganda". African Studies Review, April 1972.

GENERAL STUDIES

01-4c GERSHENBERG, IRVING, and KIGGUNDU, SULEIMAN. "The economic situation under Amin". Paper at the Uganda Workshop, Dartmouth College Public Affairs Center, May 1979.

01-5 HAZLEWOOD, ARTHUR. The economy of Kenya: the Kenyatta era. Oxford University Press, London, 231pp.
A general survey of the economic structure and policies from independence in 1963 to the late 1970s.

01-6 HELLEINER, G.K. "Economic collapse and rehabilitation in Uganda". U.S.A. African Studies Association meeting, Philadelphia, Oct. 1980.

01-7 JANSEN, S. "Regional economic atlas mainland Tanzania". BRALUP, Research Paper No. 1. University of Dar-es-Salaam, June 1968, 72pp.
Highlights the regional variations in development and opportunities in Tanzania with a view to assisting in the decentralization of planning.

01-8 KAPLAN, IRVING (ed.). Tanzania: a country study (2nd ed.). American University, Washington, D.C. Foreign Area Studies, Washington D.C., 1978, 322pp.
Contains discussion of the historical, political, physical, and social setting, the economy, and national security of Tanzania.

01-9 "Kenya: an economic survey". New African Development, Vol. 11, No. 3, March 1977, pp. 209-224.
Argues that Kenya has adopted a mixture of private and state enterprise which pulls in foreign investment, but maintains the gulf between rich and poor.

01-10 "Kenya: survey". New Africa, Vol. 127, March 1978, pp. 39-61.
Finds that small farmers produced more than the large farmers in 1977. But many farms are too small to produce a surplus for marketing. On tourism, Kenya banned big game hunting, Tanzania closed the border, and East African Airways collapsed. It is hence suggested that the tourist industry needs rebuilding.

01-11 "Kenya survey". African Business, No. 19, March 1980, pp. 39-65.
Contains eight short articles on the current state of the Kenyan economy. Topics include foreign trade and aid, transport, the motor vehicle assembly industry, and population growth. Similar surveys have appeared at approximately annual intervals during the past decade in this publication and its predecessor, African Development.

01-12 "Kenya's 1974-78 development plan". Standard Bank Review, April 1974, pp. 8-14.

01-13 KILLICK, TONY. Policy Economics. Heinemann, London, 1980, 336pp.
Following several chapters on economic policy principles, the book discusses a range of policy issues: population growth, poverty, unemployment, balance of payments management, etc.

01-14 ___, (ed.). Papers on the Kenyan economy. Heinemann, London, 1981.
A collection of 35 chapters dealing with (a) economic performance and structure, (b) public finance, money, and the balance of payments, (c) development strategies and planning, (d), income distribution, (e) population, labour and factor proportions, (f) the economics of education, and (g) agriculture and industry.

01-15 KIM, KWAN S.; MABELE, ROBERT B.; and SCHULTHEIS, MICHAEL J. Papers on the political economy of Tanzania. Heinemann, Nairobi and London, 1979, 294pp.
A collection of 29 papers by various authors arranged in the following sections: I--background to socialist development in Tanzania; II--planning for development; III--industrial development; IV--money and banking; V--international economic relations; VI--rural development; VII--human resources and development.

01-16 LEMA, HELEN. Comparative agricultural strategies of Kenya and Tanzania. M.A. thesis, University of Nairobi, 1977.

01-17 LIVINGSTONE, IAN, and ORD, H.W. Economics for Eastern Africa (rev. ed.). Heinemann, London, 1980.
Revised edition of the A-level textbook first published in 1968.

01-18 MABELE, R.B., et al. "Economic development of Tanzania". Scientific American, Vol. 243, No. 3, Sept. 1980.

01-19 MARTIN, ESMOND B. Zanzibar tradition and revolution. Hamish Hamilton, London, 1978.
A socio-economic and political history of Zanzibar and the Pemba Islands. Includes topics such as agriculture, fishing, hunting, development projects, traditional Islamic practices, and tourism, and an appraisal of changes that have taken place since 1963.

GENERAL STUDIES

01-20 MUTALIK-DESAI, PRIYA (ed.). Economic and political development of Kenya. Himalaya Publishing House, Bombay, 1979, 197pp.

01-21 PRATT, R. CRANFORD. "Tanzania: the development debate--a comment". African Affairs, July 1980, pp. 343-347.

01-22 STEIN, LESLIE. "Transforming the Tanzanian economy: a review covering the first decade of independence". African Social Research, No. 27, June 1979, pp. 541-564.
Argues that by 1971, Tanzania had not completed the necessary groundwork to ensure itself continuous development. But through the Ujamaa movement, Tanzania's experience demonstrates that even if a country sets out from a situation of structural dependency that, given appropriate leadership, it can surmount many of these obstacles.

01-23 Tanzania Notes and Records: Special Issue No. 76. A decade of progress 1961-1971. The Tanzania Society, 1975, 202pp.
An attempt to cover some of the dynamic changes that have taken place in Tanzania during the first decade of independence. An overview of economic progress of Tanzania during the decade.

01-24 THOMAS, H.B., and SCOTT, ROBERT. Uganda. Oxford University Press, London, 1935, 559pp.
A general survey of the political, economic, and social conditions in Uganda during the colonial period up to 1935.

01-25 UNITED NATIONS. Economic survey of Africa. Vol. 3. East African sub-region. United Nations, New York, 1971, 133pp.
Attempts to give the main economic data for twelve countries in the eastern Africa sub-region including their economic progress from 1950-1965 and the plans that most of them have made to enhance the growth of the economies.

02--Political economy and economic independence

02-1 AMSDEN, A.H. "A review of Kenya's political economy since independence". Journal of African Studies, Vol. 1, 1974.

02-2 ANYAN'G NYONG'O, P. "The development of a middle peasantry in Nyanza". IDS Working P 380, 1981.
Argues that the intrusion of international capital into Nyanza has led to the stagnation of middle-peasant agriculture. Examines the historical-social forces that have made the establishment of such agriculture difficult.

02-3 AWUONDO, C.O. "Social indicators of marginilisation in a

changing pastoral economy: the case of commercialized fishing in Turkana." Department of Sociology Seminar Paper, University of Nairobi, July 1980, 23pp.
Examines the trend of pastoral transformation and development in a traditional pastoral economy. The analysis is based on data collected on the role of Turkana Fishermen's Co-operative Society in the development of Turkana district.

02-4 BERMAN, B.J. "Changing modes of production and the colonial state in Kenya". Paper presented to the Institute of Commonwealth Studies, London, 1978.

02-5 ___ and LONSDALE, J.M. "Crises of accumulation, coercion and the colonial state: the development of the labour control system in Kenya, 1919-1929". Can J Afr Studs, Vol. 14, No. 1, 1980, pp. 55-81.
Describes how African labourers were recruited into the settler estates and the instruments then used to lure African labourers to work. Analyses the application of official coercion through the state and provincial administration.

02-6 BERNSTEIN, H. "African peasantries: a theoretical framework". Journal of Peasant Studies, Vol. 6, No. 4, July 1979, pp. 421-443.
Outlines and illustrates concepts for the analysis of contemporary peasantries, with specific reference to Africa and to Tanzania in particular. Concludes that there is no single and essential peasantry. Similar paper appears as ERB Occasional Paper 78.2, University of Dar-es-Salaam.

02-7 BIENEFELD, M.A. "The informal sector and peripheral capitalism: the case of Tanzania". IDS Bulletin, Vol. 6, No. 3, Feb. 1975, pp. 53-73.

02-8 CAMPBELL, H. "The so-called national bourgeoisie in Kenya". Ufahamu, Vol. 9, No. 2, 1979, pp. 86-118.

02-9 CARLSEN, JOHN. Economic and social transformation in rural Kenya. Scandinavian Institute of African Studies, Uppsala, 1980.

02-10 CHILUNGU, S.W. "Kenyan values in national development". Historical Association of Kenya, 1977, 13pp.
Tries to define what and whose values to use in national development, and discusses how these values are related to the reader's own national identity.

02-11 CLAYTON, E.S. "A note on the alien enclave and development".

GENERAL STUDIES

EAER, Vol. 10, No. 1, June 1963.
Claims that the alien farming enclave in Kenya has done little to establish a springboard for the development of the economy.

02-12 CLIFFE, LIONEL. "Rural class formation in East Africa". Journal of Peasant Studies, Vol. 4, No. 2, Jan. 1977, pp. 195-224.
Basically focuses on the formation of rural classes resulting from the interaction of an imposed capitalistic mode of production on the pre-existing social structure.

02-13 COULSON, A.C. "A simplified political economy of Tanzania". ERB Paper 74.9, University of Dar-es-Salaam, 1974.

02-14 COWEN, M., with F. MURAGE. "Notes on agricultural wage labour in a Kenya location" (mimeo). Nairobi, n.d. (ca. 1972).
Based on a partial analysis of one location in Nyeri district. Argues that it is not disproven that the formation of groups of agricultural labourers could constitute on embryonic agricultural proletariat, and argues that the wage labourer in agriculture and the hirerer of such labourers are often different persons.

02-15 COWEN, M., and KINYANJUI, K. "Some problems of capital and class in Kenya". IDS Occ P 26, University of Nairobi, 1977, 99pp.
The authors move beyond the simple formulations of inequality and class formation in Kenya to an analysis of how some types of labour have been devalued (in terms of labour power) through wage guidelines and the Industrial Court. The analysis incorporates international capital penetration and the local accumulation of capital by the salaried class.

02-16 ELKAN, WALTER. Migrants and proletarians: urban labour in the economic development of Uganda. Oxford University Press, London, 1960, 149pp.
An analysis of how in Uganda, despite the flow of labour between town and country, there are few signs of the growth of an urban working class.

02-17 GATHERU-WANJOHI, N.A. Socio-economic inequalities in Kenya: the case study of Rift Valley province. M.A. thesis, University of Nairobi, 1976, 459pp.
Argues that in order to effectively implement the ILO Report on the issue of land subdivision as a means of reducing inequality the entire land policy must be overhauled, the necessary prerequisite for which is nationalization.

02-18 GOTTLIEB, MANUEL. "The process of differentiation in Tanzanian agriculture and rural society". ERB Seminar Paper, University of Dar-es-Salaam, n.d.

02-19 GUTKIND, PETER, and WATERMAN, PETER. African social studies: a radical reader. Monthly Review Press, New York, 1977.
Contains essays on African society from the radical perspective covering six areas: methodology, history, economy, social structure, ideology, and politics. Several pertain specifically to East Africa.

02-20 HARBESON, JOHN W., and ROTHCHILD, DONALD. "The political economy of rehabilitation in Uganda". U.S.A. African Studies Association meeting, Philadelphia, Oct. 1980.

02-21 HEBLUND, HANS. "Contradictions in the peripheralization of a pastoral society: the Maasai". Review of African Political Economy, Nos. 15-16, May-Dec. 1979, pp. 15-34.
Examines the relations of production in pastoral societies. Shows important aspects in the transformation of the Maasai from a pre-capitalist economy to a periphery with an underdeveloped capitalist mode of production. Analyses how external forces have changed the old reproductive patterns by creating a deterioration of the reproductive foundation of the society both regarding economy and means of production.

02-22 HENLEY, J.S. "Capitalist accumulation in Kenya--straw men rule OK?". Review of African Political Economy, No. 17, Jan.-April 1980, pp. 105-108.
A critique of R. Kaplinsky's discussion in the same issue of this journal.

02-23 HOLMQUIST, FRANK. "Class structure, peasant participation and rural self help". In J.D. BARKAN and J.J. OKUMU (eds.), Politics and public policy in Kenya and Tanzania. Praeger, New York, 1979, pp. 129-153.
Explains why both Tanzania and Kenya experienced high rates of self-help development just after independence. discusses the differing trends of self-help programmes in the two countries.

02-24 HOUSE, W.J., and KILLICK, T. Social justice and development policy in Kenya's rural economy. WEP, ILO, 1980.

02-25 INTERNATIONAL LABOUR ORGANIZATION. Social classes and the government in Kenya: a comparison between the ILO report and the government's response. WEP, ILO, Geneva, 1975.

GENERAL STUDIES

02-26 JAMAL, V. "Asians in Uganda, 1880-1972: inequality and expulsion". Economic History Review, Vol. 29, No. 4, Nov. 1976, pp. 602-616.

Deals with the historical background of the Asian control of the economy and of events up to 1972. Attempts to quantify the extent of inequality in Uganda, the reasons for it, and governmental policies.

02-27 JORGENSEN, J.J. Structural dependence and economic nationalism in Uganda 1888-1974. Ph.D. dissertation, McGill University, 1977, 631pp.

DAI, Vol. 38, p. 4350A.

02-28 ___. "The political economy of the Obote regime". In T.M. Shaw and K.A. Heard (eds.), The politics of Africa: dependence and development. Africana, New York, 1979, pp. 43-72.

02-29 KAMAU, C.M. "The search for economic independence in Kenya". IDS (unnumbered paper), n.d. (ca. Sept. 1972), 38pp.

Argues that the low status of Africans in Kenya was of more importance in the search for independence than the economic and political dependence of Kenya on overseas capitalist economies. Consequently the search for economic independence has been concentrated in raising the relative economic level of Africans.

02-30 KAPLINSKY, RAFAEL. "Capitalist accumulation in the periphery --the Kenyan case re-examined". Review of African Political Economy, No. 17, Jan.-April 1980, pp. 83-105.

A discussion of Colin Leys's 1978 article "Capital accumulation, class formation and dependency: the significance of the Kenyan case", which re-assesses his own book, Underdevelopment in Kenya (1975), as to the relationship of the Kenyan indigenous industrial bourgeoisie to foreign capital. Kaplinsky presents data in considerable detail to argue that Leys was correct in his book and not in his 1978 reassessment.

02-31 KARIOKI, JAMES N. "Socialism in Africa--the Tanzanian experience". Civilizations, Nos. 23-24, 1-2, 1973-1974, pp. 31-47.

02-32 ___. Tanzania's human revolution. Pennsylvania State University Press, University Park, 1979.

02-33 KING, K.J. "The politics of agricultural education for Africans in Kenya". Education in Eastern Africa, Vol. 5, No. 1, 1975, pp. 1-12.

Argues that schools are a very limited instrument of

social change and that what may be educationally progressive can be politically reactionary.

02-34 KITCHING, GAVIN. "Modes of production and Kenyan dependency". Review of African Political Economy, No. 8, Jan.-April 1977, pp. 56-74.

02-35 ___. Class and economic change in Kenya: the making of an African petite bourgeoisie 1905-1970. Yale University Press, New Haven, 1980, 479pp.

Historical analysis of the basic changes in the Kenyan economy since the growth of colonialism, and relates that to the growth of the petite bourgeoisie. Theoretical discussion of its implications for such issues as the type of class analysis which is appropriate for the country, role of state in capital accumulation and class formation, and the relevance of Marxist value theory to the analysis of exploitation in Kenya.

02-36 KOSGEI, SALLY J. "Some thoughts on the Kipsigis colonial economy". Department of History Staff Seminar Paper, University of Nairobi, Feb. 1979, 8pp.

Gives a brief survey of the pre-capitalist society before discussing the process of capitalist penetration into the Kipsigis society.

02-37 KWERI, BALAMU A.C.D. "Domestic self-reliance". Vol. 39, 1980, pp. 75-81.

Analyses the relevant ideas and concepts of self-reliance, and identifies its qualitative essence as being basically social.

02-38 LAMB, G.B. "Peasants, capitalists and agricultural development in Kenya". EA USSC Conference, Nairobi, Dec. 1972, pp. 153-162.

Argues that a heavily subsidized and protected capitalist agricultural sector, in which the nascent bourgeoisie have strong interests, is becoming, to an uncertain extent, vulnerable to pressure from peasant unemployment and land need.

02-39 ___. "The neocolonial integration of Kenyan peasants". Development and Change, Vol. 8, No. 1, Jan. 1977, pp. 45-59.

Examines the social categories which are not in any meaningful sense self-contained communities, and their political roles as well as their effects on the capacity of the Kenyan state to service, control, or otherwise cope with their political presence.

GENERAL STUDIES

02-40 LANGDON, STEVEN. "The state and capitalism in Kenya". Review of African Political Economy, No. 8, Jan.-April 1977, pp. 90-98.

Focuses on state-MNC relationships as they affect the interaction of indigenous and international capital, drawing upon specific case materials.

02-41 LEVINE, R.A. "Wealth and power in Gusiiland". In P. Bohannan and G. Dalton (eds.), Markets in Africa. Northwestern University Press, Evanston, 1962, pp. 520-536.

02-42 LEYS, COLIN T. "Politics in Kenya: the development of peasant society". British Journal of Political Science, Vol. 1, No. 3, 1971.

02-43 ____. Underdevelopment in Kenya. Heinemann, London, 1975.

Tries to apply the underdevelopment theory to the Kenyan case. Starts by describing the meaning of the underdevelopment theory; proceeds to argue that the present state of underdevelopment in Kenya is due to external influence that started to affect Kenya as early as the middle of the 19th century.

02-44 ____. "Capital accumulation, class formation and dependency--the significance of the Kenyan case". In R. Miliband and J. Saville, The Socialist Register 1978. Merlin Press, London, 1978, pp. 241-266.

Clarifies some of the issues that have been posed in the theoretical debate about dependency and reconsiders the evidence from Kenya in the light of this clarification.

02-45 ____. "Kenya: what does dependency explain?". Review of African Political Economy, No. 17, Jan.-Apr. 1980, pp. 108-113.

A reply to Rafael Kaplinsky's critique of his book Underdevelopment in Kenya and his article "Capital accumulation, class formation and dependency: the significance of the Kenyan case". Kaplinsky's critique appears in the same issue of this journal.

02-46 LEYS, COLIN; BORGES, JANE; and GOLD, HYAM. "State capital in Kenya: a research note." Can J Afr Studs, Vol. 14, No. 2, Aug. 1980, pp. 307-317.

Discusses the direct participation of the state in the process of capitalist production in Kenya through such state enterprises as the Industrial and Commercial Development Corporation (lCDC), Development Finance Company of Kenya (DFCK), Industrial Development Bank (IDB), and other agencies.

02-47 McHENRY, DEAN E., Jr. "The underdevelopment theory: a case study from Tanzania". J Mod Afr Studs, Vol. 14, No. 4, Dec. 1976, pp. 621-636.

Assesses the validity of three propositions in the underdevelopment theory using data from the "dargaa" industry in Tanzania. Finds discrepancy between the propositions and the data.

02-48 MAMDANI, M. Politics and class formation in Uganda. Heinemann, London, 1976, 339pp.

Explains the politics of Uganda in the period between independence (1962) and the Asian expulsion of 1972.

02-49 MBILINGI, M.J. "The transition to capitalism in rural Tanzania". ERB Paper 74.7, University of Dar-es-Salaam, 1974.

02-50 MOHIDDIN, AHMED. "Reflections on Socialist Tanzania". EAJ, Vol. 9, No. 11, Nov. 1972.

02-51 ___. African socialism in two countries. Croom Helm, London, 1980, 208pp.

Argues that, after independence, Kenya proclaimed socialism while practising capitalism. The encouragement of an emergent African bourgeoisie has produced rapid growth in Kenya, but at the cost of heavy dependence on continuing foreign investment and a satellite relationship with richer powers. In contrast, Tanzania made a substantive break with the colonial pattern and accepted the slow rate of economic growth that self-reliance entails. The key policy documents examined are the Kenyan Sessional Paper No. 10 of 1965 and the Arusha Declaration.

02-52 MUSOKE, ISSA KABOKA. Imperialism, social structure and class struggles in Tanzania: an analysis of labour processes in a dependent economy. Ph.D. dissertation, Michigan State University, 1978, 487pp.

DAI, Vol. 39, p. 4530A.

02-53 MWANSASU, B., and CRANFORD, P. Towards socialism in Tanzania. University of Toronto Press, Toronto.

02-54 MWANZI, H.A. "The roots of underdevelopment in Kenya". Historical Association of Kenya, 1978, 10pp.

Argues that underdevelopment in Kenya is externally created with its roots to be found in Europe. Opposed to the idea that underdevelopment was locally generated.

02-55 NELLIS, JOHN R. A theory of ideology: the Tanzanian example.

Oxford University Press, Nairobi, 1972, 217pp.
A fundamental assumption of this work is that by the manipulation of the wealth, production, and distribution mechanisms a government can, to a certain extent, induce either behaviour change or the maintenance of existing behaviour patterns. Develops a model where all actors are assumed to be rational economic maximizers, only the material appeal is powerful and only the economic appeal is capable of inducing behaviour alteration. Applies the model to Tanzania.

02-56 N'GAN'GA, MUKARU D. "Differentiation of the peasantry and the development of capitalism in the central province of Kenya: 1880-1970". Kenyatta University College Department of History Staff Seminar, Nairobi, Nov. 1977, 18pp.
Argues that various factors were at work in the Kikuyu pre-colonial society which facilitated the process of individual accumulation and differentiation while at the same time hindering members of the society from being excluded from the means of production.

02-57 ___. "What is happening to the Kenyan peasantry". Department of History Staff Seminar Paper, University of Nairobi, Oct. 1978, 16pp.
Contends that accumulation leading to social differentiation was not a result of the implantation of colonialism in Kenya, but rather it took place through the agency of the peasant-bourgeoisie who benefited mainly through the intervention of international capital.

02-58 NJONJO, A.L. "The Kenyan peasantry: a re-assessment". Department of Government Staff Seminar Paper, University of Nairobi, Feb. 1979.
Shows that neither the extensive entry of the peasantry into the commodity frontier nor its participation in the land frontier has led to the survival of the peasantry. Rather, in both instances the apparent maintenance of the peasantry on the land has been shown to be only the specific form taken by the development of capitalism in Kenya.

02-59 NYERERE, J. Man and development. Oxford University Press, London, 1974.
A selection of speeches and writings made by Julius Nyerere re-affirming the need to recognize in action the fundamental unity and quality of all human beings regardless of colour, race, religion, or sex.

02-60 O'KEEFE, P. Gakarara: a study in the development of undevelopment. Ph.D. dissertation, University of London, 1978, 426pp.

02-61 OXALL, I.; BARNETT, T.; and BOOTH, D. (eds.). Beyond the sociology of development: economy and society in Latin America and Africa. Routledge and Kegan Paul, London, 1975, 295pp.
Includes John Weeks, "Imbalance between the centre and periphery and the 'employment crisis' in Kenya", and R. Feldman, "Rural social differentiation and political goals in Tanzania".

02-62 PINYCWA-GINGERA, A.G.G. "Some aspects of the politics of resource allocation in northern Uganda before independence". EA USSC Conference, Nairobi, Dec. 1969.
Examines the factors other than economic that influenced the allocation of public offices and educational opportunities in northern Uganda during the pre-independence period.

02-63 PRATT, R. CRANFORD. The critical phase in Tanzania 1945-1968: Nyerere and the emergence of a socialist strategy. Cambridge University Press, Cambridge, 1976, 309pp.
Inquires into the political strategies of both the colonial and the independent governments of Tanzania and discusses ideas on shaping of political institutions to meet government requirements and achieve long-term development goals.

02-64 PREWITT, KENNETH (ed.). Education and political values: an East African case study. East African Publishing House, Nairobi, 1971, 249pp.
Essays on how various educational experiences in the three East African countries influence political values and citizenship behaviour. Examines what citizenship behaviours are produced by educational practices inherited from colonial times.

02-65 RAIKES, PHILIP. "Rural differentiation and class formation in Tanzania". Journal of Peasant Studies, Vol. 5, No. 3, April 1978, pp. 285-325.
Relates various specific processes of differentiation of rural Tanzania to the overall emergence of classes within the Tanzania social formation and to Tanzania incorporation within the international capitalist system.

02-66 ROSENBERG, DAVID. "Some myths on the African working class: the construction of social science theory and the political function". IDS working P 294, Dec. 1976, 27pp.
The paper talks about two issues: migrant labour and labour aristocracy. The author argues that migration is cuased not only by economic factors but also by social and political factors, using Uganda as an example. As for

GENERAL STUDIES

labour aristocracy, Rhodesia and South Africa are taken as case studies.

02-67 RYAN, SELWYN D. "Economic nationalism and socialism in Uganda". Journal of Commonwealth Political Studies, Vol. 11, No. 2, July 1973, pp. 140-158.
Discusses Uganda's post-independence political economy strategies and possible future ones.

02-68 RYAN, T.C.I. "A rejoinder to Dr. Clayton's article on the alien enclave". EAER, Vol. 10, No. 1, 1963, pp. 43-46.

02-69 SAMOFF, JOEL, and SAMOFF, RACHEL. "The local politics of underdevelopment". Afr Rev, Vol. 6, No. 1, 1976, pp. 69-97.
Argues that while impressive strides have been made toward the implementation of the economic components of a self-reliance development strategy in Tanzania, the restructuring of the political order that is required has received less attention and has been less successful.

02-70 SAMOFF, JOEL. "Underdevelopment and its grassroots in Africa". Can J Afr Studs, Vol. 14, No. 1, 1980, pp. 5-36.
Examines underdevelopment of Africa from a distinctly local perspective and argues that there is no disjunction between studies of underdevelopment and studies of local politics. There are local studies from Muranga, Kilimanjaro, and Kigoma regions to show how the process of underdevelopment occurs and how it looks to those subjected to it.

02-71 SAUL, JOHN S. The state and revolution in eastern Africa. Monthly Review Press, New York, 1979.
Discusses the post-colonial experiences of Kenya, Uganda, Tanzania, and Mozambique and compares the levels of external control and internal inequality.

02-72 SENDER, JOHN. "Some preliminary notes of the political economy of rural development in Tanzania, based on a case study in the western Usambaras". ERB Paper 74.5, 1974.

02-73 SHIVJI, ISSA G. Class struggles in Tanzania. Monthly Review Press, New York; Heinemann, London; 1975, 182pp.
Gives an outline sketch of the class struggles in Tanzania since independence, indicating the course of these struggles. Briefly discusses the concept of class and the theory of class struggles before applying them concretely to the Tanzanian situation. Argues that the fact that Tanzania's economy continues to be part of the international capitalist system is reflected in its external structures and domestic formations.

02-74 STICHTER, S. "The formation of a working class in Kenya". In R. Sandbrook and R. Cohen (eds.), The development of an African working class. Longman, London, 1975, pp. 21-49.

02-75 STOCKTON, R.R. (ed.). "Local leadership in Kenya". Rural Africana, Vol. 3, 1979.

02-76 SWAINSON, NICOLA. "The role of the state in Kenya's post-war industrialization". IDS Working P 275, Sept. 1976, 82pp.

Evaluates the nature of industrial growth in Kenya in the context of worldwide concentration of capital after the Second World War. Examines the activist role of the post-war colonial state in supporting the participation of industrial capital in colonial enterprises.

02-77 ___. "State and economy in post-colonial Kenya, 1963-1978". Can J Afr Studs, Vol. 12, No. 3, 1978, pp. 357-381.

Examines some aspects of capitalist development in post-colonial Kenya between 1963-1978. Shows how the state has tried to encourage private accumulation of capital and the instruments and policies it has pursued. There is a case study of the tea industry.

02-78 ___. The development of corporate capitalism in Kenya 1918-1977. Heinemann, London, 1980, 371pp.

02-79 SZENTES, TAMAS. "Socioeconomic effects of two patterns of foreign capital investments, with special reference to East Africa". In P.C.W. Gutkind and I. Wallerstein (eds.), The economy of contemporary Africa. SAGE, Beverly Hills, London, 1976, pp. 261-290.

Discusses the pattern of foreign investment in developing countries with some examples from Tanzania and Kenya. Suggests that the international division of labour is becoming one between centres of scientific and technological progress and the periphery of countries that rely on regular imports of such technical achievements and scientific results. This pattern may result in a wider gap between centre and periphery than heretofore. Suggests greater reliance on loan rather than direct foreign investment capital, but a structural transformation of the rural economy is necessary if dependence is really to be decreased.

02-80 TAMARKIN, M. "The roots of political stability in Kenya". African Affairs, Vol. 77, No. 308, July 1978, pp. 297-320.

Examines the source of Kenya's political stability during the Kenyatta era. Concluded that the stability did not rest on Kenyatta's personality but on a strong state apparatus and a solid social basis.

GENERAL STUDIES

02-81 THOMAS, CLIVE Y. Dependence and transformation; the economics of the transition to socialism. Monthly Review Press, New York, 1974, 327pp.
Analyses certain economic aspects of dependence and underdevelopment in order to indicate how these factors interact in societies struggling to develop their productive forces during the "transition to socialism". It attempts to develop an economic strategy to cope with the problems encountered during the process of transforming the mode of production. Draws heavily on the Tanzanian experience.

02-82 VAN ZWANENBERG, R.M.A. "The European economy in Kenya 1919-1939: an example of primitive capital formation". IDS Staff P 46, 1969.
Tries to show how capital was accumulated and discusses the role of financial institutions in giving credit.

02-83 ___. "Anti-slavery, the ideology of 19th century imperialism in East Africa". Historical Association of Kenya, 1972, 33pp.
Concerned with relating anti-slavery to the imperial development of the 19th century. Gives a brief account of Britain's overseas economic expansion and the ideas which supported these movements.

02-84 VON FREYHOLD, MICHAELA. "The post-colonial state". Review of African Political Economy, No. 8, 1977, pp. 75-89.
Using the Tanzanian state as an illustration, the paper argues that to analyse the post-colonial state it is necessary to know not only generally which classes influence it, but the effect these classes have on the state and society and the relative position of each.

02-85 WACHTEL, ELANOR. "The urban image: stereotpyes of urban life in Kenya". African Urban Notes, Series B., Vol. 1, No. 3, 1975, pp. 77-92.
Shows the importance of the interplay of image and social reality in urban development in Kenya. The main body of the paper discusses one significant source of urban stereotypes --contemporary Kenyan fiction and especially the Kenyan urban novel.

02-86 WAWERU, E.M. "Captial accumulation and alienation at the shop-floor level: the Kenyan situation". Journal of Eastern African Research and Development, Vol. 9, No. 2, 1979, pp. 102-112.
Looks into alienation as defined by Karl Marx and its manifestations in Kenya. Also examines Kenya's capital accumulation strategy and its implications for alienation.

02-87 WOLFF, R.D. The economics of colonialism: Britain and Kenya, 1870-1930. Yale University Press, New Haven, 1974, 218pp.
Shows that the British colonial development strategy made economic sense, did operate, and caused transformations in Kenya. Focuses on the total reorganization of the Kenyan economy that British policy makers carried out.

03--Bibliographies and research programmes

03-1 ALLEN, CHRIS. "A bibliographical guide to the study of the political economy of Africa". In P.C.W. Gutkind and I. Wallerstein (eds.), The political economy of contemporary Africa. SAGE Publications, Beverly Hills, London, 1976, pp. 291-313.
A review of writing on underdevelopment by those with a radical political commitment, and includes a twelve-page bibliography that contains some items published as recently as 1975.

03-2 BOALT, C., and MYERS, D. Kenya. Vol. 2 of Bibliography on human settlements (draft). University of Lund, Lund, Sweden, 1980.
For volume on eastern Africa, see M. Curutchet. Final version to be ready in 1981. Vols. 3-4 concern Mozambique and Zambia.

03-3 COLLINSON, R.L. Uganda. Clio Press, Santa Barbara, California, ca. 1980.
An item in the World Bibliographical Series.

03-4 CURUTCHET, MIRINA. Developing countries with emphasis on Eastern Africa. Vol. 1 of Bibliography on human settlements (draft). University of Lund, Lund, Sweden, 1980.
For volume on Kenya, see C. Boalt and D. Myers.

03-5 DARCH, COLIN. "Russian writings on Tanganyika, Zanzibar and Tanzania: a guide to the published materials". BRALUP, University of Dar-es-Salaam, 1976, 68pp.
Entries in twenty classifications with annotations.

03-6 DORLING, M.J. (ed.). "Contemporary agricultural economics research in Kenya: future needs". Department of Agricultural Economics, University of Nairobi, 1979?, 94pp.
A collection of 13 papers from a seminar in June 1977. Papers discuss current agricultural economics research activities and future research needs and priorities.

03-7 EAST AFRICAN STATISTICAL DEPARTMENT. "A bibliography of

GENERAL STUDIES

articles published in the Economic and Statistical Review since December 1961". Econ Stat Rev, No. 58, March 1976, 148pp.
Lists titles, authors, issue number, and date of publication, and includes those articles dealing with economic matters of East African significance.

03-8 GRAY, B.A. Uganda: subject guide to official publications. U.S. Library of Congress, Washington D.C., 1977, 271pp.
Coverage of official documents from 1893 to 1974.

03-9 GUTKIND, P.C.W. "Bibliography on unemployment". Manpower and Unemployment Research in Africa, Vol. 8, No. 1, April 1975, pp. 67-83.
An outline of books and journal articles on unemployment in Africa in general, with some East Africa coverage.

03-10 HOWELL, JOHN BRUCE. East African Community: subject guide to official publications. U.S. Library of Congress, Washington, D.C., 1976, 272pp.
Subject guide to official publications of the East African Community and its predecessors for the period 1926 to 1974. Subject categories include commerce and trade, economics and finance.

03-11 ___. Tanganyika African National Union: a guide to publications by and about TANU. U.S. Library of Congress, Maktaba Afrikana Series, Washington, D.C., 1976, 52pp.
Contains references to official documents, books, articles, and dissertations.

03-12 ___. Kenya: subject guide to official publications. U.S. Library of Congress, Washington, D.C., 1978, 423pp.
A subject guide to official publications of Kenya for the period 1886 to 1975. Includes citations to official documents of the Republic of Kenya (1963-1975), the Kenya Colony and Protectorate (1920-1963), East Africa Protectorate (1895-1920), Great Britain (1886-1975), and the East African Community and its predecessors (1926-1975). Includes economics publications on the East African economies and Kenya in particular.

03-13 KILLICK, TONY. The economies of East Africa. G.K. Hall, Boston, 1976, 150pp.
Annotated bibliography covering English-language materials on all aspects of the economies of Kenya, Tanzania, and Uganda. Includes approximately 1,000 items, and includes only a few items published later than 1974.

03-14 ___. "Past and future research on the East African economies". EAER, Vol. 8, No. 1, June 1976, pp. 51-61.
Based upon Killick's annotated bibliography The economies of East Africa for the three East African Community countries. Comments on the coverage of the project, surveys the literature, and makes suggestions about future research strategies.

03-15 ___. "Trends in development economics and their relevance to Africa". J Mod Afr Studs, Vol. 18, No. 3, Sept. 1980, pp. 367-386.
Argues that research into the special problems of small, open, early-stage developing countries that are not rich in natural resources would be highly relevant to the circumstances of much of the African continent.

03-16 KOCHER, J.E., and FLEISCHER, B. "A bibliography on rural development in Tanzania". Rural Development Paper No. 3, Michigan State University, East Lansing, 1979.
Earlier version appeared as Harvard Institute for International Development Discussion Paper No. 17, 1977.

03-17 KRUMMES, DANIEL C. Transportation in East Africa: a bibliography. Vance Bibliographies, Monticello, Illinois, 1980, 27pp.

03-18 LIVINGSTONE, IAN. "The relationship between research and planning in development." The Uganda Economic Journal, Vol. 1, No. 1, Dec. 1971, pp. 71-93.
A discussion of the organizational structure of research institutes in East Africa. Calls for increased exchange of ideas between the three East African countries in respect of university research organization.

03-19 LULA, N.L. "Guide to articles in East African agricultural and forestry journal". Ministry of Agriculture Library, Dar es Salaam, 1976, 79pp.

03-20 MOORE, M.; CONNELL, J.; and LAMBERT, C.M. (eds.). Village studies data analysis and bibliography. Vol. 2. Institute of Development Studies, University of Sussex, Brighton, 1978.
Contains approximately seven bibliographic items for Kenya, eleven for Uganda, and forty for Tanzania. Items generally published between 1960 and 1972.

03-21 MUNGEAM, G.H. Kenya: select historical documents 1884-1923. East African Publishing House, Nairobi, 1980, 610pp.

03-22 MUREITHI, L.P. "Writings on the economy of Kenya". In Ole

GENERAL STUDIES

Nørgaard (ed.), Kenya in the social sciences: an annotated bibliography. Kenya Literature Bureau, Nairobi, 1980, pp. 365-369.

03-23 NILSEN, ODD. A bibliography of the mineral resources of Tanzania. Scandanavian Institute of African Studies, Uppsala, 1980, 92pp.

03-24 NØRGAARD, OLE. Kenya in the social sciences: an annotated bibliography. Kenya Literature Bureau, Nairobi, 1980.
Intends to serve as a practical tool to individuals interested in Kenya and problems of development. Includes L.P. Mureithi, "Writings on the economy of Kenya".

03-25 NZIOKI, MUTUKU. "Bibliography of Kenya agriculture 1979-80". Egerton College Agricultural Bulletin, Vol. 4, No. 2, Sept. 1980, pp. 71-79.

03-26 OKIDI, C. ODIDI. "Conservation and development of coastal and off-shore resources in Eastern Africa: agenda for research". IDS Working P 368, June 1976, 31pp.
Outlines national and international interests at stake in the negotiations at the third U.N. law of the sea conference and relates them to Kenya and its neighbours.

03-27 SCHEVEN, YVETTE. Bibliographies for African studies 1976-1979. African Studies Association, Crossroads Press, Waltham, Massachusetts, 1980, 142pp.

03-28 SIMS, MICHAEL. United States doctoral dissertations in third world studies 1869-1978. Crossroads Press, Waltham, Massachusetts, 1980, 435pp.

03-29 SMITH, J.G. "Regional economic cooperation and integration in Africa: some bibliographical references". Centre for Developing-Area Studies, McGill University, Montreal, 1973, 22pp.

1--ECONOMIC DEVELOPMENT, PLANNING, AND STABILIZATION

10--Growth and development: measurement and experiences

10-1 ALIBARUHO, GEORGE. "Production structure and income generation in Uganda: pathfinder of the current negative growth rate in the economy". IDS Working P 188, n.d. (ca. Aug. 1974), 20pp.
Provides background information necessary for an analysis of the negative growth of the economy in the fiscal year 1973/74.

10-2 ASETO, OYUGI. "Captial growth and development policy: the Kenyan experience." IDS Working P 311, June 1977, 18pp.
Concludes that capital investment is a necessary but not sufficient condition for the growth of the economy and that capital investment has little or no correlation with growth in some sectors.

10-3 ___. "The measurement of growth rates and trends in Kenya, 1964-1974". IDS Working P 312, June 1977, 9pp.
Discusses and compares the various methods available for measuring economic growth and applies them to the Kenyan economy in 1964-1974.

10-4 BLUE, R.N., and WEAVER, J.H. "A critical assessment of the Tanzanian model of development". Reprint No. 30, Agricultural Development Council, New York, 1977.

10-5 CAMPBELL, DAVID J. "Development and decline: resources, land-use and population growth in Kajiado District". IDS Working P 352, March 1979, 24pp.
Examines the nature of the relationship between the increasing subsistence demands of the growing population of Kajiado District and the capacity of the environment to support these demands.

10-6 COLLIER, P., and LAL, D. Poverty and growth in Kenya. World Bank Working Paper No. 389, Washington, D.C., 1980, 178pp.
An account of the trends in poverty, income distribution, and growth in Kenya between 1963 and about 1977. Gives some strategies for alleviating rural poverty.

10-7 GREEN, REGINALD H. "Annex: redistribution with growth: Tanzania". In Hollis Chenery et al., Redistribution with Growth. Oxford University Press, London, 1974, pp. 268-273.
Discusses Tanzanian government instruments of redistribution and central government objectives in economic growth. Problems encountered in trying to achieve government objectives are analysed.

10-8 IKIARA, G.K. Structural changes in the Kenyan economy 1953-1973. M.A. thesis, University of Nairobi, 1977.

10-9 ___. "Zimbabwe economic path: lessons from the Kenyan experience". Zimbabwe Economic Symposium, Harare, Sept. 1980, 87pp.
A study of the Kenyan development experience with a view to defining a viable economic policy for Zimbabwe. Includes a thorough discussion of the Kenya government participation in the development process.

GENERAL STUDIES

10-10 ___, and KILLICK, T. "Structural changes in the Kenyan economy". In T. Killick (ed.), Papers on the Kenyan economy. Heinemann, London, 1981.

10-11 INSTITUTE FOR DEVELOPMENT RESEARCH. Dualism and rural development in East Africa. Copenhagen, 1973, 209pp.
Report of a seminar, the keynote paper of which argues that theories and models of dualism may have great descriptive value but lack explanatory power.

10-12 INTERNATIONAL LABOUR OFFICE. Report to the government of Tanzania on the past, present and future incomes policy in Tanzania. Geneva, 1975.

10-13 KILLICK, TONY. "Application of science and technology to Kenya's development: an economist's view". Journal of Eastern African Research and Development, Vol. 9, No. 2, 1979.
Describes how economists view scientific and technological research and the ways in which it might fit into the overall development of Kenya's economy. Highlights the advantages Kenya and other developing nations have since such knowledge is already in stock for their utilization.

10-14 KUUYA, P.M. "Inflation: Tanzania's dilemma". Economic Research Bureau Paper 75.8, University of Dar-es-Salaam, 1975.

10-15 MORAWETZ, DAVID. "Economic lessons from some small socialist developing countries". World Development, Vol. 8, May-June 1980, pp. 337-369.
Examines economic performance of Burma, Cuba, Sri Lanka, and Tanzania with respect to per capita income growth, income distribution, unemployment, fulfilment of basic needs, self-reliance, and economic independence.

10-16 MUREITHI, L.P., and RUKWARO, G.K. (eds.). "Summary proceedings of a seminar on alternative patterns of development and lifestyles in Eastern Africa" (mimeographed). Society for International Development, Nairobi, 1979, 50pp.
Summary of SID conference held in Nairobi 10-13 July, 1979.

10-17 NYERERE, JULIUS K. "The Arusha declaration ten years after". International Development Review, Vol. 19, No. 1, 1977, pp. 2-7.

10-18 RWEGASIRA, DELPHIN. "Inflation and the structure of the

Tanzanian economy, the 1966-73 evidence". ERB Paper, 76.9, University of Dar-es-Salaam, 1976, 54pp.

Examines three issues of the structure of the economy significant to inflation: the agricultural sector; the capacity to import; and imported inflation. Concludes that there is a significant relationship between recent movements in prices and balance of payments and the structure of the economy, even though different factors assumed differing importance at different times.

10-19 ___. "Inflation and economic development: some lessons from the Tanzanian experience". Africa Development, Vol. 2, No. 3, 1977, pp. 29-49.

Argues that inflationary pressures could also arise from an unsatisfactory agricultural export performance which in many less developed countries is the medium and long-term determinant of national import capacity.

10-20 SHARMA, K.L. "Relative rates of growth of agricultural and non-agricultural sectors in Kenya". Kenyan Economic Association, Nairobi, 1979, 8pp.

An empirical study of the rates of growt of the economy during three development plans, 1964-1978 and provides projections for the period 1979-1983 based on that experience.

Argues that agriculture and industry are interdependent in the process of economic development. The growth of agriculture should be consistent with the demand for industry.

10-21 SHARPLEY, JENNIFER. Intersectoral capital flows and economic development: evidence from Kenya. Ph.D. dissertation, Northwestern University, 1976, 228pp.

Found evidence of a large net capital outflow from the agricultural sector between 1964 and 1972, an outflow which persistently increased in size throughout this period and represented a high proportion of total gross fixed capital formation in the economy.

10-22 ___. "Intersectoral capital flows: evidence from Kenya". Journal of Development Economics, Vol. 6, No. 4, Dec. 1979, pp. 557-571.

Argues that upon examining the composition of intersectoral commodity flows in Kenya, it was found that outflows of goods used for consumption and intermediate inputs by the non-agricultural sector increased at a faster rate than did agricultural exports.

10-23 SZENTES, TAMAS. "The second five year plan of Tanzania". Studies for Developing Countries, No. 46, Centre of

ECONOMIC DEVELOPMENT

Afro-Asian Research of the Hungarian Academy of Sciences, Budapest, 1970, 50pp.

11--General development strategies and policies

11-1 ANDERSON, M.B. Self reliant development: a comparison of the development strategies of Ghandi, Mao and Nyerere. Ph.D. dissertation, University of Colorado, 1978, 338pp.
DAI, Vol. 39, p. 6867.

11-2 ASAHINA, J., and NGAN, K.H. "ILO report on Kenyan employment, incomes and equality: a critique". York University, Toronto, 1974, 23pp.

11-3 BANUGIRE, F.R. "Uganda's development patterns--an historical and prospective analysis". SID Seminar on Patterns of Development and Lifestyles for Eastern Africa, Nairobi, July 1979, 60pp.
After stating some key elements of alternative development strategies, the paper examines the transition from colonial capitalism to post-independence tendencies toward greater state control of the economy and emphasis on social infrastructure, the socio-economic consequences of Amin's regime of repression, and the prospects for self-sustained and self-reliant economic development.

11-4 BARKAN, J.D., and OKUMU, J.J. (eds.). Politics and public policy in Kenya and Tanzania. Holt-Saunders Ltd., Praeger, New York, 1979, 297pp.
An examination of the Kenyan and Tanzanian experience which assesses each country's performance in different aspects of public policy. Illustrates both countries' approaches to urban and rural development, education, and foreign relations, including their potential for power and regional diplomacy.

11-5 BIBANGAMBAH, J.R. Contemporary problems and issues in rural development. Makerere Institute of Social Research, Kampala, 1978, 71pp.

11-6 CALLENDER, C.V. "Uganda's new government seeks recovery of economy with broad stabilization plan". IMF Survey, 3 March 1980, pp. 66-67.
Includes presentation of major economic indicators for Uganda since 1970, and balance of payments and government finance statistics for 1975-1979.

11-7 CLARK, EDMUND W. "Socialist development in an underdeveloped

country: the case of Tanzania". World Development, Vol. 3, No. 4, April 1975, pp. 223-228.
Comments on the socialist investment strategy adopted in Tanzania, particularly its emphasis on rural development.

11-8 ___. Socialist development and public investment in Tanzania, 1964-1973. University of Toronto Press, Toronto, 1978, 295pp.
Provides data on levels and articulation of ministerial and parastatal investment and attempts to relate party political goals and investment allocation decisions.

11-9 COLLINS, P.D. "The institutionalisation of basic needs for rural development". International Seminar on Basic Needs, Peshawar, 1979, 69pp.

11-10 DAMACHI, UKANDI G.; ROUTH, GUY; and TAHA, ABDEL-RAHMAN E. ALI (eds.). Development Paths in Africa and China. Macmillan, London; Westview, Boulder, 1976, 251pp.
Includes Guy Routh, "Development paths in Tanzania", and Frances Stewart, "Kenya: strategies for development".

11-11 EBANGIT, Z.O. The Chinese conception of economic development: its influence on development strategy in Tanzania. Ph.D. dissertation, University of Texas, Austin, 1977.

11-12 ECONOMIC COMMISSION FOR AFRICA. "Alternative patterns of development and lifestyles: the case of Tanzania". Economic Commission for Africa Seminar on Alternative Patterns of Development and Life Styles for the African Region, Addis Ababa, March 1979, 17pp.
Looks at Tanzania's institutional framework from independence to decentralization in 1972, and the policies and strategies from independence to the Arusha Declaration and after. Argues that Tanzania is seriously pursuing her declared policy of socialism and self-reliance.

11-13 FREEMAN, B. DONALD. "Development strategies in dual economies: a Kenyan example". African Studies Review, Vol. 18, No. 2, Sept. 1975, pp. 17-33.
Argues that government planning efforts aimed at generating change in the traditional sector should make conscious use of existing contacts between the traditional and modern sectors. Describes such an interaction complex for Kenya.

11-14 GAILE, GARY L. "Processes affecting the spatial pattern of rural-urban development in Kenya". African Studies Review, Vol. 19, No. 3, Dec. 1976, pp. 1-16.

Argues that urban-based spatial investment strategies will result in an exacerbated pattern of rural-urban development inequity. Calls for planners to weigh the efficiency of urban-based investments versus the inequity which results.

11-15 GHAI, DHARAM; GODFREY, MARTIN; and LISK, F. Planning for basic needs in Kenya. ILO, Geneva, 1979.

11-16 GHAI, DHARAM. "Basic needs: from words to action". International Labour Review, Vol. 119, No. 3, May-June 1980, pp. 367-379.

Proposes a simple methodology for the practical application of some of the ideas associated with a basic-needs approach. Argues that in most private-enterprise market economies there exist certain programmes and projects which display basic-needs characteristics but that they generally remain marginal to the central thrust of the development effort. Concludes that even though basic need activities represent a considerable advance over conventional programmes in terms of objectives, technology and organization, and in their impact on poverty, the very poorest groups sometimes remain beyond their reach.

11-17 GODFREY, MARTIN. "Prospects for a basic needs strategy: the case of Kenya". IDS Bulletin, Vol. 9, No. 4, June 1978, pp. 41-44.

Concludes that if the basic needs-redistribution option were chosen as a future strategy this would imply a programme similar to the unimplemented part of the ILO (1972) report.

11-18 GREEN, REGINALD H. "Redistribution with growth and/or transition to socialist development: some jottings on Tanzania 1961-74". IDS Bulletin, Vol. 7, No. 2, Aug. 1975, pp. 22-28.

Examines Tanzania's 1961-1974 political economic experience with exphasis on strategic themes, major changes, critical obstacles, and the pace of change. Considers the political aspect and the relevance of Tanzania's experiences to other economies.

11-19 ___. Toward socialism and self reliance: Tanzania's striving for sustained transition projected. Research Report No. 38, Scandinavian Institute of African Studies, Uppsala, 1977.

Argues that Tanzania's commitment to self-reliance does not mean a quest for autarchy or a refusal to import and adapt ideas.

11-20 ___. "Tanzanian political economy; goals, strategies and result". Institute for Development Studies, Sussex, n.d.

11-21 HARWITZ, M. "On Improving the lot of the poorest: economic plans in Kenya". African Studies Review, Vol. 21, No. 3, Dec. 1978, pp. 65-73.
Describes the dimensions of the problem of poverty in 1969 and deals with the economics of the World Bank and ILO/UNDP reports. Discusses the differences and the possible effects of both plans.

11-22 HYDEN, GORAN. "Policy-making for development: Tanzania in comparative perspective". EA USSC Conference, Kampala, Dec. 1974, 29pp.
Argues, with specific reference to Tanzania, that the key factor in the policy-making process is not planning but power, and that only by realizing this can one find models which will be of value to those who make and study policies.

11-23 INTERNATIONAL LABOUR OFFICE. Time for transition--a mid-term review of the Second United Nations Decade. Geneva, 1976.
Discusses the seriousness of the world unemployment problem. Attention is drawn to the report of ILO's inter-agency Mission to Kenya and the importance it laid on the informal sector.

11-24 ___. Towards self-reliance. Addis Ababa, 1978.

11-25 KILLICK, TONY. "Strengthening Kenya's development strategy: opportunities and constraints". EAER, Vol. 8, No. 2, Dec. 1976, pp. 1-33.
Critiques the strategy of "redistribution through growth" presented in the 1974-1978 development plan in order to identify ways in which the strategy and policies could be improved for the future. Argues that there are large political obstacles in the way of implementing a more effective strategy.

11-26 KONTER, J.H. "Economic imperatives for socialist development in the rural economy of the Nyakyusa (Tanzania)". Cultures et Development, Vol. 10, No. 3, 1978, pp. 409-431.

11-27 LEYS, COLIN. "Development strategy in Kenya since 1971". Can J Afr Studs, Vol. 13, Nos. 1-2, 1979, pp. 297-320.
Analyses development strategy in the 1970s in terms of the general character of Kenyan development: as an expression of the balance of class forces. Identifies the social forces which are purported to determine the real scope and effect of the official development policies.

11-28 LIVINGSTONE, IAN. "The non-economic factor in economic development". Conference on the teaching of economics in East

ECONOMIC DEVELOPMENT

Africa, Dar-es-Salaam, 1969, 16pp.
Argues that with existing resources and market opportunities, the less developed countries are capable of greatly increased outputs through increased supply of effort and "determination to develop".

11-29 MALIMA, KIGHOMA A. "Planning for self-reliance: Tanzania's third five-year plan." African Development, Vol. 4, No. 1, Jan.-March 1979, pp. 37-55.

11-30 MORAWETZ, D. "Economic lessons from some small socialist developing countries". World Development, Vol. 8, Nos. 5-6, 1980.

11-31 MOSLEY, PAUL. "Implicit models and policy recommendations: policy towards the 'informal sector' in Kenya". IDS Bulletin, Vol. 9, No. 3, Feb. 1978, pp. 3-10.
Uses report of the ILO employment mission to Kenya to show how a shift from using partial models of labour markets in favour of broader interdisciplinary models has implications for policies recommended.

11-32 MSEKWA, PIUS. "Self-reliance as a strategy for development; the meaning of self-reliance". ERB Paper 76.6, University of Dar-es-Salaam, 1976, 24pp.

11-33 MUKUI, JOHN K. Price controls in Kenya. M.A. thesis, University of Nairobi, 1978.

11-34 ___. "The impact of price controls on inflation and the distribution of real income in Kenya". IDS Seminar on Price and Marketing Controls in Kenya, University of Nairobi, March 1979, 31pp.
Gives background information to price controls, why the controls were introduced, and their coverage. Makes an attempt at empirical analysis of the effectiveness of the price controls, their impact on growth, distribution of income, and observance and evasion of controls by traders.

11-35 MUREITHI, L.P. "Some alternative development strategies in Africa: an overview". Proceedings of the African-American trade union symposium on employment. African-American Labour Centre, New York, 1978.

11-36 NURSEY-BRAY, P.F. "Tanzania: the development debate". African Affairs, Vol. 79, No. 314, Jan. 1980, pp. 55-78.
A commentary upon the debate over the limitations, success and potential of Tanzania's development strategy.

11-37 RICE, ROBERT C. "The Tanzania price control system: theory, practice and some possible improvements". In K.S. Kim, R.B. Mabele, and M.J. Schultheis (eds.), Papers on the political economy of Tanzania. Heinemann, Nairobi, 1979, pp. 95-110.

Analysis of the theory of the present price control system under the jurisdiction of the National Price Commission, and its successes and shortcomings. Deals with the determination of the prices of both imported and local goods. Initially appeared as ERB Paper 76.4.

11-38 ROUTH, GUY. "Development paths in Tanzania". In U. Damachi et al. (eds.), Development paths in Africa and China. Macmillan, London; Westview, Boulder, 1976, pp. 10-38.

Looks at the problems Tanzania inherited at independence, and how three problems are being solved by Tanzania's "socialist path". Stresses importance of dedication for determining results of development path.

11-39 SOGGA, G.E. The developmental consequences of the Arusha Declaration on the Tanzanian economy. Ph.D. dissertation, University of Pittsburgh, 1979, 204pp.

DAI, Vol. 40, p. 2794-A.

11-40 STEWART, FRANCES. "Kenya: strategies for development". In U. Damachi et al. (eds.), Development paths in Africa and China. Macmillan, London; Westview, Boulder, 1976, pp. 80-111.

That the strategies of development in Kenya are linked to the past development events and the current world economic system. That government represents those who have benefited during the past and therefore its strategies are bound to be biased in their favour.

11-41 STRAGE, HENRY. "Decentralisation for development: a study of Tanzania's experience". International Technical Cooperation Centre Review, Vol. 4, No. 2, Oct. 1975, pp. 52-60.

11-42 SURUMA, E. "The patterns of change in Uganda's economic structure". EA USSC Conference, Kampala, Dec. 1974, 15pp.

Suggests that the development of agricultural capital technology will come from the urban elite and the government, and that this will in turn lead to the industrialization of the country.

11-43 ___. An evaluation of international interaction as a source of change in economic structure with special emphasis on Uganda. Ph.D. dissertation, University of Connecticut, 1976.

ECONOMIC DEVELOPMENT

11-44 "Tanzania: decade of socialism". International Technical Cooperation Centre Review, Vol. 6, No. 2, April 1977, pp. 110-112.
Reviews Tanzania's achievements in the ten years since the Arusha Declaration. Covers a brief discussion of progress in industrialization, importance of agriculture and some required changes to save the country's faltering economy.

11-45 TSCHANNERL, GERHARD. "Periphery capitalist development--a case study of the Tanzanian economy". Utafiti, Vol. 1, No. 1, 1976, pp. 5-46.
Looks at Tanzania's shift in official policy toward socialism with the aim of eliminating monopoly capitalism. Argues that to develop a balanced economy with less dependence requires a break with the international capitalist system.

11-46 UGANDA MINISTRY OF INFORMATION AND BROADCASTING. Uganda's economic war. Government Printer, Kampala, Jan. 1975, 40pp.
Designed and illustrated for a wide readership, provides background information, describes the economic war and its consequences. Three speeches by President Amin are reproduced as appendices.

11-47 WORLD BANK. Kenya: into the second decade. Johns Hopkins Press, Baltimore, 1975, 533pp.
A World Bank country economic report. Proposes increased emphasis on agriculture and other domestic resource-based industries and calls for a change in key factor prices. Presents a macro-economic model of the economy and surveys such areas as fiscal policy, planning, aid, and agriculture.

12--Development planning and implementation

12-1 ASETO, OYUGI. "The application of the concept of comprehensive and integrated regional planning to the development of Lake Victoria basin". IDS Working P 338, March 1979, 35pp.
Stresses that the planning and development authority charged with the responsibility should be autonomous and independent. There is also need for detailed information of the existing natural and human resources. The author cautions against the weaknesses of a regional development plan, for example, externalities, political problems, etc. He concludes that the government should be fully involved in the scheme.

12-2 BAVU, IMMANUEL KILIMA. Tanzanian experience of self-reliance: a possibility for the development of the poor societies. Ph.D. dissertation, University of Southern California, 1975.

12-3 BELSHAW, D.G.R. "Decentralised planning and poverty-focused rural development: intra-regional planning in Tanzania". In K.S. Kim, R.B. Mabele, and M.J. Schultheis (eds.), Papers on the political economy of Tanzania. Heinemann, Nairobi, 1979, pp. 47-64.

Centres on inter-regional differences in performance and planning tasks and alternative experiences in regional planning methodologies in Tanzania. Two-stage integrated regional planning methodology and the integrated rural development procedures are evaluated.

12-4 BIRGEGARD, LARS-ERIK. The project selection process in developing countries. Economic Research Institute, Stockholm School of Economics, Stockholm, 1975, 307pp.

A study of the public investment project selection process based on 14 agricultural project studies in Kenya plus supplementary material from Zambia and Tanzania. Shows these processes to be highly simplified with little search for, or comparison between, alternatives.

12-5 COLLINS, P.D. "Decentralisation and local administration for development in Tanzania". Institute of Development Studies Discussion Paper 94, University of Sussex, Brighton.

12-6 COULSON, A.C. "The inadequacy of project appraisal--and an outline alternative method for choosing projects". EA USSC Conference, Kampala, 1974, 15pp.

Proposes social-cost benefit analysis as a better alternative to profitability analysis in project appraisal. Argues that the latter alternative allows the project analyst to include benefits that cannot be quantified.

12-7 CURRY, STEVE. "Project appraisal accounting prices and underdevelopment". ERB Paper 78.1, University of Dar-es-Salaam, 1979.

12-8 GREEN, R.H. "Relevance, efficiency, romanticism and confusion in Tanzania planning and management". Afr Rev, Vol. 5, No. 2, 1975, pp. 209-234.

Examines the relevance and efficiency of planning and development management in the Tanzanian economy. Examines their success, weakness, and failures.

12-9 HYDEN, GORAN. "'We must run while others walk': policy-making for socialist development in the Tanzania-type of polities". ERB Paper 75.1, Feb. 1975, 48pp.

Reviews the literature on policy-making and planning with specific focus on Tanzania. Argues that the literature has

ECONOMIC DEVELOPMENT

shifted from concern with policy or plan formulation to the issues of policy or plan execution.

12-10 KABWEGYERE, T.B. "Time and planned change". IDS Working P 155, April 1974, 21pp.
Concludes that the planning process needs to be re-examined so as to incorporate time as a scarce resource.

12-11 KILLICK, TONY. "A political-economy explanation of the failure of development planning". EA USCC Conference, Kampala, Dec. 1974.
Focuses more narrowly on "comprehensive development planning", as practiced in low-income countries. Believes that development planning in practice has achieved few of the benefits that its advocates expected from it.

12-12 ___. "'By their fruits ye shall know them': the fourth development plan". In Tony Killick (ed.), Papers on the Kenyan economy. Heinemann, London, 1981.
Discusses arguments in favour of development planning and problems of implementation, and then provides an overall assessment of Kenya's 1979-1983 development plan.

12-13 KINYUA, J.K. Plan implementation in Kenya 1974-78. M.A. thesis, University of Nairobi, 1978.

12-14 KILLICK, T., and KINYUA, J.K. "On implementing development plans". ODI Review, 1980-1981, pp. 30-47.

12-15 LITTLE, I.M.D., and SCOTT, M.FG. (eds.). Using shadow prices. Heinemann, London, 1976, 254pp.
Includes G.A. Hughes, "Low income housing: a Kenyan case study", D.M.G. Newbery, "The social value of private investment in Kenya".

12-16 MALIMA, KIGHOMA A. "Planning for self-reliance: Tanzania's third five year development plan". ERB Paper, University of Dar-es-Salaam, 1978, 31pp.

12-17 MASAKHALIA, Y.F.O. "Development planning in Kenya in the post-independence period". Econ Bull Afr, Vol. 12, No. 1, 1976, pp. 19-44.
Discusses development planning as the government's major tool for initiating and promoting economic and social progress. Looks at development objectives subject to a number of limiting constraints. Concludes that while development in the post-independence period has been satisfactory and the longer-term prospects look bright, the present economic situation certainly causes concern.

12-18 MUREITHI, L.P. "Economic development, planning and employment in English-speaking East and West Africa". International education materials exchange, International Institute for Labour Studies, Geneva, 1978.

12-19 PAPANDREOU, ANDREAS G., and ZOHAR, URI. The impact approach to project selection, Vol. 2. Praeger, New York, 1974, 187pp.
Presents a new methodology of project evaluation illustrated by four Kenyan case studies including cashew nut processing, fibreboard production, a range development project in the north east, and the Mumias sugar scheme.

12-20 REITHAUG , I.; MIRITI, A.M.; and ANDREOU, P. "Planning co-operative development in Kenya: a formalized and integrated approach to sector planning". J Admin Overseas, Vol. 17, No. 2, April 1978, pp. 102-117.
Discusses cooperative potentials and possibilities. Determines cooperative priorities and the strategy toward the achievement of stated targets given limited resources. Provides the basis for an assessment of continued foreign assistance to the co-operative sector. Concludes that planners should prepare a long-range plan for the cooperative sector and to institute the development planning function as an integrated and basic part of an information system for the co-ordination, planning, and control of the cooperative sector. Also appears as chapter in I. Reithaug, A.M. Miriti, and P. Andreou, Cooperative institutions and economic development; some lessons from advanced and developing countries, Nairobi, East African Literature Bureau, 1977, pp. 300-328.

12-21 RWEYEMAMU, A.H. Planning in Tanzania; background to decentralisation. East African Literature Bureau, Nairobi, 1974, 131pp.
Argues that the decision to decentralize administration has been interpreted as a measure of giving "more power to the people". Suggests strongly that decentralization in Tanzania is not a mechanism for "decongesting" the work load at the centre but a means of maximizing participation.

12-22 RWEYEMAMU, J.F., et al. (eds.). Towards socialist planning. Tanzania Publishing House, Dar es Salaam, 1972, 199pp.
Includes J.S. Saul, "Planning for socialism in Tanzania: the socio-political context"; J.F. Rweyemamu, "Planning, socialism and industrialization: the economic challenge"; J. Loxley, "Financial planning and control in Tanzania"; P.C. Packard, "Management and control of parastatal organisations"; L.R. Cliffe, "Planning rural development"; W.L. Luttrell, "Location planning and regional development in

Tanzania"; M. Segall, "The politics of health in Tanzania"; M.A. Bienefeld, "Planning people". Many of these papers also appear in special issue of Development and Change, Vol. 3, No. 3, 1971-1972, edited by M.R. Doornbos et al.

12-23 RWEYEMAMU, J.F. "Development planning in the United Republic of Tanzania". Econ Bull Afr, Vol. 12, No. 1, 1976, pp. 45-65.

Gives a brief history of planning in the United Republic of Tanzania. Discusses policies and strategies for solving problems of mass poverty and unemployment. Concludes that unlike many under-developed countries, Tanzania does not face serious under-employment in the rural sector. Adds that it is too early to review the effectiveness of the development policies and strategies.

12-24 SCOTT, M.FG.; MACARTHUR, J.D.; and NEWBERRY, D.M.G. Project appraisal in practice. Heinemann, London, 1976, 548pp.

Shows how a set of accounting prices was estimated for Kenya, evaluates land settlements in Kenya, and appraises the economic feasibility of intensive cattle feeding.

12-25 SURUMA, E. "The functional dependence of planned growth and economic control". EA USSC Conference, Kampala, 1974, 16pp.

Hypothesizes that plan implementation is the counterpart of the dynamics of a free market economy, such as that approximated by the United States and other Western countries. Also hypothesizes that the degree of success in plan implementation depends on controllable and uncontrollable factors, such that the higher the ratio of controlled to uncontrolled factors, the more completely plans will be fulfilled. Statistics from Kenya, Uganda and Tanzania are included in the survey.

12-26 SZENTES, TAMAS. "Economic policy and implementation problems in Tanzania". Studies for Developing Countries No. 40, Centre of Afro-Asian Research of the Hungarian Academy of Sciences, Budapest, 1970, 18pp.

12-27 THOMAS, I.D. "Planning techniques: physical indicators in Tanzania". IDS Bulletin, Vol. 8, No. 1, 1976, pp. 30-35.

Presents some indices developed in research and planning work in Tanzania with reference to the provision and location of health facilities in Iringa region.

12-28 VAN DOORNE, HANS. "Development planning and participation from below". IDS Seminar on alternative patterns of development and lifestyles, Nairobi, 1979, 30pp.

Investigates the effectiveness of the activities of extension workers in Kenya and suggests alternative measures to reach the rural farmers.

13--Macro-economic models

13-1 ASETO, OYUGI. "On protecting Kenya's future: a World Bank report". Journal of Eastern African Research and Development, Vol. 9, No. 1, 1979, pp. 1-13.
Assesses the usefulness of the Harrod-Domar growth model for development planning in Kenya.

13-2 COHEN, NEAL PETER. Structural change in a low-income country: an econometric approach using the Republic of Kenya. Ph.D. dissertation, University of Wisconsin, 1974, 121pp.
Creates a macro-economic model of Kenya which allows for and analyzes the extent and nature of structural change and assists in the analysis of the second Kenya economic development plan.

13-3 HODD, MIKE. "A design for an econometric model of the Kenyan economy". IDS Working P 171, July 1974, 19pp.
Describes the structure, equations, and data sources for a medium-sized econometric model of the Kenyan economy to be estimated from annual data for the period 1947-1972.

13-4 ____. "Aggregate supply in Kenya: production functions for four major sectors". IDS Working P 173, July 1974, 13pp.
Reports production functions for Kenya's traditional agriculture, industry, and service sectors, estimated from annual time series data over the period 1954 to 1972.

13-5 KING, J.R. "Simulating Kenya's balance of payments". IDS Working P 169, June 1974, 25pp.
A quarterly simulation model of Kenya's monetary system and balance of payments which is found to simulate changes in Kenya's foreign exchange reserves quite closely.

13-6 MAITHA, J.K. "Time-series production functions and technological progress in Kenyan industry". IDS Working P 217, n.d. (ca. May 1975), 7pp.
Estimates elasticity of substitution between capital and labour in eight main sectors of the Kenyan economy using the constant elasticity of substitution (CES) production functions.

13-7 PATEL, CHANDRA, K.R. An econometric study of the Ugandan economy: 1954-1967. Ph.D. dissertation, New York University, 1973.

ECONOMIC DEVELOPMENT

13-8 SEIDMAN, ANN W. "A note on the use of mathematical models in empirical research in East Africa". EA USSC Conference, Nairobi, Dec. 1969.
Tries to discredit the use of conventional mathematical models to analyse and/or predict the consequences of specific measures designed to contribute to reallocation of resources in the East African circumstances.

13-9 SLATER, C.S., and WALSHAM, G. "A systems simulation model of the Kenyan economy". Omega: International Journal of Management Science, Vol. 3, No. 5, 1975, pp. 557-67.
The model, while relatively primitive in monetary features, offers novel capacities to deal with income distribution and inflation policy problems. The 1974-1978 development plan is examined as well as some simulation analyses of unemployment problems. Also appeared as IDS Working P 174, Nairobi, July 1974.

13-10 SLATER, C.S.; WALSHAM, G.; and SHAH, M.M. A simulation of the Kenyan economy: a computerised systems simulation of a developing African economy, 1970 through 1978. Westview Press, Boulder, 1977, 188pp.
Describes the use of a general systems simulation model for identifying, discussing and analysing a spectrum of development problems facing Kenya and other societies. Includes a description of the Kenyan data sources and a complete listing of the computer program in Fortran with comment cards.

13-11 WHITACRE, ROBERT JAMES. "Sectoral planning in Kenya: a proposed macro-economic model". IDS Working P 216, June 1975, 21pp.
Presents a theoretical outline of a macro-economic model designed to determine whether government's stated economic objectives are actually fulfilled.

14--Public and development administration

14-1 ADU, A.L. "Service in three fields". J Admin Overseas, Vol. 13, No. 1, Jan. 1974, pp. 273-282.
Discusses the influence of British colonial administration on the economic development of some African countries. Concludes that even though the independent states have good reason to diverge from the colonial system in their institutions and in their administration systems, the traditions inherited from the British connection will continue to make contributions in the development of these economies.

14-2 ALIBARUHO, G. "Issues in administration of integrated development programmes in Kenya with reference to the special rural development programme". African Administrative Studies, Vol. 17, July 1977, pp. 23-28.

14-3 ALILA, P.O. The role of public bureaucracy in agricultural development in Kisumu district, western Kenya. Ph.D dissertation, Indiana University, 1978, 423pp.
DAI, Vol. 39, p. 5714-A.

14-4 BAGUMA, R.H. "Inefficiency, irresponsiveness, and irresponsibility in the public services--is Mwongozo to blame?" Afr Rev, Vol. 5, no. 2, 1975, pp. 195-200.
Examines problems of inefficiency in light of the Mwongozo report in Tanzania, and makes tentative suggestions to rectify the situation.

14-5 BERMAN, B.J. Administration and politics in colonial Kenya. Ph.D. dissertation, Yale University, 1978.

14-6 BEWAYO, E.D. Central-Local relations in Kenya: the local government experience in relation to national development. Ph.D. dissertation, State University of New York at Albany, 1978, 411pp.
DAI, Vol. 39, p. 5715-A.

14-7 BROKENSHA, D., and NELLIS, J. "Administration in Kenya--a study of the rural division of Mbere". J Admin Overseas, Vol. 13, Oct.-Nov. 1974, pp. 510-523.
Attempts to answer the question of how the Kenya government administers one particular rural locale--the Mbere division of Embu district, in Eastern province. Discusses rural development in Mbere division and has a section devoted to discussion of Mbere Special Rural Development Programme.

14-8 ___. "Administration in Kenya, a study of Mbere--Part II". J Admin Overseas, Vol. 14, No. 1, January 1975, pp. 17-29.
Examines departmental endeavours in Mbere, in particular the all-important role of agricultural and ancilliary staff. In conclusion the authors seek briefly to consider how far the Kenya administration is really developmental when confronted with the conflict between tradition and innovation.

14-9 CHAMBERS, ROBERT. "Managing rural development". IDS Bulletin, Vol. 6, No. 1, Sept. 1974, pp. 4-12.

14-10 CHEGE, M. "Systems management and the plan implementation process in Kenya". Afr Rev, Vol. 3, No. 4, 1973, pp. 595-609.

ECONOMIC DEVELOPMENT

Attempts to assess how appropriate are the various approaches of systems programming in the plan implementation process. Kenya is used to illustrate the kind of administrative behaviour which results from using limits set by uncertainty on the general development policy as the point of departure. Appraisal of logic underlying such behaviour and suggestions by which latent advantages in the process can be harnessed to better plan implementation.

14-11 COLEBATCH, HAL. Local services and the government process in Kenya. Ph.D. dissertation, University of Sussex, 1974.

14-12 ___. "Local councils and local services". IDS Bulletin, Vol. 6, No. 1, Sept. 1974, pp. 13-24.

14-13 EL NAMAKI, M.S.S. Problems of management in a developing environment. Free University, Brussels, 1977.
Discusses the Tanzanian experience.

14-14 MAYO-SMITH, IAN. Administration and management in Africa: thirty-one problem case studies. Kenya Institute of Administration, Nairobi, 1970?, 316pp.
Includes problem case studies, as opposed to descriptive ones, all based on actual events. The material is drawn from East and West Africa, mostly Kenya and Nigeria, from civil service, politics, local government, and public and private enterprise.

14-15 MPANDE, L.D. "Management by objectives: problems and prospects in the Kenya public sector". Kenya Institute of Administration, Nairobi, 1975, 12pp.
Examines the reasons for negative attitudes expressed by management course participants at Kenya Institute of Administration toward the "management by objective" system of operation. Evaluates the gains the government recieved from the use of this system.

14-16 MURUGU, J.K. Requirement for short-term economic management in Kenya. M.A. thesis, University of Nairobi, 1978.

14-17 MUTAHARA, G. "The effect of changes in the Tanzanian public service system upon administrative productivity 1961-72". Afr Rev, Vol. 5, No. 2, 1975, pp. 201-208.
Examines developments in the Tanzanian public service (exclusive of those in parastatal organizations) system since 1961 and gives an assessment of their contribution to overall national development.

14-18 NAIYA, PETER WANJOHI. Public participation in planning process in Kenya: a case study of Githunguri division. M.A. thesis, University of Nairobi, 1977.

14-19 NYANGIRA, NICHOLAS. Relative modernization and public resource allocation in Kenya. East African Literature Bureau, Kampala, 1975, 169pp.

Attempts to relate the concept of relative modernization to public resource allocation as experienced in agriculture, commerce, education and self-help projects in Kenya. Introduction and discussion of the concept of modernization.

14-20 OBASO, J.H. "Administrative process in rural development". Seminar on law and rural development in East Africa, Kisumu, July 1977, pp. 447-456.

Highlights the role of the government administration in rural development.

14-21 ODIT-MAFUTA, F.T. "The rule of thumb, promotion by crisis, and the role of the personnel administration in future promotional decision making in institutions of higher learning in Uganda". EA USSC Conference, Kampala, 1974, 17pp.

Exposes the major limitations of the present promotion policies and practices prevailing in institutions of higher learning in Uganda.

14-22 OEBOECK, GUIDO, and KINSEY, BILL. "Managing information for rural development: lessons from Eastern Africa". World Bank Staff Working Paper 379, Washington, D.C., March 1980.

14-23 OGANG, M., and WALLACE, J. "Computer policy in developing countries: the East African experience". EA USSC Conference, Kampala, 1974, 30pp.

Discusses the role of social scientists in influencing the use of computers in developing countries.

14-24 OKOTH-OGENDO, H.W.O. "Development and legal process in Kenya: an approach to the analysis of law and rural development administration". Seminar on law and rural development in Eastern Africa, Kisumu, July 1977, pp. 144-233.

Investigates how law can contribute positively to rural development.

14-25 OYUGI, OUMA W. "Assessing local administrative capacity for development purposes: a Kenyan case". Afr Rev, Vol. 5, No. 3, 1975, pp. 341-352.

Attempts to show empirically that the administrative capacity in the Kenyan sub-district of Migori was too weak to sustain any conceivable development programme.

ECONOMIC DEVELOPMENT

14-26 ___. "Agricultural administration in Kenya: a review". IDS Working P 256, Dec. 1975, 31pp.
Discusses Christopher Trapman's Change in administrative structures (Overseas Development Institute, London, 1974) and evaluates some of his conclusions.

14-27 ___. "Local government and development in Kenya since independence". Department of History Staff Seminar Paper, University of Nairobi, March 1977, 19pp.
Examines historically the role that local government has played in the development process in Kenya since independence. Also sketches the experience of the colonial local authorities in the field of development.

14-28 ___. "Bureaucracy and rural development in Africa". University of Sussex Institute of Development Studies, Brighton, 1978, 32pp.

14-29 RASMUSSON, R. "Social emphasis of people's priorities in rural development: case studies in Kenya on results of decentralised planning". Agricultural Administration, Vol. 2, No. 4, Oct. 1975, pp. 263-284.
Finds that actual project choice in decentralized government programmes reflects pressures for social development as a national way of long-run economic development.

14-30 RWEYEMAMU, A.H. Public sector management problems in Africa. Dag Hammarskjold Foundation, Uppsala, 1975.

14-31 SCHAFFER, BERNARD. Administrative training and development. Praeger, New York, 1974.
A comparative study of East Africa, Zambia, Pakistan, and India.

14-32 SEGALL, M., et al. "Uganda district government and politics 1947-67". University of Wisconsin African Studies Program, 1979.

14-33 STEEVES, J.S. The politics and administration of agricultural development: the Kenya Tea Development Authority. Ph.D. dissertation, University of Toronto, 1975.
DAI, Vol. 39, p. 1815.

14-34 TRAPMAN, CHRISTOPHER. Change in administrative structures: a case study of Kenyan agricultural development. Overseas Development Institute, London, 1974, 108pp.
Concerned with the need for fashioning new and more appropriate administrative approaches in underdeveloped

circumstances. Describes the relationship between politicians and administrative officers. Examines how well the present organization of the formal sector serving the agricultural sector is adapted to the type of farming community in Kenya.

14-35 VON FREYHOLD, MICHAELA. "The government staff and Ujamaa villages--the Tanga experience". EA USSC Conference, Dar es Salaam, Dec. 1973, 17pp.
Analyses the effects of the independence struggle and Ujamaa villages by considering the forces which are undermining the old peasant-staff relations and the forces which will allow the peasants to re-organize themselves in a socialist way.

15--Income distribution studies

15-1 AMEY, A. Urban-rural disparities in Tanzania 1960-1975. World Bank, Washington, D.C., 1976.

15-2 ASETO, OYUGI. "A method of measuring the Gini-ratio of income inequality: the Kenyan case". IDS Working P 313, 1977, 9pp.
Discusses a method of income inequality measurement by the use of the Gini coefficient of concentration. Finds that the method is simple, precise and free from ambiguities.

15-3 ____. "Why should there be a concern with income inequality?". Kenyan Economic Association Annual Conference, Nairobi, 1977.
Argues that the question of income inequality is going to assume a role of bigger proportion in economic affairs due to its connections with major issues of policy.

15-4 BEQUELE, A., and VAN DER HOEVEN, R. "Poverty and inequality in sub-Saharan Africa". International Labour Review, Vol. 119, No. 3, May-June 1980, pp. 381-392.
Reviews the limited evidence and provides a glimpse of the situation as well as of the reasons for the persistence and, in some cases, the growing incidence of poverty and inequality in sub-Saharan Africa.

15-5 BIGSTEN, ARNE. "Regional inequality in Kenya". IDS Working P 330, Nov. 1977, 80pp.
Presents some basic facts about regional inequality in Kenya.

15-6 ____. Regional inequality and development: a case study of Kenya. Gower Press, Farnborough, 1980, 200pp.
Analyses the processes determining the development of regional income inequality in Kenya. An inter-regional

ECONOMIC DEVELOPMENT

input-output simulation model is used to analyse patterns of regional growth and various policy alternatives. Concludes that government must pursue a systematic regional policy, based on indirect stimuli or direct investment control, in order to offer any real hope to the poorer regions. Appeared under the same title, published by Nationalekonomiska Institutionen, University of Göteborg, 1978.

15-7 CHENERY, H., et al. (eds.). Redistribution with growth. Oxford University Press, London, 1974, 304pp.
Analyses policies to improve income distribution in developing countries in the context of economic growth. It concludes that distributional objectives should be treated as an integral part of development and growth strategy and that this implies a significant reorientation of development research.

15-8 COLE, JOHN. The poor of the earth. Macmillan, London, 1976, 144pp.
Examines the gap between the poor and rich countries and also between the privileged groups and the poor within the developing countries. Suggests that the solutions to the two problems are complementary. One chapter focuses on the need to develop the "informal sector", with particular reference to Kenya.

15-9 COLLIER, PAUL. Poverty and growth in Kenya. World Bank, Washington, D.C., 1980, 76pp.

15-10 COLLIER, P., and SABOT, R. "Measuring income differences between rural and urban incomes: some conceptual issues." Research Workshop on Urban-Rural Labour Market Interactions, World Bank, Washington, D.C., 1976.

15-11 CONNOLLY, J.G. Planning for equality in rural Tanzania. M.Sc. thesis, University of Swansea, 1976.

15-12 EDGREN, GUS. Population, income distribution and employment. Ministry of Labour, Nairobi, 1975.
Deals with minimum wages and tries to account for the variations in wages between firms.

15-13 EWUSI, K. "Changes in distribution of earnings of Africans in recorded employment in Uganda". Economic Bulletin of Ghana, Vol. 3, No. 1, 1973 (Second series).

15-14 FOSH, PATRICIA. "Attitudes of East African white-collar workers to income inequalities". International Labour

Review, Vol. 117, No. 1, Jan.-Feb. 1978, pp. 99-110.
Investigates the views of the former East African Community employees on pay inequality between the different ranks, organizations within the Community, manual, officeworkers and small farmers, as well as the preferred future distribution of income in East Africa.

15-15 HAZLEWOOD, ARTHUR. "Kenya: income distribution and poverty--an unfashionable view". J Mod Afr Studs, Vol. 16, No. 1, March 1978, pp. 81-95.
Argues the need to temper concern for inequality with attention to absolute levels of living. Suggests that some of Kenya's poor have become less poor and that the resulting increase in inequality is not to be deplored.

15-16 HEYER, JUDITH. "The origins of regional inequalities in smallholder agriculture in Kenya, 1920-73". EAJ Rural Devel, Vol. 8, Nos. 1-2, 1975, pp. 142-181.
Attempts to summarize the origins of the disparities in agricultural development in small farm areas in Kenya. Concentrates particularly on the growth of marketed output from different provinces and districts.

15-17 HODD, MICHAEL. "Income distribution in Kenya (1963-72)". J Dev Studs, Vol. 12, No. 3, April 1976, pp. 221-228.
Computes concentration ratios and annual wage shares to measure income distribution in Kenya. Argues that Kenyanization has improved the distribution. See also a comment by House and Killick, a reply by Hodd, and an agreed statement by these three in J Dev Studs, April 1978.

15-18 ___. "Income distribution in Kenya: a reply". J Dev Studs, Vol. 14, No. 3, April 1978, pp. 375-377.
Hodd defends his previous article in this journal (Vol. 12, No. 3, April 1976) against House and Killick's criticisms in this same issue.

15-19 HODD, MICHAEL; HOUSE, WILLIAM J.; and KILLICK, TONY. "Income distribution in Kenya: a controversy resolved". J Dev Studs, Vol. 15, No. 1, Oct. 1978, p. 117.
Presents an agreed statement as to why it is impossible to use Kenya's 1978 national accounts to estimate changes in distribution of income between labour and non-labour factors of production.

15-20 HOUSE, WILLIAM J., and KILLICK, TONY. "Hodd on income distribution in Kenya: a critical note". J Dev Studs, Vol. 14, No. 3, April 1978, pp. 370-374.

ECONOMIC DEVELOPMENT

Criticizes Michael Hodd's article in an earlier issue of this journal (Vol. 12, No. 3, April 1976, pp. 221-228).

15-21 HUNT, DIANA M. "Methodological issues and selected findings of an analysis of the distribution of wealth and income in Mbere division, Eastern Kenya". IDS Working P 212, Mar. 1975, 50pp.
Finds that threr is a notably unequal distribution of economic status in Mbere and that the main cause of this is variations in the formal educational attainments of household heads.

15-22 ___. "Growth versus equity: an examination of the distribution of economic status and opportunity in Mbere, eastern Kenya". IDS Occ P 11, 1975.
Examines the potential conflict between promotion of two economic objectives, growth and equity, in a rural division of eastern Kenya. Focus is on response of the relatively poor and relatively wealthy farmers to agricultural innovations recommended by extension workers. Concludes that only wealthy farmers can be expected to supply the necessary resources for, and to carry the risks of, innovations; hence innovations lead to increased economic inequality.

15-23 JOHNSON, G.E. "Notes on wages, employment and income distribution in Kenya". Paper presented to a Conference of York University held in Nairobi, 1971.

15-24 KAMAU, P.N. Income distribution in Kenya. M.A. thesis, University of Nairobi, 1977.

15-25 ___. "Measurement of income inequality in Kenya". Kenyan Economic Association Annual Conference, Nairobi, 1977, 11pp.
States that little is known about the income distribution in the rural areas. Economists should therefore produce data that reveal the nature of the distribution of income in the rural areas so that efforts directed at alleviating rural poverty may have more effect.

15-26 KAPLINSKY, R. "Trends on the distribution of income in Kenya, 1966-76". IDS Working P 336, May 1978, 28pp.
Using a number of indicators, the paper summarizes the evidence available on income distribution in Kenya between 1966 and 1976.

15-27 KMIETOWICZ, T., and WEBLEY, P. "Statistical analysis of income distribution in the Central province of Kenya". EAER, Vol. 7, No. 2, Dec. 1975, pp. 1-25.

Using data collected in 1963-1964, various parameters are calculated and a Lorenz curve is plotted. After fitting the log-normal distribution on the observed distributions, a tentative predictive model is developed and tested.

15-28 LAMB, G. "Distributive policies in Tanzania". Workshop on Distributional Issues in Development Planning, Bellagio, 1977.

15-29 MACARTHUR, J.D. "Appraising the distributional aspects of rural development projects: a Kenya case study". World Development, Vol. 6, No. 2, Feb. 1978, pp. 167-193.

Attempts to illustrate methods of increasing sophistication by which the question of distribution weighting may be handled. A conventional shadow-pricing method of revaluing all project inputs and outputs in terms of the economic opportunity cost of the primary resources involved has been applied.

15-30 NG'ETHE, NJUGUNA. "Some problems of income distribution in Kenya: report of a workshop held at the Institute for Development Studies, University of Nairobi". IDS Working P 308, April 1977, 16pp.

The workshop was based on a paper the authors of which intended "to move beyond the simple formulations of inequality and class formation in Kenya without proposing to formulate a general theory".

15-31 PHILLIPS, A.O. "Review of income distribution data: Ghana, Kenya, Tanzania and Nigeria". Discussion Paper No. 58, Princeton University, Princeton, 1975, 43pp.

For the four countries, the paper attempts to survey existing income distribution studies; appraise the availability of data for future studies; and give indications as to desirable areas of emphasis in future studies of income distribution problems. Concludes that studies of income distribution have been insufficient, and size distribution has reeived scant attention. Also that relevant data are greatly lacking, especially in Kenya and Tanzania, and that much future research activities must be orientated toward generating the required distributional data.

15-32 RWEYEMAMU, J.F. (ed.). Industrialization and income distribution in Africa. Zed Press, London, 1980, 240pp.

15-33 VAN GINNEKEN, WOUTER. Rural and urban income inequalities in Indonesia, Mexico, Pakistan, Tanzania and Tunisia. ILO, Geneva, 1976, 67pp.

Argues that urban inequality of household expenditure is

greater than rural inequality in these countries where the share of total expenditure attributable to the group of households able to incur the heaviest expenditure os larger in the urban than in the rural areas.

16--Consumption and saving studies

16-1 DAVID, M. "Marketing of food crops and purchase of industrial commodities by Nyanza smallholders, 1970-1971". IDS Working P 247, Dec. 1975, 42pp.
Considers the allocation problem of a rural household and says that consumption allocation depends heavily on demographic composition of the households. Emphasizes the effect of changing household composition on the allocative choices made.

16-2 HENNING, PETER. "A description of a survey taken in the area surrounding Kariobaing market". IDS Working P 239, Sept. 1975, 16pp.
Provides data necessary to estimate the degree of self-sufficiency of the economy of a low income area of Nairobi. Useful for a preliminary analysis of demand elasticities for informal sector products and services.

16-3 HUMPHREY, DAVID H., and OXLEY, HOWARD S. "Expenditure and household-size elasticities in Malawi: urban-rural comparisons, demand projections and a summary of East African findings". J Dev Studs, Vol. 12, No. 2, Jan. 1976, pp. 252-269.
In section seven of the article results are given of several different elasticities studies conducted in Eastern Africa including Kenya, Uganda, and Tanzania.

16-4 KAPUNDA, S.M. "An econometric analysis of consumer's behaviour in selected areas of Tanzania". ERB Paper, University of Dar-es-Salaam, 1977, 42pp.

16-5 LILLYDAHL, JANE HANDY. Economic and demographic influences on household saving in urban Kenya. Ph.D. dissertation, Duke University, 1976.

16-6 MIRACLE, M.P.,; MIRACLE, D.S.; and COHEN, L. "Informal savings mobilization in Africa". Econ Dev Cult Change, Vol. 28, No. 4, July 1980, 23pp.
A review of institutions by which resources are mobilized in the informal sector of African economies. Focuses mainly on the savings accumulated through clubs and associations but also surveys the evidence of mobile banks operating in African market places.

16-7 OSTBY, I. "An econometric study of demand patterns in Dar-es-Salaam: preliminary review". <u>ERB Paper 68.5</u>, University of Dar-es-Salaam, 1968, 7pp.
Presents estimates of demand functions in Dar-es-Salaam based on a sample of 108 wage-earner households.

16-8 RYAN, T.C.I., and BIGGS, T.S. "A theory of dynamic lifestyles in a transitional economy". SID seminar on alternative patterns of development and lifestyles in Eastern Africa, Nairobi, July 1979.

16-9 SMITH, L.D. "Low income smallholder marketing and consumption patterns analysis and improvements, policies and programmes". FAO Marketing Project, Rome, 1978.

16-10 UGANDA, MINISTRY OF PLANNING AND ECONOMIC DEVELOPMENT STATISTICS DIVISION. <u>The patterns of income and expenditure of coffee growers in Buganda 1962/63</u>. Government Printer, Entebbe, Jan. 1967.

16-11 WALDORF, WILLIAM H. "A comparison of savings rates in Uganda: Africans, Asians and Europeans". <u>J Dev Studs</u>, Vol. 13, No. 3, April 1977, pp. 229-237.
Concludes that the common notion that the savings rate was lower among Africans than among Asians or Europeans is not correct and that it probably arose out of casual comparison of persons in different occupational groups.

16-12 YONA, D.A.N. "Savings and credit for low cost housing: the experience of the Tanzania housing bank". <u>Savings and Development</u>, Vol. 3, No. 1, 1979, pp. 60-74.

2--FISCAL AND FINANCIAL TOPICS

<u>20--Public finance and budgeting</u>

20-1 ASETO, O. "Taxation and income inequality in Kenya". Kenyan Economic Association Annual Conference, Nairobi, 1977, 16pp.
Suggests that the government should tighten the administrative machinery of taxation to increase tax revenues. Also could change the tax structure by instituting a land tax, urban property taxation, capital gains tax, and general improvement in wealth taxation.

20-2 ___. "Republic of Kenya". In A.A. Suliman and E. de Brauw-Hay (eds.), <u>Income taxation in Eastern Africa: policies and prospects</u>. International Bureau of Fiscal Documentation, Amsterdam, 1980, pp. 67-92.

FISCAL AND FINANCIAL TOPICS

Discusses the post-independence development, the major features, and the economic effects of Kenyan income taxation of individuals and companies.

20-3 BANUGIRE, F.R. "Republic of Uganda". In A.A. Suliman and E. de Brauw-Hay (eds.), Income taxation in Eastern Africa: policies and prospects. International Bureau of Fiscal Documentation, Amsterdam, 1980, pp. 149-196.
Discusses the post-independence development, the major features, and the economic effects of Kenyan income taxation of individuals and companies.

20-4 BRENT, ROBERT J. "Shifting of the Kenyan sales tax, 1973-74". IDS Working P 290, Nov. 1976, 15pp.
Attempts to estimate the extent of shifting of the Kenya sales tax in its first year of operation. Shows the tax to be more than fully shifted.

20-5 ___. "A cross-section framework for estimating jointly the extent of shifting of sales and company income taxes with an application to Kenya". Public Finance, Vol. 34, No. 1, 1979, pp. 51-68.
Aims at establishing a general framework for estimating tax shifting to incorporate both the company income and sales taxes.

20-6 BUTT, S.A., and SOKWALA, A. An introduction to taxation in Kenya. Cassell & Co., London, 1978, 176pp.
Analyses the various forms of taxation in Kenya as of 1 Jan. 1978.

20-7 CHEGE, MICHAEL. Public expenditure in an underdeveloped capitalist state: Kenya 1964-74. Ph.D. dissertation, University of California, Berkeley, 1976.

20-8 CHOUDHRY, NURUN N. "Measuring the elasticity of tax revenue: a divisia index approach". IMF Staff Papers, Vol. 26, No. 1, March 1979, pp. 87-122.
Proposes a method of estimating the elasticity of total tax yield to national income which is then applied to Kenya and three other countries.

20-9 DAVEY, K. Taxing a peasant society: the example of graduated taxes in East Africa. Charles Knight and Co., London, 1974, 226pp.
Chronicles the defects and difficulties of mass direct taxation in a developing country, based on a detailed examination of Uganda's graduated personal tax, with some comparisons with Kenya, Tanzania, and Nigeria.

20-10 DUE, J.F. "A comparison of four manufacturers sales taxes and two retail sales taxes--Ghana, Kenya, Tanzania, Zambia, Barbados, Iceland". Bulletin for International Fiscal Documentation, Vol. 30, No. 11, Nov. 1976, pp. 464-476.
Presents information on manufacturers sales taxes in Kenya, Tanzania, Zambia, and Ghana. Compares these with the retail sales taxes of Barbados and Iceland. Finds that in a developing country a sales tax can provide significant revenue and that sales taxes at the manufacturing level can function extremely well. Also appears as IDS Disc P 251.

20-11 GHAI, DHARAM P. Income elasticity of the Uganda tax structure. Ph.D. dissertation, Yale University, 1966.

20-12 GRAY, W.J. A guide to income tax in Kenya. Longman, Nairobi, 1979, 128pp.
Covers items such as capital and investment allowances, withholding tax, capital gains, employment, income, personal reliefs, PAYE, and other aspects of taxation on income from farming and property. Discusses and interprets current tax laws.

20-13 HUANG, YUKON. "Distribution of the tax burden in Tanzania". Economic Journal, Vol. 86, No. 341, March 1976, pp. 73-86.
Uses data from a budget survey which includes in-kind consumption. Concludes that both direct and indirect taxes are progressive. Also appears in K.S. Kim, R.B. Mabele, and M.J. Schultheis (eds.), Papers on the political economy of Tanzania.

20-14 INTERNATIONAL BUREAU OF FISCAL DOCUMENTATION. African tax systems. IBFD for UN Economic Commission for Africa, Amsterdam, 1979, 1500pp.
Presents a comparative survey of direct and indirect taxation in African countries for both corporations and individuals. Updated quarterly.

20-15 ITWERANDU, P.K. The effects of economic development on the base of a sales tax: a case study of Kenya. M.A. thesis, University of Nairobi, 1977.

20-16 KARIUKI, NELIUS W. Inter-governmental fiscal relations in Kenya: a case study of Nairobi City Council. M.A. thesis, University of Nairobi, 1980.

20-17 KARIUKI, NGOTHO WA. Income taxation in Kenya. Midi-Tiki Publishers, Nairobi, 1978, 281pp.
Based on the income tax Act 1973, as revised in 1977.

FISCAL AND FINANCIAL TOPICS

It combines both the theoretical analysis and the mechanics of taxation so as to understand the purpose for every section of the Act. It also discusses other economic and environmental considerations that underlie tax decisions.

20-18 KARLGÅRD, NILS OLAV. "Improvements in the budgetary procedures in Kenya". DERAP Working Paper No. 104, Chr. Michelsen Institute, Bergen, Nov. 1977, 26pp.
Offers an evaluation of an improved budgetary system introduced in 1974-1975 and suggests further improvements. The author was formerly an advisor in Kenya's Ministry of Finance and Planning.

20-19 "Kenya: budget 1980-81". Bulletin for International Fiscal Documentation, Vol. 35, No. 1, January 1981, pp. 30-34.
An extensive extract from the June 19, 1980 budget speech by Vice-President and Minister for Finance Kibaki.

20-20 MATSEBULA, M.S. "Tax ratios in Africa". South African Economic Journal, Vol. 47, No. 2, June 1979, pp. 156-167.
Tests the hypothesis that a country's tax ratio is determined by the stage of development, sectoral distribution of income, openness of the economy, and geographic situation. Uses 17 African countries (including Tanzania and Kenya) to test the hypothesis with data from 1969 to 1973. Tax ratio responds as hypothesized only to income per capita and openness of the economy.

20-21 MWASE, N. "Road user taxation in the LDC: an overview". Taamuli, Vol. 8, No. 1, 1978, pp. 28-37.
Examines the role of road user taxation in Tanzanian-type economies, particularly the role it plays as a source of public revenue.

20-22 OLE, A.M. Income elasticity of tax structure in Kenya 1962/63-1972/73. M.A. thesis, University of Nairobi, 1975, 107pp.
Shows that during the period 1962/63 to 1972/73 the tax structure in Kenya was income inelastic. Argues that the observed inelasticity of the structure was mostly a result of the inelasticity of indirect taxes.

20-23 RUPLEY, LAWRENCE A., and FINUCANE, BRENDAN P. "Kenya's 1980 budget". Bulletin for International Fiscal Documentation, Vol. 35, No. 1, Jan. 1981, pp. 24-29.
Discusses the 1980 Kenya government budget, particularly its focus on the need for additional government revenue, the necessity to deal with the balance of payments constraint on the economy, and measures to bring structural changes in the

economy such as a switch from import substitution to export promotion in manufacturing.

20-24 SCOVILL, MARY EDITH. Local taxation in Uganda, Kenya and Zambia. Ph.D. dissertation, University of Illinois, 1975, 224pp.
Examines existing local government tax structures in Uganda, Kenya, and Zambia. Evaluates the taxes on the basis of revenue potential, progressivity, effect on resource allocation, and costs of collection. Offers recommendations for achieving improved tax structures.

20-25 SMITH, R.S. "Financing cities in developing countries". IMF Staff Papers, Vol. 21, No. 2, July 1974, pp. 329-388.
Centres on urbanization process aspects with Nairobi as one of the African cities. Explains why urbanization leads to an increasing need for government revenues and expenditure. Investigates the effects that division of responsibility among governmental levels have on the provision of urban services. Examines the patterns of city finances that may originate from within.

20-26 SULIMAN, A.A., and DE BRAUW-HAY, E. (eds.). Income taxation in Eastern Africa: policies and prospects. Vol. 7 of Studies on Taxation and Economic Development, International Bureau of Fiscal Documentation, Amsterdam, 1980, 244pp.
Includes country surveys of income taxation in Kenya by O. Aseto and Uganda by F.R. Banugire, as well as in Egypt, Ethiopia, Somalia, Sudan, and Zambia.

20-27 TER WEELE, ALEXANDER J. Equity in financing education in East Africa: the cases of Ethiopia, Kenya, and Tanzania. Ph.D. dissertation, Harvard University, 1975.

20-28 WILSON, F.A., and AMANN, V.F. (eds.). Financing rural development. Makerere University, Kampala, March, 1975, 277pp.
Papers on the theme "financing rural development" of the Eastern Africa Agricultural Society conference, Lusaka, Zambia, in May 1974. Includes papers dealing with credit programmes in Kenya as well as a discussion of the Ujamaa schemes in Tanzania.

20-29 ZULU, JUSTIN BEVAN. An economic study of the postwar African experience with taxation, with special reference to the Republic of Uganda. Ph.D. dissertation, University of Colorado, 1964.

FISCAL AND FINANCIAL TOPICS

21--Domestic financial institutions and markets; money and credit

21-1 ABDI, ALI I. "Banking in Uganda since independence: comment". Econ Dev Cult Change, Vol. 24, No. 2, Jan. 1976, pp. 417-422.
A comment on article by I. Gershenberg, "Banking in Uganda Since Independence" that appeared in April, 1972 issue of this journal. Reply by Gershenberg also appears herein.

21-2 ___. Commercial banks and economic development: the experience of Eastern Africa. Praeger, New York, 1977, 148pp.

21-3 ANGWENYI, C.P. Access to credit: commercial bank lending practice in Kenya. Kenya Economic Association Annual Conference, Nairobi, 1977, 26pp.
Argues that rather than being accessible only to shareholders and friends of the rich and influential, commercial banks assist both individuals and business concerns indiscriminately.

21-4 BAMWINE, G.M. Investing for development: the East African Development Bank case. M.B.A. thesis, University of Nairobi, 1975, 148pp.
Studies various techniques for appraising capital investments in developing countries and the East African Development Bank's investment criteria and performance. Concludes that the bank would perhaps have done better as a national rather than as an inter-regional corporation.

21-5 BINHAMMER, H.H. The development of a financial infrastructure in Tanzania. East African Literature Bureau, Nairobi, 1975, 199pp.
The first two chapters concentrate on the institutional framework for providing a medium of exchange. The other chapters are more directly concerned with the transfer of the medium of exchange, and ultimately real resources, from surplus spending units to deficit spending units.

21-6 DAVID, MARTIN, and WYETH, PETER. "Kenya Commercial bank loans in rural areas a survey". IDS Working P 342, Aug. 1978, 43pp.
Presents analysis of the economic characteristics of both the loans and the borrowers.

21-7 DUE, JEAN M. "Agricultural credit in Tanzania". Journal of Southern African Affairs, Vol. 3, No. 1, Jan. 1978, pp. 99-113.
Study of the allocation of credit, and the sources of that credit, to small farmers and Ujamaa villages in Tanzania

between the 1972/73 and 1975/76 crop years. Also analyses the debtors' capacity to repay, repayment experience, and attitudes toward the credit provided in Iringa and Mbeya regions of Tanzania.

21-8 ___. "The allocation of credit to Ujamaa villages and to small private farmers in Tanzania". Savings and Development, No. 2, 1978, pp. 69-107.

21-9 "Financial education has stimulated demand for Kenya's banking facilities". Standard Chartered Review, Oct. 1977, pp. 2-4.

21-10 FREDIANI, LORENZO. The liquidity policy of deposit banks in Kenya. Cassa Risparmio Provincie Lombarde, Milan, 1975, 277pp.
Argues that the failure of deposit banks in Kenya to adopt seasonal liquidity policies seems to have been due to adjustment costs, the structure and rigidity of yields, economies of scale, and the rate of expansion of domestic money supply.

21-11 GERSHENBERG, IRVING. "The impact of independence on the role of commercial banking in Uganda's economic development, 1960-68". EA USSC Conference, Nairobi, Dec. 1969.
Analysis of the structure and investment and loan policies of Uganda's commercial banking system with the view of determining the extent to which they have managed to redirect savings from being deposited abroad and to redirect credit facilities away from the traditional pre-independence pattern.

21-12 ___. "Banking in Uganda since independence". Econ Dev Cult Change, April 1972, pp. 504-523.
An analysis of the commercial banking system.

21-13 ___. "Banking in Uganda since independence: reply". Econ Dev Cult Change, Vol. 24, No. 2, Jan. 1976, pp. 421-422.
Argues that banks in underdeveloped countries maintain a very short-run profit outlook because of the prevailing environment. Maintaining highly liquid portfolios produces an emphasis on short-run loans and advances to the commercial sector.

21-14 HOUSE, WILLIAM J., and KANOGA, EPHRAIM N. "'Grass root' savings and credit operations in Kenya". Vierteljahresberichte, No. 78, Dec. 1979, pp. 385-389.
Examines the role of rotating credit associations (RCA) in mobilizing grass-root savings in the face of inefficient formal credit to the informal sector. Concludes that RCA are more developed in the rural informal sector than in the

FISCAL AND FINANCIAL TOPICS

urban, due to the lack of closely knit, ethnically homogenous communities in the urban areas.

21-15 HUNT, DIANA. Credit for agricultural development: a case study of Uganda. East African Publishing House, Nairobi, 1975, 401pp.

Focuses on actual use made and impact of loans in certain selected areas of Uganda. Main sources of credit considered are the commercial banks, traders, other farmers, and farm labourers. Assessment of two government schemes--the progressive farmer's loan scheme and the co-operative credit scheme.

21-16 ___. "Personal savings in Africa: strengthening the institutional framework (commercial banks, post office savings banks, thrift and credit cooperatives, and savings banks proper)". IDS Working P 323, Aug. 1977, 35pp.

Analyses the concern for personal savings mobilization in Africa and places it in a wider economic perspective.

21-17 ___. "The Ugandan agricultural cooperative credit scheme". In Paris Andreou (ed.), Co-operative institutions and economic development: some lessons from advanced and developing countries. East African Literature Bureau, Nairobi, 1977, pp. 23-61.

Tries to evaluate the Ugandan agricultural co-operative credit scheme with regard to the needs it was intended to meet, the system of administration and costs of credit provision, and the impact on output, income, consumption, distribution of income, and wealth.

21-18 KAPLINSKY, R.M. "An analysis of ICDC small industrial loan commitments, 1961-1975". IDS Working P 251, Feb. 1976, 28pp.

Argues that there has been a decline in the number of loan commitments by ICDC in recent years. Gives reasons to explain this.

21-19 KARIISA, GABRIEL M.B. The process of monetization: a case study of Kenya 1922-1972. Ph.D. dissertation, Johns Hopkins University, 1976.

21-20 KANOGA, EPHRAIM N. Informal credit in Mathira, Nyeri district, central Kenya, a case study of rural informal credits in Kenya. M.A. thesis, University of Nairobi, 1978.

21-21 KENYA, CENTRAL BANK OF. The first ten years. Nairobi, 1977, 34pp.

Domestic financial institutions

21-22 KENYA, CENTRAL BUREAU OF STATISTICS. "Survey of hire purchase credit". K Stat Dig, Vol. 13, No. 2, June 1975, pp. 1-3.
A compilation of statistics on the hire purchase business written by companies operating in Kenya.

21-23 LOXLEY, J. "Principles of finance management in capitalist and socialist economies". Rasilimali: Tanzania Investment Outlook, Tanzania Investment Bank, Jan. 1973, pp. 9-15.

21-24 McCARTHY, D.M.P. "Media as ends: money and the underdevelopment of Tanganyika to 1940". Journal of Economic History, Vol. 36, No. 3, Sept. 1976, pp. 645-662.
Historical analysis of the circumstances surrounding the introduction of money. Also deals with previous media of exchange.

21-25 MEGBENU, T.F. Portfolio holdings of insurance companies in Kenya. M.B.A. thesis, University of Nairobi, 1976, 90pp.
Concludes that unless insurance companies change their conservative investment behaviour, they will continue to have no appreciable direct impact on the economic development of Kenya.

21-26 MENSAH, A. "The process of monetary decolonisation in Africa". Utafiti, Vol. 4, No. 1, 1979, University of Dar-es-Salaam, pp. 45-63.
Traces the process and mechanics of monetary decolonization from the time when many African countries became politically independent up to 1977. Argues that the establishment of central banks initiated a modification of the monetary relations between the ex-colonies and the metropoles.

21-27 MITTELMAN, JAMES H. "Underdevelopment and nationalisation: banking in Tanzania". J Mod Afr Studs, Vol. 16, No. 3, Dec. 1978, pp. 597-617.
Discusses how nationalization of the banks was achieved and the strategies the Tanzanian government and the banks adopted.

21-28 MOHELE, A.T. "The Ismani maize credit programme". In K.S. Kim, R.B. Mabele, and M.J. Schultheis (eds.), Papers on the political economy of Tanzania. Heinemann Educational, Nairobi, 1979, pp. 216-222.
The paper examines the impact of the Tanzania Rural Development Bank (TRDB) credit programme in which the bank was involved and evaluates the effectiveness of the credit programme lounched by TRDB. It investigates the problems encountered and pinpoints possible solutions. Initially appeared as ERB Paper 75.2.

FISCAL AND FINANCIAL TOPICS

21-29 MSAMBICHAKA, L.A., and MABELE, R. "Agricultural credit and the development of Ujamaa villages in Tanzania." In K.S. Kim, R.B. Mabele, and M.J. Schultheis (eds.), Papers on the political economy of Tanzania. Heinemann Educational, Nairobi, 1979, pp. 207-215.

Deals with production credit. Traces the general development of agricultural credit institutions in Tanzania from the British colonial period to the present day. Focuses on the evolution of production credit programmes designed to help small holders and on the present programme's relationship to the building of socialism in rural Tanzania. Initially appeared as ERB Paper 74.10.

21-30 MUNGA, D.N. The Nairobi stock exchange: its history, organization and role in the Kenyan economy. M.B.A. thesis, University of Nairobi, 1974, 137pp.

Found that the exchange has largely failed to respond to the local environment, which badly needs an aggressive and educational initiative in promoting investment activities. Argues that the exchange is not important source of capital, nor an important allocator of investible funds and does not provide any meaningful liquidity in securities.

21-31 MWABU, G.M. Finance in small-holder agriculture in Tharaka, eastern Kenya: a case study of small-farm finance. M.A. thesis, University of Nairobi, 1976.

21-32 MWASE, N.R.L. "Decision-making in Tanzania's National Bank of Commerce (NBC): controls and participation dichotomy". ERB Paper 75.9, Dar-es-Salaam, 1975.

Emphasizes the increase over time of wider participation in management at the expense of technocratic "one-man" controls.

21-33 NEWLYN, W.T. The financing of economic development. Clarendon Press, Oxford, 1978, 374pp.

Examines the primary role of development finance in mobilization of the national surplus. Includes a case study of the pattern of company savings in Kenya's manufacturing sector.

21-34 OKELO-OBONG, GEORGE SAMUEL. Kenya's financial development: an analysis from East African Currency Board to central banking, 1919-1971. Ph.D. dissertation, University of Nebraska, 1974, 159pp.

Enumerates characteristics profiling an efficiently functioning financial system and applies them in a comparative analysis of the performance level of Kenya's economy during the operation of the Currency Board and, subsequently, the central banking system.

21-35 OKUMU, WENGI. "Supranational effort in East Africa: the case of a bank". EA USSC Conference, Kampala, 1974, 30pp.
Discusses the intended roles of East African Development Bank (E.A.D.B.) and its principles of operation as well as sources of funds. Concludes that because EADB operates along with other financial institutions, its impact on industrial balance will be limited, and the capital limitation on EADB is a barrier to greater influence of the industrial growth of East Africa.

21-36 OLUM, O.B.O. Capital investment appraisal techniques and publicly financed investments in the private sector. M.B.A. thesis, University of Nairobi, 1976, 243pp.
Examines how two public corporations in Kenya, the Industrial and Commercial Development Corporation and the Kenya Tourist Development Corporation, have solved the problem of how to appraise joint public-private projects.

21-37 ONYONKA, ZACHARY T. "Report on the loan schedues for large scale farmers". IDS (unnumbered paper), July 1969, 47pp.
Concludes that substantial changes in the current terms of lending are one of the most powerful means immediately available for increasing the loan repayment capacity of many large-scale African farmers who are seriously in debt.

21-38 RWEGASIRA, K.S.P. "Is corporate financial information disclosure inadequate in Tanzania". Tanzania Management Journal, Vol. 1, No. 1, Autumn 1976, pp. 81-91.

21-39 ___. "The mode of financial analysis in Tanzania commercial bank short-term lending". Journal of Eastern African Research and Development, Vol. 9, No. 2, 1979, pp. 83-99.
An evaluation of Tanzanian commercial banking in a bid to improve its performance. Similar item appeared as IMF Research paper in Jan. 1977.

21-40 SINGH, DUSHYANT C. "A study of motor vehicle insurance in East Africa". Econ Stat Rev, No. 17, Dec. 1965, pp. vii-xv.
A statistical analysis of the growth of motor vehicle insurance in East Africa. Points out that the operating surpluses of this form of insurance waned while those of other non-life insurance were consolidated substantially.

21-41 TANZANIA, BANK OF. Credit for development of agriculture in Tanzania. Dar-es-Salaam, 1979, 72pp.

FISCAL AND FINANCIAL TOPICS

21-42 VON PISCHKE, J.D. "A penny saved . . . : Kenya's cooperative savings scheme and some related aspects of rural finance". <u>IDS Working P 204</u>, Jan. 1975, 49pp.
Looks at the performance of the cooperative savings scheme ince its transformation from a pilot project to an on-going savings programme. A complement to the author's <u>IDS Working P 80</u>.

21-43 ___. "A critical survey of approaches to the role of credit in smallholder development". <u>IDS Disc P 233</u>, March 1976, 21pp.
Argues that the creed that small-holder farmers need credit is based on assumptions which may not be applicable to specific rural situations. Examples on Kenya are incorporated in the critique.

21-44 ___. <u>The political economy of farm credit in Kenya</u>. Ph.D. dissertation, University of Glasgow, 1977, 540pp.
Directs its attention to questions of financial market theory, elementary aspects of financial logic, and the nature and quality of government intervention.

<u>22--Domestic fiscal, financial, and monetary policies</u>

22-1 BAHL, ROY W. (ed.). <u>The taxation of urban property in less developed countries</u>. University of Wisconsin Press for the Committee on Taxation, Resources and Economic Development, Madison, 1979, 288pp.
Tenth symposia volume of Committee on Taxation, Resources and Economic Development. Professor Bahl's paper attempts to quantify the revenue from urban property tax for fourteen less developed countries, including Kenya. Some evidence is also presented for Dar-es-Salaam.

22-2 BANUGIRE, F.R. "The first two budgets and the third 5-year development plan". <u>The Uganda Economic Journal</u>, Vol. 2, No. 2, Dec. 1972, pp. 126-153.
Examines the 1971/72 and 1972/73 Uganda government budgets and relates them to expectations in the third plan. Concludes that the best solution for the incompatibility between the third plan and the two budgets is to shift from long-run "document planning" to short-run operations-oriented planning.

22-3 BROUGH, A.T., and CURTIN, T.R.C. "Growth and stability: an account of fiscal and monetary policy". In Tony Killick (ed.), <u>Papers on the Kenyan economy</u>. Heinemann, London, 1981.

22-4 ELLIOTT, HOWARD J.C. "The Uganda budget 1971-72: an economic evaluation". Uganda Economic Journal, Vol. 1, No. 1, Dec. 1971, pp. 7-30.

Concludes that the austerity budget represented no significant change from the situation of the previous year. Suggests restricted government spending and increased tax collection.

22-5 HAMMOND, ROBERT C. Fiscal harmonization in the East African Community. International Bureau of Fiscal Documentation, Amsterdam, 1975, 137pp.

A reappraisal of the 1967 treaty for East African Cooperation in the light of subsequent experience.

22-6 KING, J.R. Stabilisation policy in an African setting: Kenya 1963-1973. Heinemann, London, 1979, 115pp.

Utilizes Kenyan experiences to test the usefulness of Kenyesian and monetary macro-economic models. Emphasizes the importance of relationships between domestic credit and foreign exchange reserves; and between the exchange rate and the domestic price level.

22-7 MUIRU, J.S. The effectiveness of Kenya's monetary policy during the period 1967-1976. M.A. thesis, University of Nairobi, 1977.

22-8 NDIRANGU, S. Fiscal incentives for industrial development in Kenya. M.A. thesis, University of Nairobi, 1977.

22-9 RWEGASIRA, DELPHIN. "Inflation and monetary expansion: the 1966-73 Tanzanian experience". In K.S. Kim, R.B. Mabele, and M.J. Schultheis (eds.), Papers on the political economy of Tanzania. Heinemann, Nairobi, 1979, pp. 143 154.

Develops an integrated discussion of monetary, balance of payments, and national product developments since the founding of the Tanzania Central Bank in 1966. Discusses the relationship of monetary expansion to inflationary pressures. Initially appeared as ERB Paper 76.8.

3--INTERNATIONAL TRADE AND PAYMENTS

30--International trade and trade relations; terms of trade

30-1 BAILEY, MARTIN. "Tanzania and China". African Affairs, Vol. 74, No. 294, Jan. 1975, pp. 39-50.

Examines the evolution of international economic relations between China and Tanzania since 1961. Suggests that Chinese aid has increased Tanzania's capacity to pursue an independent foreign policy.

INTERNATIONAL TRADE

30-2 BIENEFELD, M.A. "Special gains from trade with socialist countries: the case of Tanzania". World Development, Vol. 3, No. 5, May 1975, pp. 247-272.
Suggests that Tanzania has not derived any special benefits from its trade with the socialist countries, other than gaining access to additional export markets.

30-3 BOWLES, B.D. "Export crops and underdevelopment in Tanganyika, 1929-61". Utafiti, Vol. 1, No. 1, 1976, pp. 71-86.
Considers crops exported from Tanganyika during the periods of colonialism from the point of view of a theory of underdevelopment as a process.

30-4 CHILESHE, JONATHAN H. The challenge of developing intra-African trade. East African Literature Bureau, Nairobi, 1977, 258pp.
Shows that developing Africa not only accepts the challenge of development and economic growth but realizes the relevance of basing it on the principle of African self-reliance expressed through promoting and expanding intra-African trade, which requires a collective and coordinated assault by all developing African countries.

30-5 EL NAMAKI, M.S.S. "Matrix organization a possible solution to the organizational problems of the Tanzanian export sector". Institute of Finance Management, Dar-es-Salaam, 1977, 12pp.

30-6 HAZLEWOOD, ARTHUR. "Inter-state trade in transfer-taxed manufactures, 1967-1970". Econ Stat Rev, No. 42, March 1972, pp. viii-xxiv.
Notes that the pattern of transfers from Kenya to Tanzania has been completely different from that of Kenya to Uganda and Uganda to Tanzania.

30-7 IBRAHIM, TIGANI E. "Prospects for export growth in an African economy: the Kenya case". Viertelsjahresberichte (Bonn), No. 80, June 1980, pp. 121-138.
Analyses export performance in the 1970s; discusses prospects and alternative export policies.

30-8 JOSEPH, G., and NSENGIYUMVA, F. "An econometric approach to the specification and estimation of import demand functions in developing countries: a case study of Tanzania". ERB Occasional Paper 78.4, University of Dar-es-Salaam, Dec. 1979, 75pp.
Develops an approach to import function specification that utilizes information from input-output tables. Estimates are made for aggregate imports, chemicals, fuels, and textiles.

30-9 MACBEAN, A.I., and NGUYEN, D.T. "Commodity concentration and export earnings instability: a mathematical analysis". Economic Journal, Vol. 90, No. 358, pp. 354-362.
An analysis of three observations which suggest that commodity concentration is unlikely in practice to be an important explanation of export earnings instability for developing countries and yet a high average degree of commodity concentration is observed to be a prevalent phenomenon in these less developed countries.

30-10 MMBAGA, W.D.S. "The pattern of Tanzanian international trade". University of New South Wales School of Economics Discussion Paper 43, Kensington, Australia, 1979, 21pp.

30-11 MULIRA, JAMES. The role of Soviet bloc countries in the political, economic and social developments of Uganda, 1945-1970. Ph.D. dissertation, Princeton Universtiy, 1974.

30-12 NABUDERE, DAN W. Essays on the theory and practice of imperialism. Onyx Press, London, 1979.
A survey of imperialism as a background to an understanding of international relations. Argues that imperialism has survived beyond colonialism despite the rising force of socialism because states in the imperialist camp have been fighting jointly against any rising forces.

30-13 NYAMBATI, S.M. The impact of trade instability on economic growth in Kenya. M.A. thesis, University of Nairobi, 1980.

30-14 ODADA, J.E.O., and MAITHA, J. "Commodity problems at the country level: Kenya". A joint report to UNCTAD, Geneva, 1979.

30-15 OLEWE-NYUNYA, JOSHUA D. The dependent nations in international interactions: emerging patterns of regional and global cooperation of the East African states. Ph.D. dissertation, University of North Carolina, Chapel Hill, 1977.

30-16 SEMBOJA, JOSEPH. "Effective rate of protection and industrialization in Tanzania". ERB Paper 78.4, University of Dar-es-Salaam, April 1978, 35pp.
Concludes that effective rates of protection in the mid-1970s were higher than nominal rates and that consumer goods are favoured over intermediate and capital goods by the protective structure. Compares several industries with respect to whether infant industries have "grown up".

30-17 STEIN, LESLIE. "Export trends in East Africa". Development

and Change, Vol. 8, No. 1, Jan. 1977, pp. 103-116.
Attempts to investigate the major factors influencing export trends in East Africa by use of statistical techniques.

30-18 ___. The growth of East African exports and their effect on economic development. Croom Helm, London, 1979, 272pp.
A development case study of Kenya, Uganda and Tanzania for the period 1959-1971 stressing the contribution of exports to development. Contains a theoretical and empirical discussion of the relationship of trade to development.

30-19 SURUMA, EZRA S. An evaluation of international interaction as a source of change in economic structure with special emphasis on Uganda. Ph.D. dissertation, University of Connecticut, 1976.

30-20 THOBANI, AKBARALI H. British entry into the European Economic Community and its implications for the East African countries' exports to Britain. Ph.D. dissertation, University of Denver, 1974.

30-21 TYLER, G.P. "The interests of East Africa in an international tea agreement". IDS Disc P 255, March 1977, 22pp.
Presents an econometric model of the international trade in tea and describes the advantages and disadvantages to East African producers of various possible agreements, as compared to a situation in which no agreement is reached and production continues unrestrained.

31--Commercial policies

31-1 BIERSTEKER, THOMAS J. "Self-reliance in theory and practice in Tanzanian trade relations". International Organization, Vol. 34, Spring 1980, pp. 229-264.

31-2 COOPER, RICHARD C. "Kenya's future as an exporter of manufactures". EAER, Vol. 6, No. 1, June 1974, pp. 44-69.
Agrues that the broad spectrum of Kenyan economic policies, though not concerned with exports, is consistently and strongly biased against exports, while the Exports Promotion Council and the "drawback system" provide very little quantitative offset to this bias.

31-3 ETHERINGTON, D.M. "An international tea trade policy in East Africa: an exercise in oligopolistic reasoning". Food Research Institute Studies, Stanford University, Vol. 11, No. 1, 1972, pp. 89-108.
Examines the trends in tea production and trade in the

East African countries. Analyses the relative costs and benefits of East Africa's participation in the international tea agreement.

31-4 FRIESEN, RONALD L. Empirical studies in import demand and tariffs: a case study of Kenya and East Africa. Ph.D. dissertation, Columbia University, 1973.

31-5 HOPCRAFT, PETER N. "Industrialization, balance of payments, and trade policy in Kenya: the effects of protectionism and government intervention on prices, exports and income distribution". Institute of Development Studies, Nairobi, 1980.
Examines the extent and consequences of Kenya's industrialization via import-substitution strategy. Also covers government participation in manufacturing firms and import licensing procedures.

31-6 JAMAL, VALI. "Effective protection in Uganda". EAER, Vol. 8, No. 2, Dec. 1976, pp. 55-74.
Calculates rates of effective protection for 22 industries for 1972. Most rates are very high, which reflects a deliberate effort to encourage industrial growth. Argues that the result is serious loss of consumer welfare and resource misallocation.

31-7 KESSEL, DUDLEY M. Effective protection rates and industrialization strategies in Tanzania. Ph.D. dissertation, Cornell University, 1969.

31-8 KOESTER, ULRICH. "National interests in international stabilization schemes". IDS Working P 332, Feb. 1978, 20pp.
Tries to show the limitations of the traditional approach to evaluating commodity stabilization schemes.

31-9 ___. "Kenya's economic policy with respect to the world coffee market". IDS Working P 333, April 1978, 34pp.
Argues that Kenya's past coffee market policy did not promote growth, income distribution, monetary stability, or employment objectives, and advocates a variable export tax to compensate for the difference between the world market price and the domestic price, with the latter set at a level to just guarantee the fulfilment of the national quota.

31-10 LOW, PATRICK. "Trade policy as a determinant of industrial structure: the case of the Kenyan pharmaceutical industry". IDS Working P 329, Nov. 1977, 23pp.
Argues that, while the pharmaceutical industry displays features of industries that require government protection,

it did not set itself behind a protectionist barrier, and explains this paradox in terms of market imperfection in the sector.

31-11 MACRAE, D.S. "The import licensing system in Kenya". J Mod Afr Studs, Vol. 17, No. 1, March 1979, pp. 26-46.
Describes the development and functions of the licensing system from colonial times. Attempts to relate such licenses to external tariffs.

31-12 McKEE, JANET W.M. Industrial protection in the Republic of Kenya. Ph.D. dissertation, University of California, Berkeley, 1970.

31-13 PAULDEN, SIDNEY. "Pooling produce for export". International Trade Forum, Vol. 10, No. 1, Jan.-March 1974, pp. 22-25, 30.

31-14 POWER, JOHN H. "Protection and employment: a memorandum to the ILO Mission in Kenya". IDS (unnumbered paper), March 1972, 25pp.
Recommends a uniform tariff partly offset by a uniform value-added tax for Kenya. Argues that the combination of uniform tariff cum uniform value-added tax would be easy to administer and could raise the revenue needed to subsidize "infants" without any of the distorting effects of "protection".

31-15 WAGACHA, BERNARD MBUI. "An analysis of the trade regime in Kenya". IDS Working P 281, Sept. 1976, 20pp.
Examines Kenya's trade policies to see whether these policies have exerted the intended effects on the economy.

31-16 ___. "International trade and agriculture: reasons for corrective policies in LDCs and MDCs". IDS Working P 293, Jan. 1977, 24pp.
Argues that, in growth, the secular problems faced by the agricultural sector of MDCs and LDCs are partly derived from the same peculiar effects of supply and demand conditions of the sector. The agricultural sector faces the same problem of relatively declining incomes as compared to industrial sector. This decline and the phenomenon behind it is in operation in both MDCs and LDCs.

32--Balance of payments experiences and policies

32-1 BHATIA, RALTAN J., and ROTHMAN, SAUL L. "Introducing the extended fund facility: the Kenyan case". Finance and Development, Vol. 12, No. 4, Dec. 1975, pp. 38-41.

32-2 FELDSTEIN, M., and HORIOKA, C. "Domestic savings and international capital flows". Economic Journal, Vol. 90, No. 358, pp. 314-329.
Compares two views of the relation between domestic saving and world capital mobility.

32-3 GRUBEL, HERBERT G., and RYAN, T.C.I. "A monetary model of Kenya's balance of payments". Department of Economics Seminar, University of Nairobi, 1979, 31pp.
Applies the monetary approach to the explanation of the balance of payments of Kenya while admitting that theoretically the country's institutions do not make the model applicable. Shows that Kenya's balance of payments has been determined primarily by the deliberate monetary policy actions of the Central Bank of Kenya.

32-4 HALL, MARSHALL. "The balance of payments of Uganda 1966-1971". Uganda Economic Journal, Vol. 1, No. 1, Dec. 1971, pp. 58-70.
Argues that a serious imbalance exists in Uganda's balance of payments. Discusses alternative policy measures and concludes that vigorous exchange control measures, devaluation-type measures and import restrictions offer the best hope of success.

32-5 HELLEINER, G.K. A world divided: the less developed countries in the international economy. Cambridge University Press, London, 1976, 299pp.
Collection of papers that includes discussion by Reginald Green of monetary aspects from the "extreme" periphery's standpoint, with specific reference to Tanzania.

32-6 KILLICK, T., and THORNE, M. "Problems of an open economy: the balance of payments in the nineteen-seventies". In T. Killick, (ed.), Papers on the Kenyan economy. Heinemann, Nairobi, 1981.

32-7 MAITHA, J.K.; KILLICK, TONY; and IKIARA, G.K. "The balance of payments adjustment process: Kenya". University of Nairobi, March 1978, 62pp and 42 tables.
A report tu UNDP/UNCTAD in two parts: (a) the main report and (b) statistical tables. Mainly concerned with the economic consequences and policy responses to the rise in oil and related prices in 1974-1975.

32-8 NYIRABU, C.M. "The International Monetary Fund, the World Bank and the third world with special reference to Tanzania". In K.S. Kim, R.B. Mabele, and M.J. Schultheis (eds.), Papers on the political economy of Tanzania. Heinemann, Nairobi,

1979, pp. 176-180.
Discusses facilities provided by the IMF for orderly exchange rate adjustments and the World Bank's role in the transfer of resources to Third World countries.

32-9 YAFFEY, M.J.H. Balance of payments problems of a developing country: Tanzania. Weltforum Verlag, Munich, 1970, 290pp.
Discusses the principle features of the Tanzanian balance of payments in relation to exports and imports, invisibles and transfers, and monetary movements and reserves. Also gives some fundamental features of Tanzania's economic relations with the developed countries.

33--Foreign investment, multinational corporations, and foreign aid

33-1 ARMSTRONG, AUBREY B. Toward a systems approach to foreign wealth deprivation in less developed countries: the Tanzanian case. Ph.D. dissertation, University of Washington, 1972.

33-2 BAILEY, MARTIN. "Chinese aid in action: building the Tanzania-Zambia railway". World Development, Vol. 3, Nos. 7-8, July-Aug. 1975, pp. 587-593.
Centres around Peking's reasons for financing the railway, the financial terms attached to the loan, and how the railway was constructed using labour-intensive techniques.

33-3 ___. Freedom railway, China and the Tanzania-Zambia link. Rex Collings, London, 1976, 168pp.
Provides an important case study of an alternative form of external assistance.

33-4 BARKER, CAROL, and WIELD, DAVID. "Notes on international firms in Tanzania". Utafiti, Vol. 3, 1978, pp. 316-339.
Presents empirical information about foreign investment in Tanzania. Gives data on firm ownership.

33-5 CARLSEN, JOHN. "Danish private investments in Kenya". Institute for Development Research project papers, Copenhagen, Jan. 1973, 59pp.
Investigates the socio-economic effects of the activities of Danish private business in Kenya and how the behaviour of the Danish companies is influenced by Kenya's policy toward private foreign investment.

33-6 EZE, OSITA. The legal status of foreign investments in the East African common market. A.W. Sijthoff-Leiden Institut Universitaire de Hautes Etudes Internales, Geneva, 1975, 353pp.

Contains a brief historical survey of the East African common market. Focuses on foreign industrial investments. Mentions some crucial theoretical and policy implications.

33-7 ___. "Multinational enterprises and local manpower in Tanzania". Journal of World Trade Law, Vol. 11, No. 5, Sept.-Oct. 1977, pp. 441-461.
Contends that ultimately it is the willingness of the proprietor of technology and know-how to effect transfer as well as the ability to absorb the information transported that will ensure that some local manpower is developed.

33-8 FEINGOLD, J.H. "Multi-national firms in the Third World: the case of Kenya". World Agriculture, Vol. 25, No. 4, March 1977, pp. 27-28.

33-9 GERSHENBERG, IRVING. "The performance of multinationals and other firms in less economically developed countries: a comparative analysis of Ugandan data". IDS Disc P 234, July 1976, 23pp.
Concludes that from the data at hand it is not clear that the operations of multinational firms in Uganda kept Ugandan industry in a state of dependancy to any significant degree.

33-10 ___, and RYAN, T.C.I. "Does parentage matter? An analysis of transnational and other firms: an East African case". J Dev Areas, Vol. 13, No. 1, Oct. 1978, pp. 3-10.
Compares the economic performance of transnational and domestically owned firms in Ugandan industrial sector, 1969. Finds transnationals to pay significantly higher wages, to be more capital-intensive and to have a superior export record.

33-11 GITELSON, SUSAN A. Multinational aid for national development and self-reliance. East African Literature Bureau, Nairobi, 1975, 308pp.
Evaluates UNDP Special Fund projects in Uganda and Tanzania. Analyses the process of selecting and implementing projects to determine how multilateral aid promotes self-reliance.

33-12 ___. "Policy options for small states: Kenya and Tanzania reconsidered". Studies in Comparative International Development, Vol. 12, No. 2, Summer 1977, pp. 29-57.
Argues that many leaders of small states do not always put into practice the policy of non-alignment because the international environment is not conducive; the leaders place a higher value on security or development than on independence, or domestic pressures influence them to search for reliable external sources of assistance.

INTERNATIONAL TRADE

33-13 GODFREY, M., and LANGDON, STEVEN W. "Partners in underdevelopment? The transnationalisation thesis in a Kenyan context". Journal of Commonwealth and Comparative Politics, Vol. 14, No. 1, March 1976, pp. 42-63.
Also given as paper at Sussex IDS in 1974.

33-14 GORDENKER, LEON. International aid and national decisions: development programs in Malawi, Tanzania and Zambia. Princeton University Press, Princeton, 1976, 190pp.
Centres on the manner in which international organizations (IBRD, FAO, UNIDO, UNDP, etc.) work in cooperation with the member Third World countries to improve the general welfare in the third world. The study analysed the role of the international organisations in the development of specific projects in Malawi, Zambia, and Tanzania.

33-15 GRAY, CLIVE S. "The impact of foreign aid for local costs on the donor's international receipts". EAER, Vol. 3, No. 1, June 1971, pp. 69-87.
Estimates that a comparatively high proportion of British local cost aid to Kenya returns to Britain. Argues that this is a function of the close links between the two economies.

33-16 GUTKIND, PETER C.W., and WALLERSTEIN, IMMANUEL (eds.). The political economy of contemporary Africa. SAGE Publications, London, 1977, 320pp.
Includes Gavin Williams, "Taking the part of peasants: rural development in Nigeria and Tanzania", and Tamas Szentes, "Socioeconomic effects of two patterns of foreign capital investments, with special reference to East Africa".

33-17 HERMAN, BARRY M. Strategies of foreign manufacturing investment in poor countries: a general theory and an application to oil refining in East Africa. Ph.D. dissertation, University of Michigan, 1974.

33-18 HOLTHAM, G.N. "Current dilemmas in aid policy: observations from British aid to Kenya". ODI Review, No. 1, 1976, pp. 34-42.
Looks at ways in which reality diverges from the ideal. Argues that attempts to solve the difficulties lead to conflicting policy prescriptions.

33-19 HOLTHAM, GERALD, and HAZLEWOOD, ARTHUR. Aid and inequality in Kenya. Croom Helm and Overseas Development Institute, London, 1976, 265pp.
Examines the impact of aid on policy-formation and economic performance. Concludes that, while British aid has facilitated

Kenya's inegalitarian growth process and distorted administrative procedures, the net effect on general living standards has been strongly positive.

33-20 HOWARD, G.A. Host country-transnational corporation relations: Kenya control over foreign enterprizes. Ph.D. dissertation, Catholic University, Washington, D.C., 1978, 332pp.
DAI, Vol. 39, p. 5708.

33-21 IBANDA, MARGARET. A case of multinational investments in East Africa: the soft drinks industry in Kenya. M.A. thesis, University of Nairobi, 1979.

33-22 JORGENSEN, J.J. "Multinational corporations and the indigenization of the Kenyan economy". Afr Rev, Vol. 5, No. 4, 1975, pp. 429-450.
Looks at foreign control of the Kenyan economy. Reviews the de-indigenization of the economy during the pre-independence period and subsequent Africanization in the post-independence period.

33-23 KAPLINSKY, RAPHAEL, and CHISTI, S. "Technical change and the multinational corporation: some British multinationals in Kenya and India". IDS Working P 266, May 1976, 70pp.
Compares the behaviour of seven Kenyan subsidiaries with that of eight Indian subsidiaries. A follow-up of IDS Working P 228.

33-24 KAPLINSKY, RAPHAEL (ed.). Readings on the multinational corporation in Kenya. Oxford University Press, Nairobi, 1978, 316pp.
A collection of papers covering such subjects as the history of foreign investment in Kenya, its dominance in the manufacturing sector, its technology choices, its reliance on import substitution, its links with the political system, its profitability, the advantages of local ownership, and the emergence of Kenyan multinationals.

33-25 ___. "Export-oriented growth: a large international firm in a small developing country". World Development, Vol. 7, Nos. 8-9, Aug.-Sept. 1979, pp. 825-834.
Argues that a large international firm operating in a small developing country is able to negotiate very favourable conditions for itself and is then able to manipulate prices and intra-firm payments to reduce taxes.

33-26 KENYA. Compendium on development assistance to Kenya as of December 1979. Government Printer, Nairobi, July 1980.

INTERNATIONAL TRADE

Summary of all commitments on development assistance entered to by the Kenya government. Includes information on donors, projects and objectives, amount and type of assistance, etc.

33-27 LANGDON, STEVEN W. "Multinational corporations, taste transfer and underdevelopment: a case study from Kenya". Review of African Political Economy, No. 2, 1974.
Argues that international corporation investment has resulted in increasing unemployment and regional inequality, has made little contribution to the balance of payments, and has failed to make linkages with the resources of the local economy. The promotion of taste transfer has reinforced the transfer of inappropriate technology. Covers period to 1972.

33-28 ___. "Multinational firms and the state in Kenya". IDS Bulletin, Vol. 9, No. 1, July 1977, pp. 36-41.
Discusses evidence about state-multinational relationships in Kenya based on research during 1972-1973. Examines the role of the state in this set of relationships.

33-29 ___. Multinational corporations in the political economy of Kenya. Macmillan, London, 1980, 240pp.
Examines the result of giving foreign firms a central place in the development plans of Kenya in the late 1960s and early 1970s. Includes a comparison of local and multinational firms in two industries (soap production and shoe manufacturing). The conclusions are then tested against interview results from most other large multinationals active in Kenya. Discussion is set in a framework of political economy analysis.
The author's Ph.D. dissertation at University of Sussex in 1975 bears the same title.

33-30 LAWRENCE, PETER R. "Socialism, self-reliance and foreign aid in Tanzania: some lessons from the socialist experience". UNIDEP Paper (May 1972), University of Dar-es-Salaam, 1974?, 21pp.

33-31 MAZZEO, DOMENICO. Foreign assistance and the East African common services, 1960-1970. Weltforum Verlag, Munich, 1976, 235pp.
Attempts to assess the role of foreign assistance provided to the common services during the 1960s, particularly in transport, communication, training, and research.

33-32 MOSHI, H.P.B. "Multilateral corporate finance and third world economies and freedom". Journal of International Relations (Dar-es-Salaam), Vol. 3, No. 2, June 1980, pp. 9-24.
An account of development strategies open to Third World countries: either alliance or non-alliance with the developed countries. Examines the role of multinational corporations.

33-33 NEERSØ, PETER. "Selected aspects of Tanzania's policies on foreign investment". World Development, Vol. 2, No. 2, Feb. 1974, pp. 139-144.
Discusses government control of parastatals, provision of know-how for industrial projects, management contracts, taxation of foreign companies, and remittance of profits.

33-34 NELLIS, J.R. "Expatriates in the government of Kenya". Journal of Commonwealth Political Studies, Vol. 11, No. 3, Nov. 1973, pp. 251-264.
Concludes that technical assistance personnel especially prominent, though perhaps declining in members, in planning positions in Nairobi ministries. Argues that their presence and assignments reflect a general Kenyan acceptance of Western economic theories and methods. Also appeared as an IDS unnumbered paper in 1974.

33-35 OSITA, C. EZE. "Multinational enterprises and local manpower in Tanzania". Journal of World Trade Law, Vol. 11, No. 5, Sept./Oct. 1977, pp. 441-461.
Deals with the effects of the activities of multinational enterprises in Tanzania in respect of the transfer of technology. Explains the reasons for the lack of benefits to the developing country and suggests ways in which the situation may be improved.

33-36 RADETZKI, MARIAN. Aid and development: a handbook for small donors. Praeger, 1973, 323pp.
Theoretically analyses aid and development as regards optimal foreign aid use in the case of limited supply. Focuses on the Swedish aid program to Kenya and Tanzania.

33-37 RASMUSSON, RASMUS. "On optimal assistance with special reference to the second Kenyan and Tanzanian five year plans". Studies on Developing Countries No. 67, Centre for Afro-Asian Research of the Hungarian Academy of Sciences, Budapest, 1973.
For these two countries, the author examines what forms of foreign aid would be optimal in the sense of mitigating conflicts between the targets in the development plans.

33-38 ROOD, LESLIE L. "Foreign investment in African manufacturing". J Mod Afr Studs, Vol. 13, No. 1, Dec. 1975, pp. 19-34.
Gives figures on private foreign direct investments in the LDC including East African economies, looks at the nature and amounts of investments in these countries, the influence of the size of the market, the risk of take-over by nationalization, Africanization, and indigenisation. Concludes that

INTERNATIONAL TRADE

investments in manufacturing by multinationals are relatively safe.

33-39 SHIVJI, ISSA G. "Capitalism unlimited: public corporations in partnership with multinational corporations". Conference on Public Corporations in Africa, Accra, May-June 1973, 24pp.
Analysis of how public corporations in LDCs form partnerships with multinational corporations and the losses and benefits that are incurred by the LDCs.

33-40 SINGER, HANS W. "Technical assistance to Kenya: some thoughts on flows and programming". University of Sussex Institute of Development Studies, Brighton, 1969, 8pp.
Discusses means of improving aid efficiency.

33-41 SINGER, HANS D., and ANSARI, JAVED. Rich and poor countries. George Allen and Unwin, London, 1977, 228pp.
Examines some fundamental aspects of the relationships between rich and poor countries, such as trade, aid and factor flows, against the background of current economic crisis. Examines import-substitution industrialization strategy. Includes a chapter on the East African common market.

33-42 STEVENS, CHRISTOPHER. The Soviet Union and black Africa. Macmillan, London, 1976, 236pp.
Analysis of the development of economic and political relations between the U.S.S.R. and African countries, including Kenya and Tanzania.

33-43 SWAINSON, NICOLA. "The history of investment in Kenya before 1945". IDS Working P 242, Oct. 1975, 77pp.
Examines aspects of capitalist development in Kenya before 1945. Aims to show the competitive relations of capitalist production when applied to the control of a particular commodity, for instance, tea.

33-44 ___. "Company formation in Kenya before 1945, with particular reference to the role of foreign capital". IDS Working P 267, May 1976, 89pp.
Concludes that investment in manufacturing concerns before 1945 was limited due to small markets in East Africa and the desire of British industrial capital to discourage manufacturing for export.

33-45 ___. Foreign corporations and economic growth in Kenya. Ph.D. dissertation, University of London, 1977, 372pp.
Examines the impact of foreign investment on the Kenyan economy and how the country has been integrated into the world capitalist system since the early 1900s. For three

historical periods the analysis illustrates the interaction between domestic and foreign capital in Kenya.

33-46 TANDON, Y. (ed.). Technical assistance in East Africa. Dag Hammerskjold Foundation, Uppsala, 1973, 209pp.

33-47 WANJOHI, N.G. "Multinational corporations and regional co-operation in developing countries: the East African experience 1947-1977". Department of History Staff Seminar, University of Nairobi, May 1978, 12pp.
Tries to show the relationship between multinational corporations and the institution, preservation, and ultimate collapse of the East African Community.

33-48 WEINSTEIN, WARREN, and HENRIKSEN, THOMAS B. Soviet and Chinese aid to African nations. Praeger, New York, 1980, 184pp.

33-49 WIDSTRAND, CARL (ed.). Multi-national firms in Africa. Scandinavian Institute of African Studies, Uppsala, 1975, 425pp.
Includes J.J. Jorgensen, "Multinational corporations and the indigenization of the Kenyan economy", and P. Neersø, "Tanzania's policies on private foreign investment".

33-50 WOOD, ROBERT, and MORTON, KATHRYN. "Has British aid helped poor countries?--Five African cases". ODI Review, No. 1, 1977, pp 40-67.
Reviews the studies of British aid which ODI had carried out. Focuses upon various features of developing countries as they relate to British aid policy.

34--East African cooperation and the East African Community

34-1 AKIWUMI, A.M. "The East African Community". Journal of World Trade Law, Vol. 6, No. 2, March 1972, pp. 203-226.
Describes the issues at stake in preserving economic co-operation after independence and gives a detailed analysis of the Treaty of East African Co-operation.

34-2 CHARKINS, RALPH J. The theory of economic integration in a development setting: East Africa. Ph.D. dissertation, University of North Carolina, Chapel Hill, 1971.

34-3 DOIMI DI DELUPIS, J. The East African Community and common market. London, 1970, 184pp.
Analyses the functioning of the East African Community and its common market. Also endeavours to analyse the association agreement with the EEC in comparison with other

INTERNATIONAL TRADE

agreements on association with African countries concluded by the EEC, such as the Yaoundé Convention and the agreement with Nigeria.

34-4 "East African Community--special survey". African Development, Vol. 8, No. 2, Feb. 1974, pp. EA 3-54.

34-5 EKEN, SENA. "Breakup of the East African Community". Finance and Development, Vol. 16, No. 4, Dec. 1979, pp. 36-40.
Examines the main problems of regional integration with specific reference to the factors that led to the breakup of the East African Community. Apart from problems of state sovereignty, other problems are seen as ideological differences, unequal development, and trade imbalance among the three member countries.

34-6 GATELY, D. "Sharing the gains from customs unions among less developed countries: a game theoretic approach". Journal of Development Economics, Vol. 1, No. 3, Dec. 1974, pp. 213-233.
Uses game theory as a framework to illustrate the division of benefits from the East African common market.

34-7 GHAI, D.P. "State trading and regional economic integration: the East African experience". J Comm Mkt Studs, Vol. 12, No. 3, Sept. 1974, pp. 296-318.
Investigates the impact of the growth of state trading enterprises in the partner states on the operation of the East African common market.

34-8 GHAI, YASH P. "East African industrial licencing system: a device for the regional allocation of industry?". J Comm Mkt Studs, Vol. 12, No. 3, Sept. 1974, pp. 265-295.
Examines the record of the system since its establishment. Focuses on the law and institutions of the system, on the institutional constraints, and on how its powers and functions have been interpreted.

34-9 ___. "Reflections on law and economic integration in East Africa". Scandanavian Institute of African Studies Research Report No. 36, Uppsala, 1976, 47pp.

34-10 HAZLEWOOD, ARTHUR. "The end of the East African Community: what are the lessons for regional integration schemes?". J Comm Mkt Studs, Vol. 18, No. 1, Sept. 1979, pp. 40-58.
Explains the background of the Treaty for East African Cooperation, outlines some main features of the Treaty, and analyses the issues which arose between the partner states.

34-11 KASSUM, AL NOOR. "The future of the East African Community". Utafiti, Vol. 2, No. 1, 1977, pp. 7-23.
A speech in which the situation of the Community is outlined and some suggestions are made.

34-12 KIM, KWAN S. "An appraisal of the East African economic integration scheme: critical issues and possibilities". In K.S. Kim, R.B. Mabele, and M.J. Schultheis (eds.), Papers on the political economy of Tanzania. Heinemann Educational, Nairobi, 1979, pp. 181-188.
Examines the structural characteristics of East African economic integration, the impact of integration, and the application of the transfer tax system in these states. Evaluates the coordination of plans for industrialization in economically integrated regions. Initially appeared as ERB Paper 76.7.

34-13 MAHIGA, A.P. "The extent of integration and disintegration in the East African Community". EA USSC Conference, Nairobi, Dec. 1975.

34-14 ___. "The pitfalls and promises of regional integration in East Africa". Utafiti, Vol. 2, No. 1, 1977, pp. 25-42.
Argues that attempts to cope with unequal distribution of benefits may be helpful in resolving temporary crises, but a long-term solution would have to tackle the root causes of underdevelopment.

34-15 MBOGORO, D.A.K. "The common market concept and economic development: Tanzania's experience in the East African common market". ERB Paper 77.8, University of Dar-es-Salaam, 1978, 35pp.

34-16 MEHRETU, ASSEFA. Regional integration for economic development of greater East Africa: a quantified analysis of possibilities. Uganda Publishing House, Kampala, 1973, 150pp.
A discussion of possibilities of integration in eastern Africa centered mainly on spatio-economic considerations. The analysis is based on Ethiopia, Kenya, Somalia, Sudan, Tanzania, and Uganda.

34-17 MUGAMBA, AGRIPPAH T. "Regional organisations and African underdevelopment: the collapse of the East African Community". J Mod Afr Studs, Vol. 16, No. 2, June 1978, pp. 261-272.

34-18 MURIUKI, GODFREY. "The breaking up of the East African Community". Department of History Staff Seminar Paper, University of Nairobi, 1978-1979, 11pp.

INTERNATIONAL TRADE

A history of the rise and fall of the East African Community, whose collapse is associated with the colonial heritage, political differences, and different approaches to economic problems within the three East African states.

34-19 MWASE, NGILA. "Regional economic integration and unequal sharing of benefits: background to the disintegration and collapse of the East African Community". African Development, Vol. 4, Nos. 2-3, April-Sept. 1979, pp. 1-29.

Emphasizes the role of regional economic integration to save developing countries from heavy dependency (technological, financial, markets, entrepreneurial, etc.). Differing levels of economic development have brought distributional problems of the benefits, with the largest share accruing to the partner able to attract more investments.

34-20 NAHAMYA, SAM GAHIIRE. Regional economic disintegration: tensions, conflicts and causes: the case for the EAC. Ph.D. dissertation, Colorado State University, 1980, 149pp.

DAI, Vol. 41, p. 2238-A.

34-21 OKIDI, C. ODIDI. "The Lake Victoria and Nile basins: an evaluation of the means for co-operative development". University of Nairobi, IDS, May 1980, 103pp.

An analysis of the inter-state agreements that have been concluded on the consumptive uses of the waters of the Nile drainage basin, including Lake Victoria and the Nile river. Intends to suggest whether such inter-state agreements provide an adequate framework for co-operative development among those states.

34-22 POTHOLM, C.P. "The breakup of the East African Community". World Affairs, Vol. 142, No. 1, 1979, pp. 45-56.

34-23 RAKE, ALAN. "East Africa's Community splits apart". African Development, Vol. 9, No. 11, Nov. 1975, pp. 20, 21, 25.

34-24 ROBSON, PETER. Economic integration in Africa. Allen and Unwin, London, 1968, 320pp.

Includes a chapter on economic integration in East Africa. The chapter covers the 1967 Treaty for East African Cooperation.

34-25 ROSBERG, C.G., Jr., and SEGAL, A. "An East African federation". International Reconciliation, No. 543, May 1963, 72pp.

Highlights the benefits that can be derived from the formation of a large and viable East African federation (Kenya, Uganda, and Tanganyika) through a common market. Argues that due to historical, political, and geographical features the formation of such a union would present no serious problems. However, the smooth running of the union would be hindered by problems related to the sharing of the benefits from the common market, among others.

34-26 ROTHCHILD, DONALD. Politics of integration: an East African documentary. East African Publishing House, Nairobi, 1967. 343pp.
Documentary materials on the politics of unification in East Africa, from the 1920s to the 1967 Treaty.

34-27 SEGAL, DAVID. East African common market inequalities of the 1960s: an arbitration scheme. Ph.D. dissertation, Yale University, 1969.

34-28 ___. "On making customs union fair: an East African example". Yale Economic Essays, Vol. 10, No. 2, 1970, pp. 115-160.

34-29 TIBAZARWA, CLEMENS MARTIN. Economic impact on Tanzania of the East African common market. Ph.D. dissertation, Claremont Graduate School, 1975, 219pp.
Attempts to delineate the variables which reflect the integration impact and examines the Tanzanian industrial sector for effects of the common market. Evaluation is aimed at assessing the common market as an alternative strategy for economic development in Tanzania.

34-30 UNITED NATIONS DEPARTMENT OF ECONOMIC AND SOCIAL AFFAIRS. Economic cooperation and integration in Africa: three case studies. United Nations (ST/EAC/109), New York, 1969, 144pp.
Includes "Economic co-operation in Eastern Africa", which attempts to indicate the character of the difficulties confronting the Eastern African integration scheme that aimed to bring about structural transformation and rapid industrialization.

34-31 WEBER, ADOLF, and HARTMANN, THOMAS T. "A comparative study of economic integration with special reference to agricultural policy in the East African Community". Zietschrift für Ausländische Landwirtschaft (Quarterly Journal of International Agriculture), Vol. 15, No. 2, April-June 1976, pp. 110-127.
Points out that total trade, as well as agricultural trade, decreased in 1967-1974. Special emphasis is placed on the divisive results of the fiction of exchange rates fixed at par within the Community, which hampered an increase in intra-community trade.

Appeared also in T. Dams and K.E. Hunt (eds.), Decision-making and agriculture (1976 conference), Agricultural Economics Institute for International Association of Agricultural Economists, Oxford, 1977, pp. 379-395.

34-32 WERE, J.M. "The geography of international trade for East Africa". Makerere University Department of Geography Occasional Paper No. 56, Kampala, 1974, 49pp.

Argues that trade between the East African countries and their trading partners is mainly a function of economic affiliation and that the process of integration has brought some increase in the diversification of exports of the East African Community.

4--THE AGRICULTURAL SECTOR

40--Structure and organization

40-1 ARMOR, T.; HONADLE, G.; OLSON, C.; and WEISEL, P. "Organizing and supporting integrated rural development projects: a twofold approach to administrative development". J Admin Overseas, Vol. 18, No. 4, Oct. 1979, pp. 276-286.

Argues that problems in rural development project management must be approached from two analytic viewpoints: the development administration point of view and/or the organizational development point of view. Both approaches are valid and necessary.

40-2 BARKAN, JOEL D.; GACHUKI, DAVID; HOLMQUIST, FRANK; and MIGOT-ADHOLLA, S. "Is small beautiful? The organisational conditions for effective small-scale self-help development projects in rural Kenya". IDS Working P 364, March 1980, 27pp.

The authors feel that small scale self-help development projects are no panacea for overcoming the obstacles to development among the rural poor. There is need to probe more deeply into the web of social relations which constitute the structures of underdevelopment and the organizational mechanisms for breaking down these structures among those for whom development is supposed to occur.

40-3 CAMPBELL, JOAN M. Agricultural development in East Africa: a problem in cultural ecology. Ph.D. dissertation, Columbia University, 1971.

40-4 COWEN, M.P. "Wattle production in the Central Province: capital and household commodity production 1903-1964". Conference on the Political Economy of Kenya, 1929-1952, Trinity College,

Cambridge, July 1975, 107pp.
Shows how the survival of estate production in wattle commodity production depended upon the intrusion of international capital; also how the expansion of household commodity production proceeded in the face of imminent depression of estate production.

40-5 GOTTLIEB, MANUEL. "The extent and character of differentiation in Tanzanian agricultural and rural society, 1967-1969". EA USSC Conference, Dec. 1972, 36pp.
Argues that clearcut lines of socio-economic stratification, separating some households into an upper class and others into a lower class, do not run through Tanzanian society.

40-6 GSAENGER, HANS G., and SCHMIDT, GUENTER. "Decontrolling the maize marketing system in Kenya". Zietschrift für Ausländische Lanwirtschaft (Quarterly Journal of International Agriculture), Vol. 16, No. 3, Sept. 1977, pp. 268-284.
An assessment of the major deficiencies of the present maize marketing system. Discusses the implications of a completely decontrolled maize market and suggests a price stabilization scheme with buffer stock operations to regulate the maize market. Also appears as IDS Disc P 254 of March 1977.

40-7 KURIA, M. CHEGE. "The role of cooperatives in agricultural development to small scale farmers". In Paris Andeou, Co-operative institutions and economic development: some lessons from advanced and developing countries. East African Literature Bureau, Nairobi, 1977, pp. 127-134.
Analyses the role played by co-operatives in small-scale farming agricultural development in aspects such as finance, education, etc. Concludes that cooperatives in Kenya are expanding rapidly and are here to stay since farmers attach great importance to them.

40-8 MAFEJE, ARCHIE. "Large-scale farming in Buganda". In D. Brokensha and M. Pearsall (eds.), The anthropology of development in sub-Sahara Africa. University Press of Kentucky, Lexington, 1969.

40-9 MBAWALA, PIUS PAUL. "Irrigation development in mainland Tanzania: the issue of farmer local organisation--a suggestion". Agricultural Administration, Vol. 6, No. 2, April 1979, pp. 99-108.
Focuses on the issue of local organization of Tanzanian small-scale irrigation projects. Suggests models of

organizing and operating the small-scale irrigation systems based on the Tanzanian formal village organization.

40-10 MOODY, ANTHONY A. "Peasant agriculture, commercial production and employment in Kenya". Africa Development, Vol. 1, No. 2, Sept. 1976, pp. 62-72.
Argues that some of the recent emphasis placed upon intensified cash crop production by small holders is over-optimistic in its hopes to increase rural employment. Examination of the relative importance attached to subsistence production shows that it is competing heavily with cash crop production for scarce productive resources.

40-11 MSAMBICHAKA, L.A. "A theoretical analysis of the fundamentals of agricultural development in a non-capitalist developing Tanzania in the state sector and agricultural producer co-operatives". ERB Paper 74.12, University of Dar-es-Salaam, 1974.

40-12 MVANO, VEN. Farm planning in Kenya: a systems simulation approach. M.B.A. thesis, University of Nairobi, 1975, 83pp.
Investigates the planning environment of a modern farm in Kenya and the planning tools that could be used in selecting farm programmes with desirable financial returns.

40-13 NDAWULA-KAJUMBA, S. "Socioeconomic aspects of an African plantation system: the Tanzanian sisal plantation case". ERB Paper 77.1, University of Dar-es-Salaam, 1977.

40-14 ONCHERE, S.R. Structure and performance of agricultural product and input markets in the Northern division of Machakos district, Kenya. M.Sc. thesis, University of Nairobi, 1976, 195pp.
Observes that farm output per household is so low that it does not satisfy subsistence needs over the year, and that the use of purchased inputs in food production is of negligible importance.

40-15 OPIO-ODONGO, J.M.A. "Agricultural productivity in Uganda; a social organizational perspective". EAJ Rural Devel, Vol. 8, Nos. 1-2, 1975, pp. 118-128.
Discusses the problem of the slow pace in modernizing agriculture in terms of the impact of the organization of the social units on agricultural productivity.

40-16 PRITCHARD, BRIAN. Tanzania's agricultural economy in brief. U.S. Department of Agriculture Economic Research Service, Washington, D.C., 1974, 22pp.

40-17 SHARMA, K.L. "Agriculture and structural transformation in a developing economy--the Kenyan experience". SID Seminar on patterns of development and lifestyles for Eastern Africa, Nairobi, July 1979.
Discusses the role of agriculture in Kenya's development, and provides an empirical study of the declining contribution of agriculture to GDP.

40-18 WALKER, HANS H., and WOLFGANG, GRAF ZU CASTELL. "The contribution of organisation analysis to the appraisal of development projects--the example of the Ahero pilot irrigation scheme in Kenya". Zietschrift für Ausländische Landwirtschaft (Quarterly Journal of International Agriculture), Vol. 18, No. 1, Jan.-Mar. 1979, pp. 49-68.
Basic elements of organization analysis are introduced and applied as a necessary component of the traditional cost-benefit analysis.

40-19 WOLGIN, J.M. "Resource allocation and risk: a case study of smallholder agriculture in Kenya". American Journal of Agricultural Economics, Vol. 57, No. 4, Nov. 1975, pp. 622-630.
Finds that farmers in Kenya are relatively efficient in their allocation of resources. Argues that they would reduce their risk aversion with increased credit.

41--Sample, locality, and farm studies

41-1 AKENDA-ONDOGA, V.J. An economic study of production organization and labor use among smallholders in Nill province, Uganda. Ph.D. dissertation, Cornell University, 1980.
DAI, Vol. 41, p. 2698-A.

41-2 ALILA, PATRICK O. "The role of public bureaucracy in agricultural development in Kisumu district--western Kenya". IDS Working P 277, Aug. 1976, 35pp.
Discusses government policy on agricultural development and how it influences the distribution of resources and services both at the macro and micro levels. The major finding from farmer responses on the distribution of goods and services such as loans and crop demonstration is that they disproportionately benefit the better farmers.

41-3 ANUSIONWU, EMMANUEL C. A framework for a regional study of African agricultural rural economy: a case study of Kigizi district in western Uganda. Ph.D. dissertation, Cornell University, 1977.

THE AGRICULTURAL SECTOR

41-4 ATENG', B.A. Linear programming: an application to the identification of the best existing farming strategy for peasant farmers in Kenya. M.A. thesis, University of Nairobi, 1977.

41-5 BERRY, L., et al. "Human adjustment to agricultural drought in Tanzania: pilot investigations". BRALUP Research Paper No. 13, University of Dar-es-Salaam, Sept. 1972, 56pp.
Reports on a number of pilot investigations into the problem of drought in Tanzania with a view to estimation of the optimal set of adjustments in relation to the economic and social setting.

41-6 BOESEN, J. "Development and class structure in a small-holder society and the potential of Ujamaa". Institute for Development Research Paper A 72.16, May 1972, Copenhagen, 100pp.
Concludes from a study of Ngara that villagers are a homogenous group of small-holder farmers and that the major socio-economic differentiation is found between the small-holder society on one side and people engaged in the industrial, commercial, and bureaucratic sector on the other side.

41-7 CHAMBERS, ROBERT, and MORIS, JON (eds.). Mwea: an irrigated rice settlement in Kenya. Weltforum Verlag, Munich, 1973, 525pp.
Includes Jane Hanger and Jon Moris, "Women and the household economy"; T.J. Aldington and L.D. Smith, "The scheme and rice marketing in Kenya"; and Stephen Sandford, "An economic evaluation of the scheme".

41-8 CONYERS, D.; NGUMBULU, P.J.; and RAJAB, A.R.M.S. "Agro-economic zones of Dodoma and Singida". BRALUP Research Report No. 47, University of Dar-es-Salaam, Oct. 1971, 75pp.
A provisional attempt to divide the districts of Dodoma and Singida regions into agro-economic zones in which agricultural conditions are sufficiently similar to warrant the adoption of a single agricultural policy at the district level.

41-9 CONYERS, D. "Agro-economic zones of Tanzania". BRALUP Research Paper No. 25, University of Dar-es-Salaam, Aug. 1973, 85pp.
Brings together the information derived from various district agro-economic zoning surveys in order to facilitate planning at the national level, and in particular to provide a basis for cross-tabulation of such data.

41-10 COWEN, M.P. "Differentiation in a Kenya location". EA USSC Conference, Nairobi, Dec. 1972, pp. 33-65.
Argues that as long as colonial estate production was not

sufficiently strong to destroy totally the means of survival for the mass of households as units of production, in an area such as Magutu, then differences between households in accumulation and the compulsion to engage in wage labour must be sought in the interaction of the peasant and colonial systems.

41-11 ___. "Concentration of sales and assets: dairy cattle and tea in Magutu 1964-1971". IDS Working P 146, March 1974, 88pp.
Focuses on the mode of inequality in the command over assets and distribution of income from the production of the major enterprises in the small-scale agriculture of Magutu, Kenya.

41-12 DAMS, THEODOR, and HUNT, KENNETH E. Decision-making and agriculture. Papers and Reports of 16th International Conference of Agricultural Economists, Nairobi, Kenya, 1976. Agricultural Economics Institute for International Association of Agricultural Economists, Oxford, 1977, 603pp.
Includes A. Weber and T.T. Hartman, "A comparative study of economic integration with special reference to agricultural policy in the East African Community".

41-13 EXETER, J. "A comparison of the intensity of cultivation on large and small farms in Kenya". Statistics Division, Kenya Ministry of Finance and Economic Planning, Nairobi, 1972.

41-14 FISHER, PATRICIA M. Risk aversion by small farmers; can it be measured? Results of a survey, Kirinyaga district. M.A. thesis, University of Nairobi, 1977.

41-15 FOYE, S.H.C. "A report on ox-cultivation in Uganda". Department of Agriculture, Entebbe, 1966.

41-16 GOLD, A.E. "Cultivation versus herding in southern Nandi, ca. 1840-1914". Department of History Staff Seminar Paper, University of Nairobi, March 1977, 24pp.
Data is derived from oral interviews with forty-five individuals who spent their childhoods within southern Nandi.

41-17 HEYER, JUDITH. "A preliminary report on farm surveys: tractor and ox-cultivation in Makueni and Bugoma". Farm Equipment Workshop Paper, 1975?, 28pp.

41-18 HOGG, RICHARD. "Pastoralism and improverishment: the case of Isiolo Boran of northern Kenya". Disasters, Vol. 4, No. 3, 1980, pp. 299-310.

THE AGRICULTURAL SECTOR

41-19 HUNT, DIANA M. "Chayanov's model of peasant household resource allocation and its relevance to Mbere division, Eastern Kenya". J Dev Studs, Vol. 15, No. 1, Oct. 1978, pp. 59-68.
Concludes that in most respects Chayanov's model explains household resource allocation in Mbere but notes that the dominant determinants of variations in per capita income in Mbere are formal education and access to full-time off-farm work, variables which Chayanov did not consider. Also appeared as University of Nairobi IDS Working P 276.

41-20 KAKENYA, MAKOTO. "Subsistence ecology of the Tongwe, Tanzania". Kyoto University African Studies, Vol. 10, 1976, pp. 143-212.
Focuses on the Tongwe tribe that makes its living on shifting cultivation, hunting, fishing, and honey collecting. The survey tries to clarify the relationship between man and nature and how this is related to the subsistence activities, dietary life, social organization, and super-natural beliefs and practices.

41-21 KAMUZORA, C. LWECHUNGURA. "Constraints to labour time availability in African smallholder agriculture: the case of Bukoba district, Tanzania". Development and Change, Vol. 11, No. 1, Jan. 1980, pp. 123-135.
Examines the effect of constrained labour supply on the output of small-holdings in agriculture, which are by nature labour intensive. Economic incentives such as a rise in crop prices or reduction of costs of crop production could lead farmers to substitute socialisation for work.

41-22 KENYA MINISTRY OF ECONOMIC PLANNING AND DEVELOPMENT. "A report on economic studies of farming in Nyanza province, Kenya". Farm Economic Report No. 26, Government Printer, Nairobi, Nov. 1969.

41-23 KONGSTAD, P., and MONSTED, M. Family labour and trade in western Kenya. Scandinavian Institute of African Studies, Uppsala, 1980, 186pp.
Presents evidence of the reporduction of labour in selected rural communities of Nyanza, Western and Rift Valley provinces The analysis concentrates on different farm activities because all activities in rural areas are related to farming. Trade is analysed in relation to agriculture and family obligation, and in relation to the possibilities for income earning or accumulation.

41-24 KUHN, J., and STOFFREGEN, H. How to measure the efficiency of agricultural cooperatives in developing countries: case study--Kenya. FAO (Access No. 28950), Rome, 1975, 108pp.

41-25 LARSEN, A. "Agriculture in Sukumaland/Tanzania". Landbrugsoekonomiske Studier No. 5, Copenhagen, 1974, 93pp.

41-26 LEO, CHRISTOPHER. "The failure of the 'progressive farmer' in Kenya's million-acre settlement scheme". J Mod Afr Studs, Vol. 16, No. 4, Dec. 1978, pp. 619-638.
Looks at the position of both "progressive" and "non-progressive" farmers in the scheme. Shows that the "progressive" is no better than the "non-progressive".

41-27 LIVINGSTONE, IAN. "Economic irrationality among pastoral peoples: myth or reality?". Development and Change, Vol. 8, No. 2, April 1977.
Analyses the mode of life of the pastoralists and the subsequent effects on economic underdevelopment among such communities with special reference to East African pastoralists, namely Kalenjin, Somali, and Maasai.

41-28 McCORD, G.S. Economics of improved management for transforming the forage livestock system in Tanzania: a simulation model. Ph.D. dissertation, Texas A. & M. University, 1979, 222pp.
DAI, Vol. 40, p. 4682-A.

41-29 McLOUGHLIN, PETER F.M. (ed.). African food production systems: cases and theory. Johns Hopkins University Press, Baltimore, 1970, 318pp.
Includes Priscilla Reining, "Social factors and food production in an East African peasant society: the Haya" and Neville and Rada Dyson-Hudson, "The food production system of a semi-nomadic society: the Karamojong, Uganda".

41-30 MAXON, R.M. "The early years of the Gusii coffee industry in Kenya, 1933-1946". J Dev Areas, Vol. 6, No. 3, April 1972, pp. 365-381.
Observes that the successful coffee cultivation in Gusiiland is illustrative of the fact that the introduction and development of cash crops could be accomplished from above without an initial strong, pervasive demand on the part of the people; and of the utility of cooperative organization in the development of cash crop agriculture among small holders.

41-31 MAYER, T., and JUNEINGER-DITTEL. "Producer income instability and farmers risk response: the case of major Kenyan export crops". Working Paper No. 101, Kiel Institute of World Economics, March 1980, 20pp.
Quantifies the effects of producer income instability on farmers' planting and long-run supply decisions in coffee, tea, and sisal production in the Kenyan large-farm sector.

THE AGRICULTURAL SECTOR

41-32 METSON, J. "Discussion of the base line survey for the evaluation of the foot and mouth disease control programme in Narok and Kajiado districts". IDS Working P 207, Jan. 1975, 10pp.
Presents data on education, employment, and agricultural activities. Highlights the major problems that confront planners in the development of pastoral areas.

41-33 MUKASA-KINTU, SAM. A study of the development problems in the southern counties of Kyaggwe district. M.A. thesis, University of Nairobi, 1975, 109pp.
Examines the problems of the likely population overspill, uneven distribution of incomes, services, and infrastructure, and the impact on the pattern of life that the increased population would have on the human activities and resource use.

41-34 MWANGI, WILFRED M. Farm level derived demand responses for fertilizer in Kenya. Ph.D. dissertation, Michigan State University, 1978.

41-35 NDAWULA-KAJUMBA, S. "Socio-economic aspects of an African plantation system". ERB Paper, University of Dar-es-Salaam, 1977, 57pp.

41-36 NSUBUGA, H.S.K. Dairy farming in Busoga, East Mengo and West Mengo districts in Uganda. M.Sc. thesis, Makerere University, 1970.

41-37 NYANKORI, JAMES C.O. Forecasting with a market oriented model: the spatial and temporal price and allocation models of the East African grain economy. Ph.D. dissertation, University of Illinois, 1977.

41-38 OBOLER, REGINA SMITH. "Work and leisure in modern Nandi: preliminary results of a study of time allocation". IDS Working P 324, Sept. 1977, 30pp.
Concludes that the Nandi work relatively short hours in agriculture as compared with many other Kenyans. Argues that increased production of crops would require land more valuable to them as pasture.

41-39 OKAI, MATTHEW. "The development of ox cultivation practices in Uganda". EAJ Rural Devel, Vol. 8, Nos. 1-2, 1975, pp. 191-214.
Aims at reawakening and stimulating interest in the use of ox-drawn equipment by indicating the potential of the technique in modernizing the agriculture of Uganda.

41-40 O'KEEFE, P., and WISNER, B. "Development or underdevelopment: a Kenyan case study". African Environment, Vol. 2, Nos. 1-2, 1976, pp. 107-120.
Attempts to combine community ecology and political economy as the appropriate methodology for analyzing the cuases of underdevelopment. Uses data gathered in the Kenyan village of Gakarara.

41-41 OTHIENO, T., and BELSHAW, D.G.R. "Technical innovation in two systems of African peasant agriculture in Bukedi district, Uganda". East African Institute of Social Research Conference Paper, Jan. 1965, 24pp.
Examines farmers' attitudes to improvements in production standards and techniques. Studies the major obstacles to agricultural change and the effectiveness of official policies in promoting new practices.

41-42 PORTER, P.W. "Food and development in the semi-arid zone of East Africa". African Studies Series 32, Syracuse University, 1979, 107pp.

41-43 RAEBURN, J.R. "Some economic aspects of African agriculture". EAER, Jan. 1959, pp. 41-49.
Focuses on conditions of production, choice of products, combination of factors, and the structure of organization.

41-44 RALD, JORGEN, and RALD, KAREN. Rural organization in Bukoba district, Tanzania. Scandinavian Institute of African Studies, Uppsala, 1975, 122pp.
A study of how the Bahaya people in Bukoba organize their life in society with respect to time and space.

41-45 RUKANDEMA, F.M. "Some economic arithmetic of poverty: preliminary farm data from Bukura and Shitoli sub-locations of Kakamega district, western Kenya". IDS Working P 253, Dec. 1975, 10pp.
Shows that the effective labour stock is insufficient to provide adequate subsistence for farm families plus a significant surplus for sale. Argues that farm tools are inadequate and reflect a low level of technology.

41-46 SANDBERG, A. "Socio-economic survey of lower Rufiji flood plain: Part I: Rufiji delta agricultural system". BRALUP Research Paper No. 34, University of Dar-es-Salaam, Oct. 1974, 59pp.
Provides background data on natural and human resources to help planners make realistic plans to further the development of peasants in the Rufiji delta.

THE AGRICULTURAL SECTOR

41-47 SHAPIRO, KENNETH H. Efficiency and modernization in African agriculture: a case study in Geita district, Tanzania. Ph.D. dissertation, Stanford University, 1974.

41-48 ___, and MÜLLER, JÜRGEN. "Sources of technical efficiency: the roles of modernization and information". Econ Dev Cult Change, Vol. 25, No. 2, Jan. 1977, pp. 293-310.
Studies cotton farmers in Geita, Tanzania, in order to explore the roles of information and modernization in achieving technical efficiency, or x-efficiency.

41-49 SMITH, L.D. "The storage of wheat on farms: an analysis of a survey of wheat farmers' attitudes to bulk storage and handling facilities". IDS (unnumbered paper), Aug. 1970, 20pp.
Concludes that the Wheat Board should not expect all farmers to convert to bulk storage and must be prepared to accept wheat in both bag and bulk form for several years to come.

41-50 STORER, J.R. "Irrigation helps former pastoralists in arid Kenya". World Crops, Vol. 28, No. 2, March-April 1976, pp. 56-60.

41-51 TUKENDA, JUN. "An ecological study of the honey-collecting activities of the Tongwe, western Tanzania, East Africa". Kyoto University African Studies, Vol. 10, 1976, pp. 213-247.
Analysis of a series of behavioral characteristics observed in the honey-collecting activities of the Tongwe with respect to how the tribe depends on the natural resources of the woodland Savanna's.

41-52 WALLACE, I.R.; BELSHAW, D.G.R.; and BROCK, BEVERLEY. The Bugisu coffee industry: an economic and technical survey. Makerere Institute of Social Research, Kampala, 1973, 387pp.
A report on the introduction and expansion of the coffee industry, the development of production and marketing policies, and their effects on the rural economy of the Gisu people.

41-53 WOLGIN, JEROME M. Farmer response to price in smallholder agriculture in Kenya: an expected utility model. Ph.D. dissertation, Yale University, 1973.

41-54 ___. "Resource allocation and risk: a case study of smallholder agriculture in Kenya: Reply." American Journal of Agricultural Economics, Vol. 61, No. 1, Feb. 1979, pp. 114-115.

Reply to Young's comment on an earlier article. Wolgin accepts the correction but maintains his earlier implications.

41-55 WORLD BANK. Tanzanian agricultural and rural development sector study. Washington D.C., 1974.

41-56 YOUNG, DOUGLAS L. "Resource allocation and risk: a case study of smallholder agriculture in Kenya: Comment." American Journal of Agricultural Economics, Vol. 61, No. 1, Feb. 1979, pp. 111-113.
Correction to Wolgin's Nov. 1975 article. Young comments critically on the mathematical derivation therein.

42(a)--Livestock studies and policies

42a-1 BAKER, RANDALL. "Pastoralism and progress". Overseas Development Group, University of East Anglia, Norwich, 1975, 104pp.

42a-2 BALDUS, ROLF D. "The introduction of cooperative livestock husbandry in Tanzania". Land Reform, No. 2, 1977, pp. 37-46.
Analyses the introduction of co-operative livestock husbandry into the various pre-existing economies.

42a-3 BATUUKA, S.K. Structure, conduct and performance of the milk marketing system in Uganda: a case study of Kyadondo county, Kampala district, 1978/79. M.A. thesis, University of Nairobi, 1979.

42a-4 CHIKAKA, C.M.B. "Milk and dairy products: production, marketing and consumption in Mara region, Tanzania". Rural Economy Research Paper No. 8, University of Dar-es-Salaam, Morogoro, 1978.

42a-5 CHUDLEIGH, P. "The use of classification and description of animal production systems in the formation of priorities for agricultural research in Kenya". Agricultural Systems, Vol. 1, No. 4, 1976, pp. 281-299.

42a-6 CREEK, M.J. "The Kenya feedlot project". FAO World Animal Review, Vol. 3, 1972.
A report on the Kenya feedlot project aimed at increasing the beef quality in Kenya. The main concern of the project is to define the input/output relationships of feeding beef cattle under commercial conditions.

42a-7 CREEK, M.J., and SQUIRE, H.A. "Kenya feedlots: from pilot project to commercial application". Span, Vol. 19, No. 3, 1976, pp. 96-99.

THE AGRICULTURAL SECTOR

42a-8 GULLIVER, P.H. The family herds: a study of two pastoral tribes in East Africa, the Jie and the Turkana. Routledge and Kegan Paul, London, 1955, 273pp.
An analysis, in two pastoral societies, of the regulations governing herds and flocks of animals as property and the interrelation of these regulations with the kinship system. The two tribes under discussion are, from the economic point of view, representative of two types of pastoralism common in Eastern Africa.

42a-9 JAHNKE, HANS E. The economics of controlling tsetse flies and cattle trypanosomiasis in Africa examined for the case of Uganda. Weltforum Verlag, Munich, 1974, 368pp.
Concludes that the tsetse and trypanosomiasis problem must be viewed as a problem of land use. This implies that it is not so much the costs of controlling tsetse flies and trypanosomiasis which are of interest, but the economics of putting land in which the problem prevails to productive use.

42a-10 ___. Tsetse flies and livestock development in East Africa: a study in environmental economics. Weltforum Verlag, Munich, 1976, 180pp.
The purpose of the study is to introduce cost-benefit thinking into the approaches to the problem of bovine trypanosomiasis and of tsetse-infested potential pastures, a problem mianly dealt with from a biotechnical standpoint.

42a-11 ___. "Livestock in economic development". International Livestock Centre for Africa, Nairobi, 1979.

42a-12 KIVUNJA, CHARLES D. The economics of cattle and beef marketing in Kenya. DLG-Verlag, Frankfurt, 1978, 138pp.

42a-13 LIJOODI, J.L. "Livestock in Kenya: developing a vital industry". Standard Bank Review, March 1974, pp. 2-7.

42a-14 LIVINGSTONE, IAN. "Improvements in Kenya's livestock economy: lessons from the SRDP". IDS Working P 226, July 1975, 46pp.
Discusses general problems of the livestock economy and of the ranching areas. Sees the problem of the Special Rural Development Programme as one of implementation, together with funding problems.

42a-15 MacKENZIE, WILLIAM. "Conflicts and obstacles in livestock development in Tanzania". ERB Paper 73.1, University of Dar-es-Salaam, 1973, 30pp.
Discusses the role of livestock in the economy; the conflict between nutrition and exports; the obstacles in buying

policy and their implications; the conflict between the market activities of the development corporation and livestock marketing procedures. Concludes that in the interest of self-sufficiency, something most be done very quickly to improve the productivity of the small herd stock of Tanzania.

42a-16 ___. "The livestock economy of Tanzania". ERB Paper 73.5, University of Dar-es-Salaam, 1973, 97pp.
Discusses the Phase II programme and its three components, all of which are intended to assist in the commercial development of the national herd. Concludes that if the Phase II programme is to be properly monitored and Phase III planned, a cattle census of considerable reliability should be taken at least every five years.

42a-17 MARO, M.A.M. "An economic survey of goat and sheep production in Tanzania". Rural Economy Research Paper No. 4, University of Dar-es-Salaam, 1977, 31pp.

42a-18 MUSANGI, R. "The utilization of improved pastures in Uganda". East African Agricultural and Forestry Journal, Vol. 34, 1969, pp. 306-311.
Describes a study of pasture ultilization by twelve Friesian and twelve Nganda steers on common tropical pastures, in an effort to determine factors affecting herbage intake and liveweight changes.

42a-19 MUTISO, G.C.M. "Kitui livestock". IDS Working P 305, Oct. 1977, 32pp.
Shows how the colonial macro policy on livestock affected Kitui's livestock marketing, leading to differentiation in wealth in the district and a deterioration of the ecosystem.

42a-20 MWEGA, FRANCIS M. An economic analysis of damage and other losses caused by ticks and tick-borne diseases, particularly in relation to East Coast Fever. M.A. thesis, University of Nairobi, 1980.

42a-21 PHIPPS, R.H. "Some aspects of supplementary feeding of dairy cows in the Lake Cresent area of Uganda". East African Agricultural and Forestry Journal, Vol. 36, 1970.
A description of experimental work aimed at determining if maintenance of a cow and milk production can be obtained from grass alone during the dry season in the lake region of Uganda.

42a-22 RAIKES, PHILIP. "Livestock development in tropical Africa: the production and state policy in Kenya and Tanzania". Centre for Development Research, Copenhagen, ca. 1980.

THE AGRICULTURAL SECTOR

42a-23 RUIGU, M.R. An economic analysis of the Kenyan milk subsystem. Ph.D. dissertation, Michigan State University, 1978, 219pp.
An account of Kenyan milk production, marketing and consumption as a subsystem of the Kenyan economy. Analyses the supply of commercial milk and evaluates the supply response of smallholder milk production in Kenya.

42a-24 SCHNEIDER, HAROLD K. Livestock and equality in East Africa. Indiana University Press, Bloomington, 1979, 291pp.

42a-25 SHERMAN, NEAL P. A political-economic analysis of Uganda dairy policy. Ph.D. dissertation, University of Wisconsin, Madison 1975.

42a-26 ZALLA, TOM M. "The herd composition and farm management data on smallholder milk producers in Kilimanjaro". ERB Paper 74.8, University of Dar-es-Salaam, 1974.

42(b)--Crop studies and policies

42b-1 ANDERSON, G.D. "Increasing coconut yields and income on the sandy soils of the Tanganyika coast". Eastern African Agricultural and Forestry Journal, Vol. 32, 1967, pp. 310-314
Deals with ways by which coconut yields could be increased on the Tanzanian coast. These include bush control, insect pest control, fertilizer application, and introduction of cover crops.

42b-2 BARNES, CAROLYN. "An experiment with coffee production by Kenyans, 1933-1948". African Economic History, No. 8, 1979, pp. 198-209.
The article analyses why the experiment was launched and provides a case study of one of the trial areas to assess the extent to which African response was directed by colonial policies.

42b-3 BARTLETT, C.D.S. "Farm information in the design of improvements for small scale agriculture: with special reference to beans in lowland areas of Morogoro region, Tanzania". Rural Economy Research Paper No. 6, University of Dar-es-Salaam, Morogoro, 1978.

42b-4 BOESEN, JANNIK, and MOHELE, A.T. The "success story" of peasant tobacco production in Tanzania. Centre for Development Research, Copenhagen, 1979, 169pp.

42b-5 BONARIUS, H. "Preliminary assessment of irrigation development in the Marsabit area". Ministry of Agriculture, Nairobi, 1975, 18pp.

42b-6 CHINN, DENNIS L. "Farmer response to foodgrain in developing countries". Quarterly Journal of Economics, Vol. 92, No. 4, Nov. 1978, pp. 697-703.

Argues that in East Africa, taking Tanzania as an example, although the objective of the maize marketing board was to establish government control over the production and marketing of maize, it has been estimated that almost 70 per cent of total maize marketed moved through private channels.

42b-7 COLLINSON, M.P. "The comparative economics of growing aromatic or Virginia tobacco on small family farms in the Tabora area of Tanzania". ERB Paper 70.7, University of Dar-es-Salaam, 36pp.

A report on the profitability of growing aromatic or Virginia tobacco on small family farms on a preliminary cost-benefit basis. The report concludes that Virginia tobacco is 18 times more profitable than aromatic tobacco.

42b-8 ETHERINGTON, D.M. An econometric analysis of small-holder tea growing in Kenya. Ph.D. dissertation, Stanford University, 1971.

42b-9 ETYANG, MARTIN. Cotton production in Busia district in the 1970s: a case study of economic factors limiting production in south Teso location. M.A. thesis, University of Nairobi, 1979.

42b-10 FORD, D.J. "Long-run elasticities in the supply of Kenyan coffee: a methodological note". EAER, Vol. 3, No. 1, June 1971, pp. 65-67.

A comment on a previous article by J.K. Maitha in this journal.

42b-11 GWYER, G.D. "Long and short run elasticities of sisal supply". EAER, Vol. 3, No. 2, Dec. 1971, pp. 19-29.

Discusses sisal's contribution to the Tanzanian economy, its short-run and long-run response to price, and output projections and their policy implications.

42b-12 HANSEL, H. "National fertilizer programming scope of decision making and implementation policies". EA USSC Conference, Kampala, 1974, 31pp.

Discusses the wide range of decision-making problems at national level that pertain to fertilizer use development, which include the major aspects of government activity, politico-economic and technical decisions, research and extension systems and market organization. The present lack of investment capital and high raw material prices may

THE AGRICULTURAL SECTOR

endanger further expansion affecting production increases for food and fibre. Deals with the case of Tanzania.

42b-13 HAZLEWOOD, ARTHUR, and LIVINGSTONE, IAN. "Complementarity and competitiveness of large-scale and small-scale irrigated farming: a Tanzanian example". OIES Bull, Vol. 40, No. 3, Aug. 1978, pp. 195-208.
Application of the linear programming technique to a problem in irrigation economics, the estimation of irrigable land, in which not land or labour but water availability in particular months forms the constraint in the linear programming problem. The choice is betwen paddy production through large state farms or through small-scale village production.

42b-14 HEIJNEN, J.D. "The mechanised block cultivation schemes in Mwanza region, 1964-1969". BRALUP Research Paper No. 9, University of Dar-es-Salaam, Dec. 1969, 44pp.
Records the main problems encountered in the block cultivation schemes in Mwanza region experimental base. However, the author points out that the shortcomings thereof are hardl either of an economic or technical nature.

42b-15 HJORT, A. "Trading miraa: from school leaver to shopowner in Kenya". Ethnos, Vol. 39, Nos. 1-4, 1974, pp. 27-43.
Explains the importance of miraa trade for the economic structure of the people from Meru town and neighbouring areas. Focuses on the opportunities the trade offers.

42b-16 HYDE, R.J. "Patterns of food crop production and nutrition in Uganda". Makerere University Department of Geography Paper, Kampala, 1974, 89pp.

42b-17 ___. "The analysis of crop distribution in Uganda". Makerere University Department of Geography Occasional Paper No. 65, 1975, Kampala, 172pp.

42b-18 INTERNATIONAL COFFEE ORGANIZATION. "Coffee in Tanzania: an economic report". New York, 1978, 47pp.

42b-19 KENYA, MINISTRY OF AGRICULTURE ECONOMIC PLANNING DIVISION. "Th effects of increased fertiliser prices on maize and wheat production costs in Kenya". Economic Review of Agriculture, Vol. 6, No. 4, April-June 1974.
Report authored by Jan Erikson.

42b-20 MALIMA, KIGHOMA A. The economics of cotton production in Tanzania: an examination of some of the factors that influence agricultural development. Ph.D. dissertation, Princeton University, 1970.

42b-21 MARITIM, L.H.K. "Analysis of produce flows to Wakulima wholesale market, Nairobi". Agricultural Economics Studies No. 3, Department of Agricultural Economics, University of Nairobi, 1977, 139pp.

Surveys the seasonal fluctuations of commodities traded at the market. Discusses the causes of congestion at the market, and provudes an econometric analysis of the quantity-price and price-quantity relationships.

42b-22 MASAYA, TICHAENDEPI R. "Spectral analysis of coffee, maize and wheat production in Kenya". IDS Working P 218, May 1975, 11pp.

Investigates the existence of periodicities in the production of these crops in Kenya and compares the lengths of some of the crop cycles with the rain-fall cycles using spectral methods.

42b-23 MBOGHO, S.G. "The potato industry of Kenya". Agricultural Economics Studies No. 1, Department of Agricultural Economics, University of Nairobi, 1977.

42b-24 MLAMBITI, M.E. "Application of production functions in maize and tobacco production". EA USSC Conference, Nairobi, Dec. 1972, 10pp.

The economic optimum quantity of nitrogen was very different from that required for maximizing gross value.

42b-25 MOODY, ANTHONY A. "A report on farm economic survey of tea small-holders in Bukoba district". ERB Paper 70.8, University of Dar-es-Salaam, April 1970, 24pp.

Reports on diversification efforts in Bukoba district, Tanzania, where small-scale tea farming was introduced to supplement coffee farming. Examines the success of the new cash crop and also assesses its future importance.

42b-26 MSUYA, M.M. Coffee in the economy of Tanzania and the implications of membership in the International Coffee Agreement. Ph.D. dissertation, University of Wisconsin, Madison, 1979, 338pp.

DAI, Vol. 40, p. 2798-A.

42b-27 MUELLER, SUSANNE D. "The agrarian question in Tanzania: the case of tobacco". Working Paper in African Studies 32, Boston University, Boston, 1980.

THE AGRICULTURAL SECTOR

42b-28 OBARA, DUNSTAN A. "Cotton production in the Lake Victoria basin in Kenya". IDS Working P 353, April 1979, 39pp.
Examines such issues as the origins of cotton and its research development, the morphology and development of the crop, cultivated commercial varieties, and uses of the crop.

42b-29 ODADA, J.E.O. Supply of Kenyan pyrethrum. M.A. thesis, University of Nairobi, 1975, 112pp.
Empirical results suggest that Kenyan pyrethrum farmers are highly responsive to price changes but that the price-elasticity of supply varies from one region to another.

42b-30 OGUTU, M.A. "The role of cotton in Nyanza: 1945-1965". EAJ, Vol. 8, No. 9, Sept. 1971, pp. 9-14.
Explores the degree to which cotton cultivation benefited the grower either economically or socially between 1945-1965 in the area.

42b-31 ___. "The economic history of maize in Nyanza province: 1939-1960". Historical Association of Kenya, Nairobi, 1973.

42b-32 PERCY, H.C. "Factors affecting cotton production in western Tanzania". Cotton Growing Review, Cot. 1975, pp. 253-277.

42b-33 SACHAK, NAJMA. "Problems ot innovation in Tanzania's crop pattern: the case of soyabeans". BRALUP Research Paper No. 26, University of Dar-es-Salaam, 1977, 65pp.

42b-34 SCHILAGE, C. "Polished versus whole maize: some nutritional and economic implications of the traditional processing of maize in north eastern Tanzania". BRALUP Research Paper No. 2, University of Dar-es-Salaam, July 1968, 18pp.
An economic assessment of the caloric losses incurred during the traditional processing of maize. Argues that the losses so incurred are equivalent to 340,000 tons of grain.

42b-35 SCHÖNHERR, SIEGFRIED, and MBUGUA, E.S. (coordinators). "Bean production in Kenya's Central and Eastern provinces". IDS Occ P 23, Oct. 1976, 69pp.
The paper is the report of a joint survey carried out by IDS and the Kenya Ministry of Agriculture's Thika Grain Legume Project. Reviews the present situation of the cultivation, storage, marketing, and pricing of beans. Discusses the basic constraints on the intensification and expansion of production both in high-rainfall small-farm areas and in dryer areas where farms are larger. Makes recommendations for extension and infrastructural support.

42b-36 ___. "Soya bean crop development in Kenya". IDS Working P 260, March 1976, 22pp.
Describes the introduction of commercial soya bean growing in Kisii, South Nyanza, and Narok. Focuses on agronomic and infrastructural problems and makes proposals for future crop development strategies.

42b-37 SMITH, J.A. "The development of large-scale integrated sugar schemes in western Kenya". IDS Working P 343, Aug. 1978, 19pp.
Examines the development of the schemes in relation to the policies of self-reliance in sugar production and promotion of rural development.

42b-38 SMITH, L.D. A wheat policy for the 1970s. IDS (unnumbered paper), Dec. 1970, 16pp.
Argues that a suitable policy would be to gear production much more closely to expected consumption, using either surpluses carried over from "good" years to overcome short-falls or, if no carryover is available, to import wheat to make up the shortfall.

42b-39 STEEVES, JEFFREY S. "Class analysis and rural Africa: the Kenya Tea Development Authority". J Mod Afr Studs, Vol. 16, No. 1, March 1978, pp. 123-132.
Argues that by 1972 it was apparent that the development of tea farmers who were non-resident, salaried, and commercially based and those who were resident full-time farmers stimulated the growth in numbers of landless and migrant wage-earners.

42b-40 TANZANIA MARKETING DEVELOPMENT BUREAU. "The current state of the coconut industry in Tanzania and proposals for the establishment of a coconut development authority". Ministry of Agriculture, Dar-es-Salaam, 1975, 44pp.

42b-41 WAKEFIELD, A.J. "Cotton experiments in Tanganyika territory under riverain conditions". Empire Cotton Growing Review, No. 8, 1931.

42b-42 WATERS, ALAN R. The cost structure of the Kenya coffee industry. Ph.D. dissertation, Rice University, 1970.

42b-43 WESTLAKE, M.J. A study of taxation as it affects the coffee industry in Kenya. IDS (unnumbered paper), Oct. 1970, 32pp.
Argues that a tax which is able to stqbilize the net revenue received by the coffee industry would both increase the industry's efficiency and, in the long-run, allow the

THE AGRICULTURAL SECTOR

government to raise a larger volume of revenue. Such a tax would have to be a function of both costs within the industry and world price.

42b-44 ZAKE, JULIUS Y.K. The effect of sulfur on the yield and quality of finger millet in Uganda. Ph.D. dissertation, Ohio State University, 1972.

42(c)--Range management studies and policies

42c-1 CAMPBELL, DAVID J. "Coping with drought in Kenya Maasailand: pastoralists and farmers of the Loitokitok area, Kajiado district". IDS Working P 337, June 1978, 56pp.
Examines the relationship between changing land use patterns, social systems, resource availability, and the ability of the Maasai to cope with drought. Concludes that if the past land use pattern is continued, their vulnerability to effects of drought will increase.

42c-2 DOHERTY, DEBORAH A. "A preliminary report on group ranching in Narok district". IDS Working P 350, Feb. 1979, 17pp.
Argues that, rather than facilitating economic development without disenfranchising large numbers of people, group ranching, together with the introduction of wheat farming, is stimulating feelings of insecurity among many Maasai herders that they will be eventually forced out of the pastoral economy.

42c-3 ___. "Factors inhibiting economic development on Rotian Olmakongo group ranch". IDS Working P 356, July 1979, 40pp.
Concludes that among principal constraints is the inability of traditional social units to generate an organizational form which would promote the development of the ranch, and it is instead subsidized by non-pastoral economic activities.

42c-4 EIJNATTEN, C.L.M. "A study of the production of wheat in the Naro Moro and Waraza settlement schemes in Kieni East, Central province, Kenya". University of Nairobi Department of Crop Science Technical Communication, Oct. 1976.
Analyzes some of the problems encountered in wheat production in a relatively dry area of medium altitude.

42c-5 HERRING, R.S. "Cattlemen and farmers: the historical pattern in northeastern Uganda". Historical Association of Kenya, Nairobi, 1977, 22pp.
Traces the historical relationship between several communities in northeastern Uganda and two of the Koten groups, the Korwakol of Jie and the Karamojong.

42c-6 JACOBS, ALAN H. "Pastoral development in Tanzania Maasailand". U.S.A. African Studies Association meeting, Philadelphia, Oct. 1980.

42c-7 LIVINGSTONE, IAN. "Cowboys in Africa: the socio-economics of ranching". IDS Occ P 17, 1976, 84pp.
Examines group ranching in West Pokot, a nomadic pastoralist area; a group ranching proposal in Kwale incorporating a co-operative element in the form of a central herd; and co-operative ranching in Mbere and Machakos districts.

42c-8 QUAM, MICHAEL D. Pastoral economy and cattle marketing in Karamoja, Uganda. Ph.D. dissertation, Indiana University, 1976.

42c-9 RIGBY, P. "Pastoralist production and socialist transformation in Tanzania". Jipemoyo, Vol. 2, 1980, pp. 32-84.

42(d)--Fisheries

42d-1 BARNES, COLIN. "A study of the peasant fishing economy in Tanzania: a case study of coastal fishing villages in Dar-es-Salaam and Coast regions". ERB Paper, University of Dar-es-Salaam, 1976, 141pp.

42d-2 CRUTCHFIELD, JAMES A. "The Uganda fisheries--aspects of government policy". South Africa Journal of Economics, Vol. 27, No. 2, June 1959, pp. 92-103.
Argues that there is steady drift toward a policy of economic maximization. Criteria applied are still encumbered by failure to distinguish overfishing in physical and economic terms. Experience indicates how far afield public policy may stray when even portions of that analysis are missing.

42d-3 FAO. Survey of the irrigation potential of the lower Tana River basin. Rome, 1968.
A report on the hydrological conditions of the lower Tana River basin.

42d-4 JANSEN, EIRIK G. "The development of the Lake Victoria fisheries and the possibilities for Norwegian participation". EAJ Rural Devel, Vol. 10, Nos. 1-2, 1977, pp. 235-268.
Discusses various development possibilities of Lake Victoria fisheries. Shows the context and circumstances under which Norwegian participation in their development will take place.

42d-5 KARUHANGA, P.N. Production functions as instruments of Lake

Victoria inshore fishery management. M.A. thesis, University of Nairobi, 1979.

42d-6 McHENRY, D.E., Jr. "A problem in development: an attempt to form a viable fisherman's co-operative society for Lake Tanganyika". EA USSC Conference, Kampala, Dec. 1969.
Deals with the Lake Tanganyika Fishermen's Co-operative Society. Presents facts concerning the key issues and the activities of those who participated in it until its demise. Provides an interpretation which can account for the demise of the co-operative society.

42d-7 NIMITZ, MAXINE L. Decision-making in the fishing industry, Bagamayo, Tanzania. Ph.D. dissertation, Indiana University, 1974.

42d-8 ODUOR-OTIENO, M.L.; KARISA, R.S.; ODHIAMBO, J.O.O.; and RYAN, T.C.I. "A study of the supply function for fish in the Kenya waters of Lake Victoria and on the Kenya coast". IDS Working P 346, Dec. 1978, 50pp.
Analyses the economic framework in which fishing decisions are made, highlighting such aspects as risk minimization, overfishing, and technological change.

42d-9 OKIDI, C. ODIDI. "Kenya's marine fisheries: a general outline of policy and activities". IDS Working P 344, July 1978, 44pp.
Examines the range of activities in the fisheries sector in which Kenya nationals and companies are involved. Also appeared as IDS Occ P 30 in January 1979.

42d-10 ROSSON, P.J. "The Tanzanian fisheries and marketing reform". EAJ Rural Devel, Vol. 10, Nos. 1-2, 1977, pp. 217-234.
Shows that modernization of the fisheries industry must affect factors beside the marketing aspects to be effective.

43--Agricultural development experiences

43-1 ALILA, PATRICK O. "Kenyan agricultural policy: the colonial roots of African smallholder agricultural policy and services". IDS Working P 327, Nov. 1977, 48pp.
Traces the evolution during the colonial period of agricultural policy and services for African small-holder sussistence areas. Addressed to the problem of what significance the colonial agricultural policies had for the present structure of agricultural services.

43-2 BARNES, CAROLYN. An experiment with African coffee growing in

Kenya: the Gusii 1933-1950. Ph.D. dissertation, Michigan State University, 1976, 266pp.

Analyses the factors within and without Gusii society which directly influenced the introduction and expansion of coffee production. It also describes the assumptions of the colonial administrators in regard to the form and structure of the industry. Also, the salient characteristics of the pioneer growers, those who adpoted coffee before 1938, are compared with a subsequent group of Gusii coffee farmers to test hypotheses on innovation.

43-3 BARRATT, J., et al. (eds.). Accelerated development in Southern Africa. Macmillan, London, 1974, 706pp.

Includes Hans Ruthenberg, "A decade of agricultural development in Tanzania and Kenya".

43-4 BUKAGILE, S.R.K. Analysis of smallholder tea development in Tanzania. M.Sc. thesis, University of Alberta, 1977, 164pp.

43-5 CLAYTON, E.S. "Kenya's agriculture and the ILO employment mission--six years after". J Mod Afr Studs, Vol. 16, No. 2, June 1978, pp. 311-318.

Also appears in Tony Killick (ed.), Papers on the Kenyan economy.

43-6 COULSON, ANDREW. "The silo project". IDS Bulletin, Vol. 10, No. 1, Aug. 1978, pp. 33-35.

An outline of negotiations that led to the acceptance of a bad project, grain storage and handling, in Tanzania, financed by the Swedish International Development Agency.

43-7 DOPPLER, WERNER. "The contributions of agricultural economists to the political decision process". Zietschrift für Ausländische Landwirtschaft (Quarterly Journal of International Agriculture), Vol. 16, No. 1, March 1977.

Deals with methodological problems, world food, and development strategies. Problems discussed in connection with the discussion on integrated rural development.

43-8 GYLLSTROM, BJORN. The organisation of production as a space modelling mechanism in underdeveloped countries: the case of tea production in Kenya. Frans Lunds Universitets Geografiska Institution, Lund, 1977, 230pp.

Examines the dependency theory with a case study of tea in Kenya. Shows how countries essentially rural in character could attain a space economy able to satisfy basic economic needs.

THE AGRICULTURAL SECTOR

43-9 HEYER, J.; MAITHA, J.K.; and SENGA, W.M. (eds.). Agricultural development in Kenya. Oxford University Press, Nairobi, 1976, 372pp.
A collection of ten essays, by various authors, discussing the structure, performance, and problems of the agricultural sector in Kenya's economy. Critically examines the major post-independence policies and programmes which the government has adopted or implemented.

43-10 HUTTON, CAROLINE. Reluctant farmers. East African Publishing House, Nairobi, 1973, 330pp.
Study of the cuases and results of unemployment in Uganda. Survey of two main industrial towns and studies of two rural-development schemes, one for peasants and one for unemployed school leavers.

43-11 JAMAL, V. "The role of cotton and coffee in Uganda's economic development". Food Research Institute, Stanford University, Aug. 1973.
Ph.D. dissertation is of same title, Stanford University, 1976.

43-12 JONES, E.L., and WOOLF, S.J. (eds.). Agrarian change and economic development. Methuen, London, 1969, 172pp.
Includes C.M. Elliott, "Agriculture and economic development in Africa: theory and experience, 1880-1914", which draws upon Kenyan and Ugandan experiences.

43-13 KENYA. Report of the select committee on the maize industry. Government Printer, Nairobi, 1973.
Gives a critical appraisal as to why Kenya has been experiencing maize shortages.

43-14 LIJOODI, J.L. Agriculture in Kenya's economy. FAO (Access No. 33183), Kabete, Kenya, 1975, 24pp.

43-15 MUKETHA, J.K. Labour absorption in Kenya's modern sector agriculture. M.A. thesis, University of Nairobi, 1976, 95pp.
Concludes that the increase in average earnings that took place in Kenya's modern sector agriculture had some negative effect on employment, that there was a high degree of substitution between labour and capital, and that the decrease in large scale farm acreage had a negative effect on labour absorption.

43-16 ODINGO, R.S. "A study of agrarian change in Kenya with special reference to Kericho district, incorporating a special study

of the Belgut and Buret divisions of Kericho district". Report for FAO, June 1973.
An assessment of the current agrarian reform programme in Kenya with special reference to Kericho district. Includes suggestions for appropriate government policies to help, encourage, and steer developments along the right channels.

43-17 RAIKES, PHILIP LAWRENCE. The development of mechanized commercial wheat production in North Iraqw, Tanzania. Ph.D. dissertation, Stanford University, 1975, 460pp.
Looks at the development of mechanized wheat production by African farmers with the purpose of drawing conclusions about the process of development and income differentiation, and the impact of government policy.

43-18 RICHARDS, A.I., and FORTT, J.M. (eds.). Subsistence to commercial farming in present-day Buganda. Cambridge University Press, 1973, 336pp.
A study of the emergence of commercial farming in a "laissez-faire" system.

43-19 VAN ZWANENBERG, PAUL. "Kenya's primitive colonial capitalism: the economic weakness of Kenya's settlers up to 1940". Can J Afr Studs, Vol. 9, No. 2, 1975, pp. 277-292.
Analyses a period when the settlers were struggling to establish large-scale farming at a time when they were short of finance and agricultural skill.

43-20 WYETH, PETER. "Economic development in Kenya agriculture". In Tony Killick (ed.), Papers on the Kenyan economy. Heinemann, London, 1981.

44--Agricultural strategies and planning

44-1 ALDINGTON, T.J. Report to the governments of Kenya, Tanzania, Uganda on agricultural cooperation in the East African Community. FAO, Rome, 1974, 37pp.
Argues that there is scope for cooperation in agricultural production and trade. This would require sector planning involving regional specialization of production, complementaries of production, and consumption in adjacent states.

44-2 COULSON, ANDREW. "Agricultural policies in mainland Tanzania". Review of African Political Economy, No. 10, Sept.-Dec. 1977, pp. 74-100.
Critically discusses the evolution of agricultural policy in Tanzania from the colonial to the present socialist era.

THE AGRICULTURAL SECTOR

44-3 DUMONT, RENE. Tanzanian agriculture after the Arusha Declaration: a report by Professor Rene Dumont. Ministry of Economic Affairs and Development Planning, Dar-es-Salaam, 1969, 62pp.
Argues that socialist development requires a high level of morality and an elite capable of promoting development and that it is not possible to omit, without major inconvenience, the stage of the "progressive farmers".

44-4 ELLMAN, A.O. "Agricultural improvements through cooperative farming in Tanzania". ERB Paper 69.23, University of Dar-es-Salaam, 1969, 10pp.
Argues that by concentrating investment of capital on groups of farmers settled in more fertile parts of the country, farming systems based on more intensive use of land would be created.

44-5 FAO. Report on FAO/NORAD seminar on agricultural sector analysis and planning, Kabete, Kenya, 11-31 August 1975. FAO (Access No. 33159), Rome, 1976, 15pp.

44-6 FAO/UNFPA. Seminar on agricultural planning and population (Rome, 1974). FAO, Rome, 1975.

44-7 GWYER, G.D. "Agricultural employment: a research proposal". IDS Staff P 93, March 1971, 15pp.
Indicates the magnitude of the employment problem by comparing recent population data with agricultural output data by region or district. Presents employment creation alternatives and the methodological approaches that appear relevant to the empirical evaluation of each of the main alternatives.

44-8 MAPOLU, H., and PHILLIPSON, G. "Agricultural cooperation and the new development of the productive forces: some lessons from Tanzania". Africa Development, Vol. 1, No. 1, 1976, pp. 42-58.
Argues that a political framework is necessary if technical processes are to bring about sustained development of productive forces. Same title appears in African Review, Vol. 6, No. 2, 1976, pp. 65-107.

44-9 MBITHI, PHILIP M. "Human factors in agricultural management in East Africa". Food Policy, Vol. 2, No. 1, Feb. 1977, pp. 27-33.
Evaluates the social and management environment of farm decision making and shows how this has led to other serious social and psychological problems. Suggests a re-orientation

in rural development strategies by a re-examination of farm management and products models and a revision of the concept of technology.

44-10 RUTHENBERG, HANS. "Outline of a strategy for agricultural development in Kenya". Zeitschrift für Ausländische Landwirtschaft (Quarterly Journal of International Agriculture), Vol. 19, No. 1, Jan.-March 1980, pp. 6-17.

44-11 THIMM, HEINZ-ULRICH. "The major agricultural policy goals of the Kenya development plan, 1974-78: some comments". Zeitschrift für Ausländische Landwirtschaft (Quarterly Journal of International Agriculture), Vol. 15, No. 2, April-June 1976, pp. 128-140.
Comments on three major agricultural policy goods of the plan. Questions the feasibility of the 6.7 per cent growth target; doubts whether the distribution of rural income will improve; argues that methods designed for aiding less favoured areas are inadequate.

44-12 ZAMAN, M.A. "Integration, decentralisation and implementation in rural development programming: the experience of Kenya". Agricultural Administration, Vol. 5, No. 4, Oct. 1978, pp. 247-252.
With special reference to Kenya's Special Rural Development Programme (SRDP), the author concludes that in Africa's approach to integrated rural development, research must be carried out to improve the lot of her people. Monitoring of projects should, in fact, begin with the initiation of the projects themselves.

45--Land use, resettlement, and tenure

45-1 ABRAHAMS, P.D. Kenya's land re-settlement story: how 66,000 African families were settled on 1325 large scale European-owned farms. Challenge Publishers, Nairobi, 1979, 76pp.

45-2 BERRY, L., and KATES, R.W. "Planned irrigated settlement: a study of four villages in Dodoma, and Singida regions, Tanzania". BRALUP Research Paper No. 10, University of Dar-es-Salaam, May 1970, 63pp.
Presents information helpful in the assessment of utilization of water and land resources in the development of irrigation farming.

45-3 BRAIN, JAMES L. "Is transformation possible? Styles of settlement in post-independence Tanzania". African Affairs, Vol. 76, April 1977, pp. 231-245.

THE AGRICULTURAL SECTOR

Describes two approaches to village settlement in the first few years after independence.

45-4 ___. "The Ulugeru land usage scheme: success and failure (Tanzania)". J Dev Areas, Vol. 14, No. 2, Jan. 1980, pp. 175-190.

45-5 BROKENSHA, D., and GLAZIER, J. "Land reform among the Mbere of central Kenya". Africa, Vol. 43, No. 3, 1973, pp. 182-206.
Outlines the social organization and the system of land rights. Describes the government's programme of land reform and assesses the probable consequences of changes in land tenure.

45-6 ___. "How land reform is affecting the Mbere of central Kenya". LTC Newsletter, No. 44, May-June 1974, pp. 8-14.

45-7 BROKENSHA, DAVID, and NJERU, E.H.N. "Some consequences of land adjudication in Mbere division, Embu". IDS Working P 320, Sept. 1977, 15pp.
Examines the claims of negative consequences of land adjudication in Mbere.

45-8 BROWN, BRACK. Political administration and rural development in Kenya: lessons from settlement and other rural programes. Ph.D. dissertation, Syracuse University, 1977.

45-9 CAMPBELL, D.J., and PALUTIKOF, J. "Allocation of land resources in semi-arid areas: a simulation based on the East African experience". IDS Disc P 262, March 1978, 54pp.
Describes a simulation model intended to integrate the socio-economic and the physical aspects of arid and semi-arid areas, particularly where there is land-use conflict between pastoralism and game rearing.

45-10 CHAMBERS, ROBERT, and MORIS, JON. "Mwea: an irrigated rice settlement in Kenya". Development Digest, Vol. 15, No. 4, Oct. 1977, pp. 75-90.
Examones the scheme's performance from an economic, administrative, technocratic, and social point of view. Extract from a book bearing the same title.

45-11 CLAYTON, ERIC S. "A comparative study of settlement schemes in Kenya". University of London Wye College Agrarian Development Unit Occasional Paper No. 3, Dec. 1978, 60pp.

45-12 COLDHAM, SIMON F.R. "Land tenure reform in Kenya: the limit of the law". J Mod Afr Studs, Vol. 17, No. 4, Dec. 1979,

pp. 615-627.
Tries to cast doubt on the assumption that changes in law necessarily produce changes in people's behaviour. It uses land adjudication in Kenya to illustrate the limits of the law.

45-13 COMMONWEALTH ASSOCIATION OF LAND SURVEYING AND LAND ECONOMY. "Seminar on the development of land resources in East, Central and Southern Africa: the role of surveying and land economy". Lusaka, 1976.

45-14 DAVIS, ROBERT K. "Prospects for joint production of livestock and wildlife on East African Rangeland: the case of Kenya". BRALUP Research Paper No. 4, University of Dar-es-Salaam, ca. 1969, 20pp.
Tries to pinpoint the optimal production programme for the rangelands of Kenya and of East Africa at large.

45-15 ___, and VON KAUFMANN, R. "An estimated trade-off between wildlife and livestock in one ranching area of Kenya". EAJ Rural Devel, Vol. 5, Nos. 1-2, 1972.
Tabulates break-even receipts required from wildlife to offset gains from the substitution of cattle.

45-16 DOORNBOS, MARTIN R. "Land tenure and political conflict in Ankole, Uganda". J Dev Studs, Vol. 12, No. 1, Oct. 1975, pp. 54-74.
Considers the origins of individual land acquisition in Ankole. Explores the socio-political effects of legalized land tenure in the area.

45-17 DORNER, PETER. Land reform and economic development. Penguin, 1972, 167pp.
Discussion revolves around the economic, social, and political importance of land tenure institutions in the development of the less industrialised countries. Emphasis is given to economies of Africa south of the Sahara. Tanzania's Ujamaa Vijijini policy is treated systematically.

45-18 FABIYI, YAKUB LAYIWOLA. Land tenure innovations in rural development: the problems in Western Nigeria with some Tanzanian comparisons. Ph.D. dissertation, University of Wisconsin, 1974, 303pp.
Attempts to identify the points of innovation and change in the customary tenure system which can serve as growing points for the modernization of traditional agriculture through the application of science and technology, investment, and accumulation of capital.

THE AGRICULTURAL SECTOR

45-19 FELDMAN, RAYAH. "Custom and capitalism: changes in the basis of land tenure in Ismani, Tanzania". J Dev Studs, Vol. 10, Nos. 3-4, April-July 1974, pp. 305-320.

45-20 FIMBO, G. MGONGO. "The right of occupancy in Tanzania: the political economy of an African land tenure system". Faculty of Law, University of Dar-es-Salaam, 1974?, 59pp.

45-21 FLEMING, J.T. "Tenurial reform as a prerequisite to the green revolution". World Development, Vol. 3, No. 1, Jan. 1975, pp. 47-58.
Draws upon Kenya's land registration experiences to explore the idea that the successful application of improved technologies depends on the existence of a sound system of land tenure.

45-22 GASTON, J.R. "Land issue in Kenya politics". Ufahamu, Vol. 9, No. 2, 1979, pp. 30-58.

45-23 GRAY, N. "Acceptance of land adjudication among the Digo". IDS Disc P 37, April 1972.
Focus is on what people hoped to gain from land demarcation, and how their expectations were formulated and supported or opposed by the commonly held values, meanings, beliefs, and understandings of the community.

45-24 HAMPSON, MARGARET. A conceptual approach to some land use problems in Kajiado district. M.Sc. thesis, University of Nairobi, 1975, 240pp.
Uses a conceptual approach to develop offtake rate formulae for the wildlife and cattle sectors. Seeks to determine the problems of defining and implementing an optimum land use pattern, which includes the utilization of wildlife as a renewable natural resource.

45-25 HERZ, BARBARA KNAPP. Demographic pressure and economic change: the case of Kenyan land reform. Ph.D. dissertation, Yale University, 1974.

45-26 HOLMES, R.S. "Land tenure and agricultural productivity in the Trans-Nzoia, Kenya". Geography, Vol. 60, No. 267, 1975, pp. 137-139.
Discusses the disadvantages, advantages, and changes due to the buying and fragmentation of former European farms.

45-27 KABWEGYERE, T.B. "Land and the growth of social stratification in Uganda". Journal of East African Research and Development, Vol. 5, No. 1, 1975, pp. 1-17.

Discusses the man/land relationship in the pre-colonial, colonial, and post-independence periods in Uganda.

45-28 KANOGO, T.M. The Kikuyu squatter phenomenon in the Nakuru district of the Rift Valley--an interpretation. Department of History Staff Seminar Paper, University of Nairobi, May 1977, 13pp.
Argues that the Kikuyu squatter community established a lucrative socio-economic structure in the settled areas, operating within and in competition with the settler economy.

45-29 KIMANI, S.M. "The structure of land ownership in Nairobi". Can J Afr Studs, Vol. 6, No. 3, 1972, pp. 379-403.

45-30 KINYANJUI, P.H.K. Land use: impact of a new road in Kikuyu division. M.A. thesis, University of Nairobi, 1976, 244pp.
Summarizes the advantages of the proximity of Kikuyu division to Nairobi as good road accessibility has made it possible for farmers supplying the city to increase productivity, a number of cummuters to find shelter in the division, and manufactured goods and other services to flow easily to the area from the city. The disadvantages are that Nairobi's expansion threatens to swallow up good agricultural land and to result in loss of food supplies.

45-31 LANGLANDS, B.W. Soil productivity and land availability studies for Uganda. Makerere University Department of Geography Occasional Paper No. 54, Kampala, 1974, 77pp.
Includes sections on soil productivity map of Uganda, soil classification by countries, cultivable land and population growth, and land use Uganda.

45-32 ___. "Geographical notes on land tenure in Uganda". Makerere University Department of Geography Paper, Kampala, 1976, 43pp.

45-33 LEO, C.P. The political economy of land in Kenya: the case of the million-acre settlement scheme. Ph.D. dissertation, University of Toronto, 1977.
DAI, Vol. 39, 4470-A.

45-34 MACARTHUR, J.D. "Benefits of hindsight: aspects of experience in the high and low density settlement programme in Kenya". EAJ Rural Devel, Vol. 8, Nos. 1-2, 1975, pp. 1-45.
Observes that during the early and middle 1960s, the most important development in Kenya's rural sector was the land transfer programmes administered by the department of settlement.

THE AGRICULTURAL SECTOR

45-35 MANNERS, R.A. "Land use, labor and the growth of a market economy in Kipsigis country". In P. Bohannan, G. Bohannan, and G. Dalton (eds.), Markets in Africa. Northwestern University Press, Evanston, 1962, pp. 493-517.

45-36 MASCARENHAS, A.C. "Resettlement and desertification: the Wagogo of Dodoma district, Tanzania". Economic Geography, Vol. 53, No. 4, Oct. 1977, pp. 376-380.
Deals with the traditional agricultural economy setting of the Wagogo and their resettlement in an Ujamaa village. Deals with their yearly cycles and the effects of drought.

45-37 ___. "Settlements and population redistribution in Dodoma". BRALUP Paper, University of Dar-es-Salaam, 1977, 35pp.

45-38 MBITHI, PHILIP M., and BARNES, CAROLYN. The spontaneous settlement problem in Kenya. East African Literature Bureau, Nairobi, 1975, 192pp.
The squatter settlements in Kenya are shown by the study to be a result of spontaneous movement of potential farmers and unemployted persons to land for which they have no legal title. The study shows that squatters are politically marginal, economically and technically backward, and a serious threat to the environment.

45-39 MKANGI, G.C. Population growth and the myth of land reform in Taita. Ph.D. dissertation, University of Sussex, 1978, 279pp.

45-40 MUKOYOGO, MWEMEZI CHRISTIAN. "Land policy and development/ underdevelopment in Tanzania: Nyarubanja tenure system: mechanics of enfranchisement". 1975?, 57pp.

45-41 MUWONGE, J.W., and RUGEGE, S. "Squatter settlements in Uganda: the case of Kampala". Seminar on Urban Planning Law in East Africa, Nairobi, April 1976, 20pp.
Concerned with laws that over the years have regulated land use in Kampala and its immediate surrounding, particularly in the urban planning area. The main legislative provisions are the Town and Country Planning Act and the Public Health Act.

45-42 OKOTH-OGENDO, H.W.O. "Land ownership and land distribution in Kenya's large-farm areas". In Tony Killick (ed.), Papers on the Kenyan economy. Heinemann, London, 1981.

45-43 PIPPING, KNUT. Land holding in the Usangu plain: a survey of two villages in the southern highlands of Tanzania. Scandinavian Institute of African Studies, Uppsala, 1976, 122pp.

45-44 POHORYLES, SAMUEL, and SZESKIN, ARIEH. "Land tenure and economic growth in Africa". Land Reform, No. 1, 1975, pp. 44-50.
Describes the types of landownership patterns according to their chronological appearance on the African scene with occasional references to the East African economies. Mentions attempts to solve the economic problems of African countries through agrarian reform, with references to the East African economies.

45-45 PRATT, D.J., and GWYNNE, M.D. Rangeland management and ecology in East Africa. Hodder and Stoughton, London, 1977.

45-46 RALD, J. "Land use in a Buhaya village". BRALUP Research Paper No. 5, University of Dar-es-Salaam, June 1969, 63pp.
Presents the results of the first of three farm-economic surveys conducted in Bukoba district.

45-47 STORRAR, A. "A guide to the principles and practice of land settlement in Kenya". Journal of Local Administration Overseas, Vol. 3, No. 1, 1964.

45-48 TAYLOR, D.R.F. "Land reform in Kenya: a reappraisal". Rural Africana, No. 23, Winter 1974, pp. 79-90.
Looks at the impact of land reform on the Kikuyu of Kenya. Says that though the reform was "revolutionary" and increased aggregate agricultural output, its impact on the nutrition of the people is undesirable and hence the reform has not brought real economic development to the rural Kikuyu.

45-49 VON HAUGWITZ, H.W., with THORWART, H. Some experiences with small-holder settlements in Kenya 1963/64 to 1966/67. Weltforum Verlag, Munich, 1972.

45-50 WASSERMAN, G. "Continuity and conter-insurgency: the role of land reform in decolonising Kenya 1962-70". Can J Afr Studs, Vol. 7, No. 1, 1973, pp. 133-148.

45-51 ___. The politics of decolonization: Kenya Europeans and the land issue 1960-1965. Ph.D. dissertation, Cambridge University, 1976.

45-52 WEST, HENRY W. Land policy in Buganda. East African Publishing House, Nairobi, 1975, 244pp.
Examines consequences of "individualization by administrative decree" in terms of land policy, land proprietary structure, and the relative importance of various institutions and influences affecting property rights. Discusses problems created by introduction of Western tenurial concepts

and legal and technological ideas, and suggests possible solutions.

45-53 YAHYA, SAAD S. Urban land policy in Kenya. Ph.D. dissertation, University of Nairobi, 1976, 499pp.
Argues that urban land policy will have to become more flexible, liberal, and development-oriented, and will also have to expand and sharpen its instruments of control. Includes four case studies. Published subsequently by Department of Real Estate Economics, Royal Institute of Technology, Stockholm, 1980.

46--Agricultural extension, technologies, and marketing and price policies

46-1 ALIBARUHO, GEORGE. Effects of marketing board policies on prices, production and income in Uganda's cotton industry. Ph.D. dissertation, University of California, Berkeley, 1973.

46-2 ___. "Resource allocation, commodity supply and income distribution aspects of agricultural pricing policy in Kenya". IDS Working P 151, March 1974, 16pp.
A research proposal underlining the importance of a micro-oriented research project which would test the efficiency of resource allocative mechanisms in the light of the goals of government policy.

46-3 ARNOLD, M.H. Agricultural research for development. Cambridge University Press, Cambridge, 1976, 353pp.

46-4 ASCROFT, JOSEPH, et al. "Does extension create poverty in Kenya?". EAJ, Vol. 9, No. 3, March 1972.
Concludes that in the short run the lop-sided distribution of extension services in a developing nation such as Kenya does not free labour for other sectors of the economy. Proposes a prototype strategy to accelerate the flow of new income-generating ideas to those farmers not yet using such ideas.

46-5 ___. "Extension and the forgotton farmer: first report on a field experiment in Kenya". EA USSC Conference, Nairobi, Dec. 1972, 40pp.
The main variable the experiment was designed to affect was the degree of adoption of productivity-increasing innovations by Tetu farmers.

46-6 ___. "The Tetu extension project: first report on a field experiment". EA USSC Conference, Nairobi, Dec. 1972, 77pp.

Describes the planning, implementation, and evaluation of the first experiment with a new strategy to promote the adoption of productivity-increasing agricultural innovation, especially among less progressive farmers in Tetu dividion of Nyeri district.

46-7 BAGER, TORBEN. Marketing co-operatives and peasants in Kenya. Scandinavian Institute of African Studies, Uppsala, 1980.

46-8 BELSHAW, D.G.R. "Economic research and agricultural development planning in East Africa". Makerere University Institute of Social Research Workshop on Rural Economy Research, Kampala, 1968.

46-9 ___. "Taking indigenous technology seriously: the case of inter-cropping techniques in East Africa". IDS Bulletin, No. 10, No. 2, Jan. 1979, pp. 24-27.

Focuses on changes in the attitudes of research workers to inter-cropping techniques over the last twenty years.

46-10 BERG, LIV. Towards village industry. Intermediate Technology Publications, London, 1978, 87pp.

46-11 BOHLEN, EBERHAR (ed.). Crop pests in Tanzania and their control. Verlag Paul Parey for Federal Agency for Economic Co-operation, Berlin, 1973, 142pp.

Pays particular attention to the problem of food crops (maize, rice, groundnuts, etc.) being attacked by pests. The work is a partial report from the Kilombero Agricultural Training and Research Institute.

46-12 BWAMBALE, H.E. Agricultural research and technology diffusion by foreign agribusiness firms. Ph.D. dissertation, Harvard, 1976, 207pp.

DAI, Vol. 39, p. 6213.

46-13 CHEGE, FRED E. "Socioeconomic constraints to the adoption and diffusion of chemical fertilisers among small-scale farmers: a Kenyan case study". IDS Working P 331, Jan. 1978, 19pp.

Aimed at identifying and quantifying, where possible, the socio-economic and other factors that constrain the adoption of fertilizer use by small-scale farmers. The study is based on a random sample of between 200 and 250 farmers located in Kirinyaga district.

46-14 CHUDLEIGH, PETER. "The improvement of resource allocation in agricultural research with special reference to animal production research in Kenya". Agricultural Administration,

THE AGRICULTURAL SECTOR

Vol. 3, No. 2, April 1976, pp. 93-107.
Attempts to identify some of the important considerations and constraints currently influencing the efficiency of resource allocation in agricultural research.

46-15 COLLINSON, M.P. "Designing agricultural technology for high rates of diffusion through farmer populations: CIMMYT's East African economics programme". IDS Working P 270, July 1976, 13pp.
Looks at the need for an interdisciplinary effort which includes social scientists in planning and designing adaptive agricultural research.

46-16 DE VRIES, J. "Has extension failed? A case study of maize-growing practices in Iringa, Tanzania". Rural Economy Department, University of Dar-es-Salaam, Research Paper No. 1, Morogoro, 1976, 25pp.

46-17 DIMA, S.A.J. "Small holder farm development through intermediate technology". Makerere University?, Kampala?, 1974, 62pp.

46-18 EROZER, SAVAS. Planning and development of extension training in rural development at the Bukura Institute of Agriculture, Kenya. Ph.D. dissertation, Harvard University, 1978.

46-19 FERGUSON, DONALD S. An economic appraisal of tick borne disease control in tropical Africa: the case of Uganda. Ph.D. dissertation, Cornell University, 1972.

46-20 FOOTE, R.J., and RØSJØ, D. "A survey of five agricultural research institutes in Tanzania, with emphasis on ways to imporve management of the research system". Rural Economy Research Paper No. 7, Department of Rural Economy, University of Dar-es-Salaam, Morogoro, 1978.

46-21 GARST, R.D. The spatial diffusion of agricultural innovations in Kisii district, Kenya. Ph.D. dissertation, Michigan State University, 1972, 280pp.
DAI, Vol. 33, p. 4334-B.

46-22 ___. "Innovation diffusion among the Gusii of Kenya". Economic Geography, Vol. 50, No. 4, Oct. 1974, pp. 300-312.

46-23 GERHART, JOHN DENEL. The diffusion of hybrid maize in Kenya. Ph.D. dissertation, Princeton University, 1975, 332pp.
Analyzes the diffusion of hybrid maize technology in western Kenya as a case study in the spread of new agricultural technology among small-scale African farmers. The

purpose is to improve understanding of factors affecting the adoption of new technology, with special attention devoted to the role of environmental factors and the perception of risk. Short paper of same title published by Centro Internacional de Mejoramiento de Maiz y Trigo (CIMMYT), 1975.

46-24 GWYER, G.D. Preliminary report on agricultural chemicals for the working party on costs of agricultural inputs. IDS unnumbered paper), Jan. 1971, 34pp.
Discusses trends in agricultural chemical use, factors affecting the demand for agricultural chemicals, characteristics of agricultural chenical manufacture, and the marketing system.

46-25 HALEY, S.D. Manipulation of agricultural marketing policy in Kenya 1922-74. M.Sc. thesis, University of Bath, 1978.

46-26 HANSEL, H.; DE VRIES, J.; and NDEDYA, P.C. (eds.). Agricultural extension in Ujamaa village development. Faculty of Agriculture, University of Dar-es-Salaam, 1975, 292pp.
Reports of a workshop held at Morogoro, Tanzania, in September 1975. Outlines the strategies to be taken in order to facilitate the growth of Ujamaa villages.

46-27 HESSELMARK, OLOF, and LORENZL, GÜNTER. "Structure and problems of the maize marketing system in Kenya". Zeitschrift für Ausländische Landwirtschaft (Quarterly Journal of International Agriculture), Vol. 15, No. 2, April-June 1976, pp. 161-179.
Pays special attention to informal trade in maize and marketing problems associated with it. Concludes that if the Maize Produce Board is to fulfill its objectives, active market participation based on better market intelligence and co-operation with the private trade are necessary.

46-28 HESSELMARK, OLOF. "The marketing of maize and beans in Kenya: a proposal for improved effectiveness". IDS Working P 300, Feb. 1977, 44pp.
Attempts to give information on the functioning of the maize marketing system and suggestions on how its functions could be improved.

46-29 HEWLETT, R., and MARKIE, J. "Cooperative farming as an instrument of rural development: examples from China, Vietnam, Tanzania and India". Land Reform, Land Settlement and Cooperatives, FAO (Access No. 35236), Rome, 1976, pp. 41-54.

THE AGRICULTURAL SECTOR

46-30 HEYER, J., and INUKAI, I. "Mechanisation and employment on small farms in Kenya: research proposal". IDS Working P 149, March 1974, 18pp.
Makes a comparison of tractor and ox-cultivation in order to identify conditions in which each of these alternatives will make the greatest contribution to agricultural production and employment in Kenya.

46-31 HOPCRAFT, PETER, and RUIGU, GEORGE. "Dairy marketing and pricing in Kenya: are milk shortages the consequences of drought or pricing policies?". IDS Disc P 237, June 1976.
Proposes an alternative milk-pricing system that recognizes that production costs and the value of additional milk are not uniform between seasons and locations.

46-32 HOPCRAFT, PETER N. (Co-ordinator). "An evaluation of the Kenya dairy production improvement programme (artificial insemination service)". IDS Occ P 20, 1976, 221pp.
Concludes that the development of artificial insemination services cannot be viewed in isolation from the complementary aspects of dairy production improvement such as the control of tick-borne disease, improved cattle management, and changes in the marketing and pricing of milk.

46-33 ___. "Milk pricing in Kenya: the case of a bulky, perishable commodity with seasonally varying production costs". IDS Disc P 266, July 1978, 15pp.
Questions the use of politicized prices that ignore the economic and technical characteristics of commodity production and consumption.

46-34 HULLS, ROBERT H. "An assessment of agricultural extension in Sukumaland, western Tanzania". ERB Paper 71.7, University of Dar-es-Salaam, Oct. 1969, 65pp.
Argues that the major reason for the failure to communicate modern agricultural technology to the majority of farmers of Sukumaland is the inadequacy of extension programme planning.

46-35 HUNT, DIANA M. Credit for agricultural development. East African Publishing House, 1975, 401pp.

46-36 JOHNSTON, B.F., and MUCHIRI, G. "Equipment and tillage innovations for small-scale farms in Kenya: some unanswered questions (with special emphasis on dryland i.e. medium potential areas)". IDS Working P 197, Nov. 1974, 7pp.
A research proposal designed to elicit facts and informed judgements concerning some specific questions related to the

potential contribution of equipment and tillage innovations to increasing agricultural productivity in Kenya.

46-37 JOHNSTON, BRUCE F. "Equipment and tillage innovations for Kenya's medium potential (semi-arid) farming regions". Farm Equipment Workshop, 1975?, 15pp.

46-38 KEMIKIMBA, CELESTIN BAMUGIMBA. The spatial diffusion of fertilizer technology in Lushoto district and the role of a change agent in Tanzanian Development. Ph.D. dissertation, University of California, Irvine, 1975, 115pp.

Argues that the diffusion of innovations is a function of the area's location, the number of social and physical barriers, and the skill of the one who brings about the innovation.

46-39 KENYA, GOVERNMENT OF. The marketing of poultry produce in the Nairobi city area. National poultry development programme survey results report, Ministry of Livestock Development, Nairobi, Jan. 1980.

Attempts to provide adequate socio-economic data about marketing and consumption of poultry in Nairobi area. Declares that the present poultry produce marketing system favours the large producers, not the small-scale poultry keepers.

46-40 KINSEY, B.H. "Economic research and farm machinery design in Eastern Africa". EAJ Rural Devel, Vol. 10, Nos. 1-2, 1977, pp. 137-157.

Focuses on the relationships between economic research and technical research on agricultural machanization. Earlier version appeared as University of East Anglia Discussion Paper No. 10, 1976.

46-41 KIVUNJA, C.D. The economics of cattle and beef marketing in Kenya. M.Sc. thesis, University of Nairobi, 1976, 222pp.

Concludes that to increase cattle numbers and beef production, aggressive strategies aimed at increasing pasture and fodder per unit of cattle in the herd must be adopted, and that the government should liberalize cattle and beef prices so that they settle at their own market levels.

46-42 KOESTLER, ULRICH. "Agricultural price policy in the case of distorted exchange rates--an empirical illustration with Kenya". Zeitschrift für Ausländische Landwirtschaft (Quarterly Journal of International Agriculture), Vol. 18, No. 4, Oct.-Dec. 1979, pp. 338-354.

Examines alternative approaches to setting agricultural

product prices that maximize the balance of payments contribution, with some illustrations from Kenya.

46-43 LEONARD, DAVID K. "Why do Kenya's agricultural extension services favor the rich farmers?". U.S.A. African Studies Association meeting, Syracuse, Oct.-Nov. 1973.

46-44 ___. Reaching the peasant farmer: organization theory and practice in Kenya. University of Chicago Press, ca. 1977, 296pp.
Applies organization theory to Kenya's agricultural extension service. Investigates factors influencing administrative performance and makes a variety of policy recommendation.

46-45 LORENZL, G., and TUI, L. The price information system for the horticultural industry in Kenya. FAO (Ken 528), Nairobi, 1974, 94pp.
Argues that the market system should supply information on short term factors, such as prices and quantities traded, mainly to the wholesale sector of the market system, which includes the processing industry. This information should be used by policymakers in order to design strategies for stabilizing the distribution of produce, improve retorns to producers, and avoid exploitation of consumers.

46-46 MacARTHUR, J.D., and SMITH, C. "Price and marketing policies on meat and eggs". IDS Paper, Mar. 1979, 33pp.
Examines the background to meat price congrol in Kenya, the government involvement in the supply and demand situation, pricing of various types of meat, and a comparison of price policies. Claims that KMC has been forced into financial difficulties, partly as a result of price controls.

46-47 McDOWELL, J. "The concept of village technology in Eastern Africa". Appropriate Technology, Vol. 2, No. 2, Aug. 1975.
Argues that the initial steps in rural development must be within the capability of the small farmer and his family.

46-48 McKIM, WAYNE. "Capitalism in a socialist environment: the rural market place in Tanzania". USA African Studies Association meeting, Philadelphia, Oct. 1980.

46-49 MacPHERSON, GEORGE, and JACKSON, DUDLEY. "Village technology for rural development: agricultural innovation in Tanzania". International Labour Review, Vol. 111, No. 2, Feb. 1975, pp. 97-118.
Describes and analyses an ILO/UNDP project in Tanzania

aimed at the improvement of farm implements most appropriate to the needs, environment, and economic constraints of small-scale subsistence farmers.

46-50 ___. "Village technology in Tanzania". Development Digest, Vol. 14, No. 1, Jan. 1976, pp. 48-55.

46-51 MAGANI, P.A. "The role of the Tanzania Rural Development Bank in fertiliser use development". In Report on the FAO/NORAD Seminar on Fertiliser Use Development in Tanzania. FAO (Access No. 30768), Rome, pp. 175-183.

46-52 MBILINYI, S.M. (ed.). Agricultural research for rural development: proceedings of the East African Academy. Vol. 9, East African Literature Bureau, Nairobi, 1973, 247pp.

Covers the historical perspective of the agrarian revolution in East Africa and research activities in crop and livestock production and marketing. Gives an insight into the land tenure systems, physical environment potential of crop/livestock production, and alternative approaches to improving rural health.

46-53 MBILINYI, S.M., and LUTTREL, W.L. "Farm implements and marketing survey in Tanzania". ERB Paper 75.10, University of Dar-es-Salaam, 1975.

46-54 MBITHI, P.M. "Issues in the transfer of useful knowledge in agricultural development in Kenya". Agricultural Administration, Vol. 1, No. 4, Oct. 1974, pp. 285-300.

46-55 MINTO, S.D., and WESTLEY, S.B. "Low-cost rural equipment suitable for manufacture in East Africa". East African Agricultural and Forestry Research Organisation Conference, 1975, 82pp.

Describes, with simple working diagrams, illustrations, and details of materials required, twenty three items of equipment which have been thoroughly tested for their suitability for small-scale farmers in East Africa.

46-56 MONGI, G.O.; URIYO, A.P.; SUDI, V.A.; and SINGH, B.R. "An appraisal of some intercropping methods in terms of grain yield, response to applied phosphorus, and monetary returns from maize and cowpeas". East African Agriculture and Forestry Journal, Vol. 42, No. 1, July 1976, pp. 66-70.

Evaluates some intercropping methods in terms of grain yeild in maize and cowpeas, their response to applied phosphorus, and monetary returns per unit area. Intercropping has significant effects on cowpeas yields but not on maize, while phosphorus affects both yields.

THE AGRICULTURAL SECTOR

46-57 MORIS, JON, and SAYLOR, GERALD (eds.). Technical innovation and farm development in East Africa. Makerere University, Kampala, 1975, 409pp.
Traces technical innovations from their point of origin in the research stations through the extension services and into problems of application within actual farming systems. Also looks at farmer's adoption of recommended practices, and the integration of innovations into the management of the farm. Includes articles by 16 authors.

46-58 MSAMBICHAKA, L.A. "Agricultural mechanization in Ujamaa villages--prospects and problems". ERB Paper 75.7, University of Dar-es-Salaam.

46-59 MUKUI, J.T. (ed.). "Price and marketing controls in Kenya". IDS Occ P 32, March 1979.
Report of a seminar on price and marketing controls in Kenya. Searches for a theoretical framework for the analysis of price and marketing controls, including illegal activities which frustrate the objectives of those policies. Outlines consumer-price data collection in rural and urban areas and describes how price controls affect the accuracy of the cost of living index. Discusses domestic price effects of industrial protection. Evaluates the role and performance of marketing boards, and of price controls on manufactured milk, maize, meat, wages, and rents. Analyses conflicts of interest and diversity of views on price and marketing control policy of trade unions, manufacturers, consumers' organizations, and the Chamber of Commerce.

46-60 MUNRO, WINTHROP H. An economic study of maize marketing in Kenya, 1952-1966. Ph.D. dissertation, University of Michigan, 1973.

46-61 MUREITHI, L.P., and ATENG', B.A. "Economic efficiency and the mechanisation of small farms". In K.A. Buigutt (ed.), Appropriate mechanisation of small farms in Africa. Kenya National Academy, Nairobi, 1980.

46-62 MWANGI, WILFRED M. Farm level derived demand responses for fertilizer in Kenya. Ph.D. dissertation, Michigan State University, 1978.
Assesses the impact of such policy variables as fertilizer subsidies, product prices and interest rates on demand functions for fertilizers. Shorter paper of same title also appeared as IDS Working P 273, July 1974.

46-63 NDUNGU, F.K. The effects of selected communications variables

on the adoption of new agricultural practices by smallholders in central Kiambu, Kenya. Ph.D. dissertation, University of Toronto, ca. 1978.
DAI, Vol. 40, p. 4726-A.

46-64 NELSON, RALPH E., and KAZUNGU, DAVID K. "An evaluation of the USAID extension saturation project in Uganda". Office of International Programs, West Virginia University, 1973.

46-65 NSEREKO, JOSEPH, and BIBANGAMBAH, J.R. "The agricultural economist, decision-making, and the man on the land, with reference to Uganda". EA USSC Conference, Dec. 1974, 28pp.
Recommends that in the short run Uganda should attempt to improve the quality of decisions made in the agricultural sector by increasing the intensity of contact between farmers and extension personnel.

46-66 OCHORO, W.E.O. Agricultural mechanisation in semi-arid areas: findings from low-land Machakos district. M.A. thesis, University of Nairobi, 1976.

46-67 ODINGO, RHODA ABONYO. Decision making in food marketing in Kenya with special reference to maize and sugar. M.B.A. thesis, University of Nairobi, 1977, 259pp.
A case study in policy formulation and implementation.

46-68 OLILA, PATRICK O. "The role of public bureaucracy in agricultural development in Kisumu District, western Kenya". IDS Working P 277, Aug. 1976, 35pp.
Major finding is that the public bureaucrqcy tends to favour progressive farmers in extension, credit, etc.

46-69 ___. "The role of public bureaucracy in agricultural development: a theoretical perspective". IDS Working P 326, Oct. 1977, 33pp.
Discusses the effectiveness of the extension bureaucracy in agricultural development.

46-70 ___. "Kenyan agricultural policy: the colonial roots of African smallholder agricultural policy and services". IDS Working P 327, Nov. 1977, 48pp.
Traces the evolution, during the colonial period, of Kenyan agricultural policy and services for African smallholder areas.

46-71 OPIO-ODONGO, J.M.A. The cotton cooperative as an institutional innovation in Uganda. Ph.D. dissertation, Cornell University, 1978, 355 pp.
DAI, Vol. 39, No. 8, 1979.

THE AGRICULTURAL SECTOR

46-72 OTIENO, A.V. "Transfer of science and technology information to rural areas in East Africa". Workshop on Science and Technology Information Transfer, Nairobi, May 1978, 14pp.

46-73 OTIENO, JAMES G. "Expanded use of manufactured and appropriate farm equipment in Kenya's strategy for rural development". Farm Equipment Workshop, 1975?, 13pp.

46-74 PARKES, M.E. "The use of windmills in Tanzania". BRALUP Research Paper No. 33, University of Dar-es-Salaam, Sept. 1974, 55pp.

Discusses the possibilities of windmill use in water supply, cattle watering, and irrigation. Also explores their use for power production to alleviate the use of petrol and other imported fuels.

46-75 RAIKES, P.L. "Fertiliser projections for Tanzania up to 1974 and 1980". ERB Paper 74.2, May 1974, 51pp.

The projections cover eight types of fertilizer material and are made for the requirements of twelve distinct crops plus fruits and vegetables, oil seeds, seed production, and research stations.

46-76 ___. The development of mechanized commercial wheat production in northern Iraqw, Tanzania. Ph.D. dissertation, Stanford University, 1975.

46-77 ROLING, NIELS. "Forgotten farmers in Kenya". Agricultural Progress, No. 49, 1974, pp. 119-127.

Reports on a field experiment which aimed at developing a replicable strategy for accelerating the adoption of income-generating innovations by farmers so far by-passed by development.

Also appeared as IDS (Nairobi) unnumbered paper in March 1974.

46-78 RUIGU, GEORGE M. "Smallholder milk production and marketing: opportunities and problems". IDS Working P 286, Oct. 1976, 25pp.

Gives primary attention to the factors that determine the net price that the Kenyan small holder receives. Also discusses the role of co-operatives in price determination.

46-79 ___. "Price and marketing controls in the Kenya dairy industry". IDS Occ P 32, March 1979, 36pp.

Paper presented at IDS seminar on price and marketing controls in Kenya (edited by J.T. Mukui). Discusses trends in Kenyan milk production, marketing channels for fluid milk and milk products, the export of dairy products, protection for the local dairy industry, and pricing policy in the Kenya dairy industry.

46-80 SAUL, JOHN S. "Marketing co-operatives in a developing country: the Tanzania case". Taamuli, Vol. 1, No. 2, March 1971, pp. 30-50.
Suggests that inefficiency and corruption hinder the realization of a fully effective cooperative movement. Concludes that cooperation can be realized via educational, political and organizational mechanisms. Also appeared as EA USSC Conference Paper, 1969, Nairobi.

46-81 SAYLOR, R.G. "A social cost-benefit analysis of agricultural extension and research services among smallholder coffee producers in Kilimanjaro district". ERB Paper, University of Dar-es-Salaam, 1974, 35pp.
Attempts to assess, ex post,, the economic payoffs of research and extension efforts on one crop in one district of Tanzania. Concludes that major adjustments in the yield performance of a major crop such as cotton or coffee can generate a sizeable social benefits stream.

46-82 SCHMIDT, G., and MBUGUA, E.S. "Aspects of marketing effectiveness for selected food crops in Kenya: proposals for further research". IDS Working P 287, Oct. 1976, 14pp.
Intends to analyse aspects of marketing effectiveness with regard to the objectives of keeping marketing risks low, improving pricing or allocative efficiency, and improving operational or technical efficiency.

46-83 SCHMIDT, GUENTER. "Maize and beans in Kenya: interaction and effectiveness of the informal and formal marketing systems". IDS Occ P 31, Nairobi, 1979.
Analyses the functioning of the Kenya domestic maize and beans marketing system with special regard to the interaction of the formal (controlled) and informal (uncontrolled) subsystems. Attempts to reduce the uncertainty as to what effects relaxation of present controls would have.

46-84 SCHONHERR, SIEGFRIED, and MBUGUA, ERASTUS S. "New extension methods to speed up diffusion of agricultural innovations". IDS Disc P 200, May 1974, 16pp.
Based on research conducted by researchers at IDS in collaboration with Kenya district agricultural offices. Its aim is to develop more efficient methods for stimulating diffusion of agricultural innovations while reducing the dualistic pattern of rural development. Concludes that

diffusion is maximized when innovations are introduced through less progressive farmers.

46-85 ___. "Managing extension staff--two experiments in Kenya". IDS Disc P 230, Feb. 1976, 30pp.
Describes a system of staff meetings, recording and reporting tested in Mbere SRDP, and inservice training and planning workshops tested in Kisii and Homa Bay. Considers both systems complementary and proposes their combination as a useful management tool.

46-86 SMITH, L.D. "Resource allocation, income redistribution and agricultural pricing policies in Kenya". EA USSC Conference, Nairobi, Dec. 1969.
Examination of the extent of income redistribution created by the existing pricing under the following flows; transfers from producers to urban consumers, transfers from consumers to producers, transfers from some producers to other producers, and transfers from overseas consumers to domestic producers. Appraisal of whether agricultural pricing system is an efficient method of achieving income redistribution.

46-87 ___, and VON KAUFMANN, R. An evaluation of the Kenya artificial insemination service: draft report. IDS (unnumbered paper), Mar. 1971, 61pp.
Stresses that the most important feature of this project since its inception in 1966 has been the foundation of a solid framework on which the artificial insemination service can be expanded in future years. Argues that its main social contribution has been to give small farmers the opportunity to enter dairy farming without the additional expense of keeping a grossly underutilized bull, while at the same time contributing to an increase in the genetic potential of the dairy herd.

46-88 TALBOTT, I.D. Agricultural innovation and policy change in Kenya in 1930s. Ph.D. dissertation, West Virginia University, 1976, 376pp.
DAI, Vol. 39, p. 4992.

46-89 TANZANIA, GOVERNMENT OF. Current problems in sugar marketing. Ministry of Agriculture Marketing Development Bureau, Dar-es-Salaam, 1975, 23pp.

46-90 TEMU, PETER E. "Maize pricing policy--the Tanzanian National Agricultural Products Board case". EA USSC Conference, Dec. 1972, 20pp.
Argues that an intra-year price review could lead to both more stable and higher producer prices than with the present

single price assessment. Proposes that buffer stock capacity should not be so large that the marginal cost of storage greatly exceeds the marginal loss from exporting.

46-91 ___. Marketing board pricing and storage policy with particular reference to maize in Tanzania. Ph.D. dissertation, Stanford University, 1975.

46-92 ___. "Marketing board pricing and storage policy: the case of maize in Tanzania. East Africa Literature Bureau, Nairobi, 1977, 141pp.

46-93 VAIL, DAVID J. The public sector as stimulus of innovation adoption in African smallholder agriculture: a case study of Jeso district, Uganda. Ph.D. dissertation, Yale University, 1971.

46-94 WANGA, MOSES A. The role of agricultural cooperatives in rural development: a case study of Kakamega district. M.Arch. thesis, University of Nairobi, 1978, 203pp.

States that the majority of cooperatives were established in the 1950s but after independence the development of the movement has tended to diversify into other areas of production and emphasis has been on management efficiency.

46-95 WESTLEY, SIDNEY B., and JOHNSTON, BRUCE F. (eds.). "Proceedings of a workshop on farm equipment innovations for agricultural development and rural industrialization". IDS Occ P 16, 1975, 238pp.

The workshop was sponsored by IDS and the Faculty of Agriculture of the University of Nairobi and the National Christian Council of Kenya in Aug. 1975. Authors and titles of papers are listed below.

1. von Hülst, H. "The role of farm mechanisation in developing countries".
2. Heyer, Judith. "A preliminary report on farm surveys: tractor and ox-cultivation in Makueni and Bungoma".
3. Otieno, James; Muchiri, G.; and Johnston, B.F. "Expanded use and local manufacture of appropriate farm equipment in Kenya's strategy for rural development".
4. Adelhelm, R.; Schmidt, H.; Frey, H.; and Bosuener, H. "Economic aspects of ox-cultivation".
5. Alexander, E. "Increasing the efficiency of the traditional systems of ox-cultivation".
6. Achiya, S., and Odundo, Gabriel. "The advantages and disadvantages of the 'Indian Method' of training and controlling oxen".

THE AGRICULTURAL SECTOR

7. Wirth, Josef. "Development, use and production of small-scale agricultural equipment in Tanzania".
8. Boshoff, Wilhelm, and Minto, D.S. "Energy requirements and labour bottlenecks and their influence on the choice of improved equipment".
9. Muchiri, G., and Johnston, B.F. "Equipment and tillage innovations for Kenya's medium potential (semi-arid) farming regions".
10. Geels, Kay; Schönherr, S.; and Mbugua, S.E. "Administrative and technical aspects of the introduction and manufacture of simple farm implements in the rural areas".
11. Latham, Paul. "Village polytechnic programmes related to the manufacture and maintenance of simple farm equipment".
12. Opoti, S. "The experience of the Soy Rural Training Centre".

46-96 WILSON, F.A., and ALDINGTON, T.J. Recent developments in cattle marketing in Kenya. IDS (unnumbered paper), Jan. 1969, 11pp.
Attempts to describe the recent history of cattle marketing in Kenya, concentrating on pastoralists to show that they have slowly been induced to produce for sale.

46-97 ZELENKA, A.T. Development plan for Kenya's horticultural industry. F.A.O. (ref. KEN 71/528), Nairobi, 1975, 148pp.
Concerned with the scope and limitations for the expansion programme for all sectors of the horticultural industry. Argues that the long-term marketing outlook for horticultural exports is sound and that the domestic market is expected to continue to expand.

47--Rural and community development, agricultural cooperatives, Ujamaa, Harambee

47-1 ALAI, S.C. Integrated rural development: a case study of Aswa county, West Acholi district, Uganda, using water resources as a base for development. M.A. thesis, University of Nairobi, 1975, 201pp.
Analyses the general resource potential that can be used in conjunction with water resources for the stimulation and the promotion of integrated rural development. Concludes that boreholes have not been successful as a means of providing good water supplies for human consumption.

47-2 ALMY, SUSAN WHITIN. Rural development in Meru, Kenya: economic and social factors in accelerating change. Ph.D. dissertation, Stanford University, 1974, 291pp.

Using data in a highly progressive area of Kenya, develops an empirical test of the relative importance of economic, social, and communicational factors in explaining individual-level change.

47-3 ANDREOU, P. "Planning of cooperative development in the economic and agricultural development of Kenya: a formalised and integrated approach to sector planning". Journal of Rural Cooperation, Vol. 6, No. 1, 1978, pp. 35-52.

47-4 ANGWAZI, J., and NDULU, B. "An evaluation of Ujamaa villages in the Rufiji area, 1968-1972". EA USSC Conference, Dar-es-Salaam, Dec. 1973, 22pp.

Tries to look at the effects of resettlement and problems of creating Ujamaa in the new village in an attempt to evaluate operation Rufiji.

47-5 ARNOLD, J. "Agrarian crisis and economic liberalisation in Tanzania". Bulletin of Tanzanian Affairs, Vol. 10, 1980, pp. 6-9.

47-6 AWITI, A. "The development Ujamaa villages and the peasant question in Iringa district: a study outline". ERB Paper 73.4, University of Dar-es-Salaam, 1973, 48pp.

Discusses the revolutionary strategy for the active mobilization of the peasantry by the government and party cadres toward the ultimate aim of socialism.

47-7 BARGHOUTI, SHAWKI M. "Reaching rural families in East Africa: a handbook for the field worker". Programmes for Better Family Living East Africa, Nairobi, 1973, 112pp.

47-8 BECKER, ROGER. "Cooperative and rural development in Africa". African Administrative Studies, Vol. 12, July 1974, pp. 151-156.

47-9 BOESEN, J.; MADSEN, B.S.; and MOODY, T. Ujamaa--Socialism from above. Scandinavian Institute of African Studies, Uppsala, 1977, 183pp.

Essay on the early development of Ujamaa in the West Lake region of Tanzania. Concludes that the potential of the Ujamaa polity to transform the existing pattern of society is "in the last instance determined by its ability to break the dominance of the neo-colonial trade relations in the economic structure and simultaneously to break the power of those who control them".

47-10 BOLNICK, BRUCE R. "Collective goods provision through community

THE AGRICULTURAL SECTOR

development". Econ Dev Cult Change, Vol. 25, No. 1, Oct. 1976, pp. 137-150.
Reports the results of data gathered in Kenya to test the paper's propositions on how voluntary collective action can succeed.

47-11 BRAIN, JAMES L. "Is transformation possible? Styles of settlement in post-independence Tanzania". African Affairs, Vol. 76, No. 303, April, 1977, pp. 231-245.
Describes two approaches to village settlement in Tanzania: one planned by former colonial service officers, heavily capitalized and bureaucratized; the other a spontaneous people's movement with minimal capital inputs and the advice of one expatriate idealist.

47-12 BRIGGS, JOHN. "Villagisation and the 1974-76 economic crisis in Tanzania". J Mod Afr Studs, Vol. 17, No. 4, Dec. 1979, pp. 695-702.
Discusses the causes of the 1974-1976 crisis in the villagisation campaign launched in late 1973.

47-13 BROWN, B. Political administration and rural development in Kenya: lessons from settlement and other rural programs. Ph.D. dissertation, Syracuse University, 1977, 375pp.
DAI, Vol. 38, No. 8, 1978.

47-14 BUGENGO, J. "Ujamaa in Mara region". EA USSC Conference, Dar-es-Salaam, Dec. 1973, 18pp.
An economic evaluation of the impact of Ujamaa in Butiama village of the Mara region of Tanzania from 1966 to 1973, with a stress on the role of cooperative development. The marked development in this region within the period in question is attributed to Ujamaa.

47-15 BUGENGO, J.; MUTANGIRA, J.P.B.; and RWELENGERA, J.B.K. "The Nyarubanja system and Ujamaa villages development in west Lake region, Tanzania". ERB Paper 76.1, University of Dar-es-Salaam, 1976.

47-16 BUNKER, STEPHEN G. The uses and abuses of power in a Uganda farmers' marketing association: the Bugisu Cooperative Union, Ltd. Ph.D. dissertation, Duke University, 1975.

47-17 CHAMBERS, R.; LONGHURST, R.; and BRADLEY, D. "Seasonal dimensions to rural poverty: analysis and political implications 1979". Institute of Development Studies, University of Sussex, Brighton, 1979, 28pp.
Examines the seasonal factors which are adverse to rural

communities, with particular emphasis on the sickness and malnutrition problems which invariably arise, when famine occurs. Covers East and West Africa and Bangladesh.

47-18 CONNEL, JOHN. "The evolution of Tanzanian rural development". Institute of Development Studies Communication No. 110, University of Sussex, Brighton, 1974, 21pp.
Briefly traces the recent history of rural development through early self-help and settlement schemes to partial integration of the two approaches in Ujamaa villages.

47-19 COULSON, ANDREW. "Peasants and bureaucrats". Review of African Political Economy, No. 3, May-Oct. 1975, pp. 53-58.
A brief account of the sequence of Ujamaa policy implementation from 1968 to 1974.

47-20 ___. "What happened to Ujamaa". New Internationalist, Vol. 48, Feb. 1977, pp. 17-19.

47-21 CRAIG, J.T. "Communication of rural development law and policy". Seminar on Law and Rural Development in Eastern Africa (Kisumu Conference Proceedings), July 1977, pp. 539-555.
Discusses the approaches that should be adopted in communicating ideas to the rural population.

47-22 DAVID, MARTIN. "SRDP in Kenya: can experiments in development succeed?" IDS Working P 254, Jan. 1976, 9pp.
Outlines four experiments associated with SRDP, assesses their value in establishing a development strategy, and explores the potential contricution of the experimental method to district development planning in Kenya.

47-23 DE VRIES, JAMES. "Ujamaa villages and problems of institutional change with emphasis on agricultural extension and development". Department of Rural Economy, University of Dar-es-Salaam, Morogoro, 1977, 33pp.

47-24 ___. Agricultural extension and the development of Ujamaa villages in Tanzania: toward a dialogical agricultural extension model. Ph.D. dissertation, University of Wisconsin, Madison, 1978.

47-25 DUE, JEAN M. Costs, returns and repayment experience of Ujamaa villages in Tanzania, 1973-76. University Press of America, Washington, D.C., 1980, 141pp.
Analyses two sets of Ujamaa villages in Iringa region. Tobacco was the major income source in one group and maize

in the other. Estimates of total social costs showed net returns to communal enterprise to be negative in 1973 but positive thereafter. Communal production of tobacco was more successful than for maize, due to high production costs of the latter. Economic viability of the villages studied requires a better package of maize inputs, more village-level choice of inputs, and higher maize prices.

47-26 ELLIOT, CHARLES. Patterns of poverty in the third world: a study of social and economic stratification. Praeger, New York, 1975, 417pp.
Includes a chapter on rural differentiation in East Africa.

47-27 ELLMAN, A. "Development of Ujamaa policy in Tanzania". Rural Development Research Committee, University of Dar-es-Salaam, 1972.

47-28 ERGAS, ZAKI. "Why did the Ujamaa village policy fail? Towards a global analysis". J Mod Afr Studs, Vol. 18, No. 3, Sept. 1980, pp. 387-410.
Argues that Tanzania in recent years has chosen to pursue rapid modernization, entailing increased dependence on foreign capital and expertise. With respect to rural sector modernization, the policy of socialist development has had to be abandoned and the new strategy entails the "control" of the peasants in the villages. The failure of the collectivization of the land and of agricultural production may illustrate that "agriculture and socialism do not mix". Concludes, however, that Tanzania remains one of the few African countries attempting to fight against injustice and inequality.

47-29 FINUCANE, JAMES R. Rural development and bureaucracy in Tanzania: the case of Mwanza region. Scandinavian Institute of African Studies, Uppsala; Africana Publishing Co., New York, 1974, 192pp.
Examines the efficiency of Tanzanian organizational arrangements in rural development in achieving a satisfactory mix of output and equity.

47-30 FULLER, COLIN. "The Special Rural Development Programme in Kenya; its use as a case-study in the Department of Administrative Studies in the University of Manchester". J Admin Overseas, Vol. 14, No. 3, July 1975, pp. 148-158.
Concludes that the use of SRDP as a frame of reference led participants to become more involved in the discussion of policies and procedures for the implementation of rural development programmes.

47-31 GORDON, JACOB U. "Ujamaa in Tanzania: problems and prospects". Current Bibliography on African Affairs, Vol. 7, No. 4, Fall 1974, pp. 360-377.

Concludes that the prospects for Ujamaa depend to a large extent on Tanzania's ability to generate local capital formation.

47-32 GREEN, R.H. "Toward Ujamaa and Kujitegemea: income distribution and absolute poverty eradication aspects of the Tanzanian transition to socialism". University of Sussex Institute of Development Studies Discussion Paper No. 66, Brighton, 1974, 92pp.

47-33 ___. "Ujamaa: success or failure?". African Development, Vol. 9, No. 1, Jan. 1975, pp. 12-13.

Argues that Tanzania's Ujamaa is the most comprehensive national effort ot raise the living standards of the ordinary peasants anywhere in Africa. But coercion has sometimes been used and there is no evidence that Ujamaa has done anything yet to increase agricultural production. In fact, Tanzania is importing more food (1975) than ever before because of drought.

47-34 HANSEL, HERMANN. "The rural development strategy of Ujamaa villages in Tanzania". Zeitschrift für Ausländische Landwirtschaft (Quarterly Journal of International Agriculture), Vol. 15, No. 2, April-June 1976, pp. 180-195.

Argues that experience shows that various problems need to be considered if the objectives of Ujamaa are to be realized. Infers some consequences of promotion measures on the basis of an anticipated change toward large-scale communal agriculture.

47-35 HARRIS, BELLE. "Survey of agricultural training institutes: implications for producing Ujamaa Vijijini extension workers". Rural Development Research Committee, University of Dar-es-Salaam, 1967.

47-36 HEYER, J.; WILLIAMS, G.; and ROBERTS, P. (eds.). Rural development in tropical Africa. Macmillan, London, 1981, 224pp.

Examines the practice of rural development by governments and international agencies. Discusses why rural development projects and programmes often fail to meet the needs of the rural poor, and even their own goals of increasing agricultural production. Examines national agricultural development since the colonial period in Tanzania, Kenya, Nigeria, Niger, and Ghana, and provides detailed surveys and critical analyses of agricultural policies.

THE AGRICULTURAL SECTOR

47-37 HJORT, ANDERS. "Socio-economic effects of rural electrification: an interim report". IDS Working P 175, July 1974, 34pp.
Preliminary results on consumption patterns in ten selected places and of business and household interviews in Isiolo on willingness to pay for electricity. Also includes interviews about people's expectations on electricity.

47-38 HOLMQUIST, FRANK W. Peasant organization, clientism and dependency: a case study of an agricultural producers cooperative in Kenya. Ph.D. dissertation, Indiana University, 1975.

47-39 HOPCRAFT, PETER N. "Integration, decentralisation and implementation in rural development programmes". IDS Disc P 252, Feb. 1977, 19pp.
Draws mainly on Kenyan experience to focus on a number of problems and issues that appear to be of importance in determining whether rural and agricultural development programmes succeed.

47-40 HUIZER, GERRIT. "The Ujamaa village program in Tanzania: a new form of rural development". Studies in Comparative International Development, Vol. 8, No. 2, Summer 1973, pp. 183-207.

47-41 HYDEN, GORAN. "Ujamaa, villagisation and rural development in Tanzania". Overseas Development Institute Review, No. 1, 1975, pp. 53-72.
Deals with 1967-1973 Ujamaa village programme which affected 15 per cent of Tanzania's population. Refers also to the present programme which has affected half of the population and discusses some implications of the country's rural development programme.

47-42 ____. Beyond Ujamaa in Tanzania: underdevelopment and an uncaptured peasantry. Heinemann, London, 1980.
Agrues that the peasant mode of production, and not capitalism, keeps African economies poor and underdeveloped. Uses an ecclectic approach and is critical of dependency and unequal exchange theorists.

47-43 INSTITUTE FOR DEVELOPMENT STUDIES. "Second overall evaluation of the Special Rural Development Programme". IDS Occ P 12, 1975, 610pp.
Evaluation was carried out by IDS at the request of the Kenya Ministry of Finance and Planning. Discusses particularly agricultural extension and farmers' training, infrastructure, and social development. The first such evaluation was carried out in 1973, and appeared as IDS Occ P 8.

47-44 JIGGINS, JANICE. "Beyond Ujamaa in Tanzania". Third World Quarterly, Jan. 1981, pp. 88-95.

47-45 KAHAMA, KABAKAMA. Rural development as a strategy of modernization: a case study of Ujamaa villages in Tanzania. Ph.D. dissertation, Claremont Graduate School, 1973.

47-46 KARANJA, EDWARD. The development of cooperative movement in Kenya. Ph.D. dissertation, University of Pittsburgh, 1974, 223pp.

Discusses the problems involved in transferring the concept of cooperative societies form Britain to Kenya. Considers the movement's potential economic, social and community contributions to society and its role in development.

47-47 KARLEN, LARS. "Co-operative development in Kenya". Review of International Co-operation, Vol. 4, 1975, pp. 137-141.

47-48 KELLER, EDMOND J., Jr. "The limits of community self-help in Kenya: a cost-benefit analysis of the Harambee movement in education". U.S.A. African Studies Association meeting, Philadelphia, Oct. 1980.

47-49 ___. "Harambee: educational policy, inequality, and the political economy of rural community self-help in Kenya". Journal of African Studies, Vol. 4, No. 1, Spring 1977.

47-50 KJEKSHUS, HELGE. "The Tanzanian villagization policy: implementational lessons and ecological dimensions". Can J Afr Studs, Vol. 11, No. 2, 1977, pp. 269-282.

Concludes that the Ujamaa policy remains in suspension because the implementational features have fundamentally undercut some of the preconditions of the programme and harmed the outcome. Doubts whether the change of settlement pattern is consistent with the fundamental requirements for economic development in Tanzanian ecology.

47-51 KNIGHT, C. GREGORY. Ecology and change: rural modernization in an African community. Academic Press, New Yori, 1974, 300pp.

Studies the processes and patterns of change among the Nyiha of Mbozi, Tanzania from four perspectives: cultural, ecological, economic, and spatial.

47-52 KONTER, J.H. Facts and factors in the rural economy of the Nyakyusa (Tanzania). Ph.D. dissertation, Hogesschool Tilburg, 1974, 346pp.

THE AGRICULTURAL SECTOR

47-53 LAMB, GEOFF. "Government, co-operatives and peasant agriculture in Kenya". IDS Bulletin, Vol. 6, No. 1, Sept. 1974, pp. 25-36

47-54 LELE, UMA. "Designing rural development programmes: lessons from past experience in Africa". IDS Dis P 213, Dec. 1974, 29pp.
The paper is based on a review of past projects in sub-Saharan Africa and rural sector surveys in Kenya and Tanzania It discusses the effects on past projects of three sets of factors: national policies, administrative systems, and overall institutional development. It then recommends planning based on the systematic acquisition of knowledge and flexibility in the course of implementations.

47-55 ___. The design of rural development: lessons from Africa. Johns Hopkins University Press, Baltimore, 1975, 246pp.
A World Bank publication that includes Kenyan and Tanzanian case materials in Chapter 9 and appendices.

47-56 ___. "A revisit to rural development in Eastern Africa". Finance and Development, Vol. 16, No. 4, 1979, pp. 31-35.
Points out the progress made in rural development policies and projects in Africa. Having the major constraints in mind, she briefly explores ways in which they can be overcome. Despite several suggested changes she still things that rural development will be a slow and difficult process in Eastern Africa.

47-57 LIVINGSTONE, IAN. "Kenya's rural industrial development programme: an evaluation of experience and proposals for action" IDS Working P 210, April 1975, 38pp.
Presents an analysis of the detailed activities of three of the four existing rural industrial centres--Nyeri, Kakamega and Embu.

47-58 ___. "Rural development in Kenya: the Special Rural Development Programme revisited". J Admin Overseas, Vol. 15, No. 3, July 1976, pp. 132-140.
Suggests that the shortcomings of the programme were partly due to incomplete government backing and failure to adhere to its objectives.

47-59 ___. "Experimentation in rural development: Kenya's special rural development programme". Agricultural Administration, Vol. 3, No. 3, July 1976, pp. 217-233.
Critically reviews Kenya's Special Rural Development Programme (SRDP).

47-60 ___. "An evaluation of Kenya's Rural Industrial Development Programme". J Mod Afr Studs, Vol. 15, No. 3, Sept. 1977, pp. 495-504.
Argues that the approaches of industrial estates and mobile assistance to an entrepreneur in his own workshop are likely to be unrewarding if pursued in their pure form, and that a system of "workshop clusters", combining elements of estates and extension, should be adopted.

47-61 LOFCHIE, MICHAEL F. "Agrarian crisis and economic liberalisation in Tanzania". J Mod Afr Studs, Vol. 16, No. 3, Sept. 1978, pp. 451-475.
Discusses Tanzania's policy of rural collectivization.

47-62 LUTTRELL, W. Towards rural cooperation. Tanzania Publishing House, Dar-es-Salaam, ca. 1980.

47-63 McHENRY, DEAN E., Jr. "The Ujamaa village in Tanzania: a comparison with Chinese, Soviot and Mexican experiences in collectivization". Comparative Studies in Society and History, Vol. 18, No. 3, July 1976, pp. 347-370.
Examines the degree of similarity in the collectivization experiences. Concludes that the construction of Ujamaa villages in Tanzania is a unique experience in collectivization.

47-64 ___. "Peasant participation in communal farming: the Tanzanian experience". African Studies Review, Vol. 20, No. 3, Dec. 1977, pp. 43-64.
Considers the degree of communal farming that has been achieved in Tanzania and the attitudes of the peasants and the leaders toward the promotion of participation in communal farming.

47-65 ___. Tanzania's Ujamaa villages: the implementation of a rural development strategy. University of California Institute of International Studies Research Series No. 39, Berkeley, 1979, 268pp.
Focuses on the struggle to implement the Ujamaa village policy in Tanzania. Provides an analysis of the Ujamaa policy, attempts at implementation, factors affecting its implementation, and an assessment of the Ujamaa village policy.

47-66 MAKERE, E.N. "Ujamaa villages in practice". Taamuli, Vol. 2, No. 2, July 1972, pp. 17-26.
Emphasizes past and present problems encountered in the development of Ujamaa villages to indicate the importance of extensive planning before and during their establishment.

47-67 MAKERERE INSTITUTE OF SOCIAL RESEARCH. "Contemporary problems and issues in rural development". Kampala 1978, 71pp.

THE AGRICULTURAL SECTOR

47-68 MAPACHU, JUMA VOLKER. "Operation planned villages in rural Tanzania". <u>Afr Rev</u>, Vol. 6, No. 1, 1976, pp. 1-16.
Argues that with over ninety per cent of its 15 million people living in rural areas and involved in agricultural production, Tanzania could not take any other more practical development route than through its rural inhabitants and their main resource potential, land.

47-69 MARKIE, JOHN. "Ujamaa villages in Tanzania: a possible solution to the problems of the rural poor". <u>Land Reform</u>, No. 1, 1976, pp. 54-76.
Focuses on income disparities in the rural areas and examines how Tanzania's development strategy is oriented towards gradual abolition of private capital, and the participation of the people in development.

47-70 MASCARENHAS, A.C. <u>Social and institutional framework for implementing integrated rural development approaches and constrants: the case of Tanzania</u>. FAO (Access No. 33981), Rome, 1976.

47-71 MATANGO, R.R. "The role of agencies for rural development in Tanzania--a case study of the Lushoto integrated development project". <u>ERB Paper 76.3</u>, University of Dar-es-Salaam, 1976, 59pp.

47-72 MBITHI, PHILIP M. "Conquering the economy through rural development". <u>Ceres</u>, Vo. 7, No. 3, May-June 1974, pp. 26-29.

47-73 MBITHI, PHILIP M., and BARNES, CAROLYN. "A conceptual analysis of approaches to rural development". <u>IDS Working P 154</u>, March 1974, 31pp.
Centres on the units of rural change and points out weaknesses in the directed planning strategy and in an integrated multi-dimensional approach in meeting the reality of the situation in rural areas.

47-74 MBITHI, P.M., and RASMUSSON, R. <u>Self reliance in Kenya: the case of Harambee</u>. Scandinavian Institute of African Studies, Uppsala, 1977, 177pp.
Stresses that to understand development in Kenya it is necessary to know something about Harambee self-help as a development strategy, a way of filling needs, and a way of working and living in Kenya. Begins with a discussion of the background and environment of Harambee and then outlines two conceptual interpretations.

47-75 MIGOT-ADHOLA, S.E. "Rural development: changing perspective and policy". Seminar on Law and Rural Development (Kisumu Conference Proceedings), July 1977, pp. 56-71.

Argues that development experts shoudl address themselves to questions concerning income distribution, social justice, democratic participation, and the satisfaction of basic needs.

47-76 MIRITI, A.M., and REITHAUG, INGE. "Cooperatives in the economic and social development of Kenya". In Paris Andreou, Co-operative institutions and economic development: some lessons from advanced and developing countries. East African Literature Bureau, Nairobi, 1977, pp. 296-309.
Analyses how the Kenya government has pursued cooperative movements as a means of bringing accelerated development of the economy and to enhance the social and economic well-being of the people.

47-77 MUKARU-NG'ANG'A, D. "Inequalities in coffee cooperative societies (The case of Muranga district)". Department of History Staff Seminar Paper, University of Nairobi, Jan. 1978, 29pp.
Discusses some aspects of socio-economic inequalities in the rural areas. Argues that one of the most prominent vehicles for eliminating socio-economic inequalities in the rural areas has been the co-operative societies, but that these societies could be a source and cause of these ineqaulities rather than a means to eliminate them.

47-78 MUSHI, S.S. "Ujamaa: modernization by traditionalization". Taamuli, Vol. 1, No. 2, March 1971, pp. 13-29.
Distinguishes between the Ujamaa of post-Arusha Declaration and the traditional Ujamaa system. Looks at the problems and prospects of implementing the three principles of Ujamaa, namely, mutual respect, sharing of joint product, and universal obligation to work.

47-79 MUSUNDI, J.J. "The development of the co-operative movement in Kenya". Review of International Co-operation, Vol. 67, No. 1, 1974, pp. 17-20.

47-80 MUTAHA, A.Z. Co-operatives in Tanzania: problems of organization building. Studies in political science, No. 4, Tanzania Publishing House, Dar-es-Salaam, 1976, 93pp.

47-81 MUTHAMO, J.K., and OTIENO, J.O. "The challenge of rural development in Kenya". African Administrative Studies, Vol. 17, July 1977, pp. 85-93.

47-82 MUTHEE, A.M. Distribution of non-farm inputs in Kenya, with special emphasis on the role of agricultural cooperatives. M.Sc. thesis, University of Nairobi, 1975, 235pp.
Argues that the possible pre-requisites for a successful non-farm input distribution system are timely estimates of

THE AGRICULTURAL SECTOR

quantities required by the group and timely procurement of adequate quantities, supported by sufficient storage and transport facilities, and reasonable credit and pricing policies.

47-83 MUTISO, G.C.M., and GODFREY, E.M. "The political economy of self help: Kenya's Harambee institutes of technology". EA USSC Conference, Nairobi, Dec. 1972, 36pp.
Concentrates on placing the institutes in their political background and on working toward a political economy of this latest Harambee phenomenon. Emphasises that the paper contains preliminary notes, set down in the hope of stimulating discussion.

47-84 MUTISO, G.C. "Kitui: the ecosystem, integration and change: an overall framework". IDS Working P 303, Oct. 1977, 32pp.
Embraces ecological, migration, and social formations variables. Recommends "comprehensive" multidisciplinary studies as bases for identifying planning alternatives for the marginal areas. Presents a view of ecosystem change and class evolution in the areas of Kitui district derived from fieldwork.

47-85 ___. "Kitui trade". IDS Working P 306, Oct. 1977, 24pp.
Applies the various explanations for the pattern of establishing trading centres to Kitui district, Eastern Province in Kenya.

47-86 MWAKA, V.M. Agricultural marketing cooperatives in Uganda. Makerere University Department of Geography, Kampala, 1978, 203pp.

47-87 MWAPACHU, JUMA V. "Operation planned villages in rural Tanzania: a revolutionary strategy for development". Afr Rev, Vol. 6, No. 1, 1976, pp. 1-16.
Concludes that decentralization of development planning and implementation powers to grass-roots level will bring speedier development.

47-88 MYERS, ROBERT B. The structure and performance of a commercial farm settlement: an economic analysis of one of Tanzania's village settlement schemes. Ph.D. dissertation, Syracuse University, 1973.

47-89 NDISSI, CHACHA. Ujamaa villages as a collective development strategy in Tanzania's economic development. Ph.D. dissertation, George Washington University, 1976.

47-90 NGETHE, N.; OKOTH-OGENDO, H.W.O.; SCHÖNHERR, S.; and WYETH, P.W. "Reaching the rural poor: lessons from the Kenyan Special Rural Development Programme". IDS Working P 296, Jan. 1977, 21pp.

Examines four aspects of actual projects, namely, extension service, credit projects, land tenure reform, and administrative decentralization. Concludes that to ensure that development reaches all sections of the community it is not simply a matter of guarding against the appropriation of development benefits by local vested interests, but also of discarding experts' notions of the "right way" to pursue development goals.

47-91 NGETHE, NJUNGUNA. "Harambee and rural development in Kenya: towards a political/administrative re-interpretation". IDS Working P 302, March 1977, 24pp.

Harambee appears to be an unsystematic and almost ad hoc response to the problems of rural poverty in Kenya. It has developed its own momentum, first from a political slogan, then to small and medium sized projects, for example, cattle dips, and finally to the present ambitious institutes of science and technology.

47-92 OBWA, OIRO. "The effectiveness of growth and service centres' policy as an instrument for rural development in Kenya". IDS Working P 317, July 1977, 26pp.

Argues that constraints on this planning exercise are past government policies, settlement patterns, and the land-tenure system.

47-93 OGUTU, M.A. "The impact of co-operative movements on the economic development of western province of Kenya 1950-1970". Department of History Staff Seminar Paper, University of Nairobi, 1977, 29pp.

47-94 OMARI, C.K. Strategy for rural development: Tanzania. East African Literature Bureau, Nairobi, 1976.

Uses Tanzania's experiences with Ujamaa to argue the need for a "frontal approach" methodology for rural development. This involves understanding social institutions in their historical and cultural perspectives.

47-95 ___. "Ujamaa cooperative farming: the way ahead". Journal of Rural Cooperation, Vol. 5, No. 1, 1977, pp. 19-28.

47-96 OUMA, SYLVESTER J. A history of the cooperative movement in Kenya. Bookwise Ltd., Nairobi, 1980, 164pp.

An account of the development and organization of cooperatives in Kenya.

THE AGRICULTURAL SECTOR

47-97 OYUGI, OUMA W. "Community development as a strategy for local development: a theoretical re-examination". IDS Working P 193, Oct. 1974, 14pp.
Argues that the traditional community development movement which emphasizes processes or mechanisms more than the output considerations is conceptionally wrong and anti-developmental.

47-98 ___. "Decentralization for integrated rural development: some lessons from Kenya". IDS Working P 255, Dec. 1975, 19pp.
Posits that since the Kenyan political system is not decentralized any attempt to decentralize planned development is faced with built-in limitations, which make it difficult for development organizations at local level to operate effectively.

47-99 PATTERSON, DOUGLAS B. "Coping with land scarcity: the pattern of household adaptations in one Luhya community". IDS Working P 360, Jan. 1980, 33pp.
Discusses several alternative responses to the land scarcity problem in one village in Kakamega district, Kenya.

47-100 RAIKES, PHILIP L. "Village planning for Ujamaa". Taamuli, Vol. 3, No. 1, Dec. 1972, pp. 3-26.
Proposes a method of local planning for Ujamaa villages. Outlines the sort of planning framework which could harmonize local and national objectives.

47-101 ___. "Economic evaluation criteria for Ujamaa villages". ERB Paper 73.3, University of Dar-es-Salaam, 1973, 36pp.
Presents for discussion some measures of success and viability which may be useful in the assessment of Ujamaa villages. Concludes that Ujamaa as a social form contains the political-economic potential to overcome the contradictions which arise during its development.

47-102 ___. "Ujamaa and rural socialism". Review of African Political Economy, No. 3, May-Oct. 1975, pp. 33-52.
Argues that some of the problems of rural planning and Ujamaa implementation are closely connected with the absence of a concerted strategy for the transformation of the Tanzanian economy.

47-103 ___. "Agrarian crisis and economic liberation in Tanzania: a comment". J Mod Afr Studs, Vol. 17, No. 2, June 1979, pp. 309-316.
Argues against Lofchie's article in the same journal, Vol. 16, No. 3, Sept. 1978.

47-104 RALD, J. "Ujamaa: problems of implementation (experience from west Lake)". BRALUP Research Report No. 10, University of Dar-es-Salaam, May 1970, 33pp.
Relates the West Lake people's attitudes, rooted in their history, with the Ujamaa policy and highlights the conflicts that arise.

47-105 REYNOLDS, ERIC J., and WALLIS, M.A.H. "Self help and rural development in Kenya". IDS Disc P 241, Nov. 1976, 27pp.
Examines six Special Rural Development Programme areas in Kenya in terms of the intensity of "economic" self-help activity versus the "social/domestic variety".

47-106 RUHUMBIKA, GABRIEL (ed.). Towards Ujamaa: twenty years of TANU leadership. East African Literature Bureau, Nairobi, 1974, 308pp.
Examination of the social, political, and economic aspects of the present Tanzanian society with respect to the post-TANU government.

47-107 RUTAIWA, FRANCIS W. Application of incentives for rural development in developing countries: a case study of Tanzania. Ph.D. dissertation, Fordham University, 1975, 435pp.
Reviews the application of incentives for rural development in developing countries. Considers the crucial institutional aspects of the Tanzanian strategy for rural development, focusing mainly on the indigenous land tenure systems and the problems of technical changes at the farm level.

47-108 SANDBERG, AUDUN. "Ujamaa and the control of environment". EA USSC Conference, Dar-es-Salaam, Dec. 1973, 23pp.
Shows how the relationship between man and his environment changes with the implementation of new ideology. The analysis is carried out in the form of a comparison between environmental processes in an "upstream" and a "midstream" area.

47-109 SCHROEDER, D.W. Rural development in Tanzania: the significance of villagisation. Ph.D. dissertation, Carleton University, 1977, 228pp.

47-110 SILBERFEIN, MARILYN. The regional impact of Tanzanian settlement schemes. Ph.D. dissertation, Syracuse University, 1972.

47-111 SUMRA, SULEMAN. "Problems of agricultural production in Ujamaa villages in Handeni district". ERB Paper 75.3, University of Dar-es-Salaam, June 1975, 19pp.
Concludes that the move to the villages does not seem to have solved the basic problems faced by the peasants in the area, that is, frequent food shortages and poor living conditions.

THE AGRICULTURAL SECTOR

47-112 TANZANIA UJAMAA COOPERATIVE DEPARTMENT. "Agricultural marketing in villages". Ujamaa Cooperative Development Department, Dar-es-Salaam, 1977, 27pp.

47-113 TEMU, P. "The Ujamaa experiment". In K.S. Kim; R.B. Mabele; and M.J. Schultheis (eds.), Papers on the political economy of Tanzania. Heinemann, Nairobi, 1979, pp. 197-201.
Explores African socialism in relation to the Tanzanian Ujamaa villages, and the administration of them.

47-114 THOMAS, BARBARA P. "Development through Harambee: who wins and who loses?". U.S.A. African Studies Association meeting, Philadelphia, 1980.

47-115 UNDP/FAO. "Iringa region Tanzania: integrated rural development proposals for the third five-year plan 1976-81". Overseas Development Group, University of East Anglia, Norwich, 19

47-116 VERHAGEN, KOENRAAD. "Changes in Tanzanian rural development policy 1975/1978". Development and Change, Vol. 11, No. 2, April 1980, pp. 285-295.

47-117 VON FREYOLD, MICHAELA. "The problem of rural development and the politics of Ujamaa Vijijini in Handeni (Tanzania)". Afr Rev, Vol. 6, No. 2, 1976, pp. 36-64.
Describes the formation of Juamaa villages in Handeni, the colonial heritage of the Handeni peasants, and stability and progress of the Ujamaa villages.

47-118 ___. Ujamaa villages in Tanzania. Heinemann, London, 1979, 244pp.
Discusses the experience since Ujamaa villages were introduced in 1967, including a collection of case studies on Tanga region villages. Concludes that Ujamaa continues to be beset with problems.

47-119 VON RICHTER, LOTHAR E. "Integrated rural development in practice". Zietschrift für Ausländische Landwirtschaft (Quarterl Journal of International Agriculture), Vol. 15, No. 4, Oct.-Dec. 1976, pp. 414-437.
Analyses the experience gained in carrying out integrated rural development projects with international assistance in ten developing countries.

47-120 WALLACE, C.C., and WEEKS, S.G. Success or failure in rural Uganda: a study of young people. Makerere Institute of Social Research, Kampala, 1976, 94pp.
Discussion based on the lives of rurally based, little educated youth. The research was done in three villages, in Buganda, Bugisu, and West Nile.

47-121 WALLACE, I.R. "Agricultural education and rural development: some problems and approaches in Kenya". Agricultural Progress, Vol. 51, 1976, pp. 131-142.

47-122 WALLIS, MALCOLM. "The community development assistant in Kenya: a study of the administration of personnel and rural development". IDS Disc P 231, Feb. 1976, 23pp.
Examines in detail the Community Development Division of the Kenya Department of Social Services. Argues that tendencies toward fragmentation within this organization are strong and are likely to weaken the self-help movement in Kenya.

47-123 ___. "Community development in Kenya: some current issues". Community Development Journal, Vol. 11, No. 3, Oct. 1976, pp. 192-198.

47-124 WATTS, E.R. (ed.). New hope for rural Africa. African Publishing House, New York. 1969.
Proceedings of a conference held at the Social Centre, Kikuyu, Kenya, in Sept. 1969.

47-125 WESTERGAARD, P. "Analysis of the accounts of the co-operative societies in Tanzania for the years 1967-1969". ERB Paper 73.2, University of Dar-es-Salaam, 1973, 48pp.
Reveals the existence of a large number of "deficit" societies and that there seems to be a need for making a thorough review of all societies in the different regions and identify those which are viable and those which are not.

47-126 WILLIAMS, DAVID. "Law and socialist rural development". Eastern Africa Law Review, Vol. 6, No. 3, 1973, pp. 193-213.
Deals with the rural development policy in Tanzania from a theoretical and legal point of view.

47-127 WILLIAMS, GAVIN. "Taking the parts of peasants: rural development in Nigeria and Tanzania". In P.C.W. Gutkind and I. Wallerstein (eds.), The political economy of contemporary Africa. SAGE, Beverly Hills, London, 1976, pp. 131-154.
Argues that food production cannot be dramatically increased by state direction of peasant producers, but only by the encouragement of peasant initiative and experience to improve their own material well-being.

47-128 WINANS, EDGAR V. "Local initiative and government response: development politics in Kenya". U.S.A. African Studies Association meeting, Philadelphia, Nov. 1972, 21pp.
Examines selected aspects of the Harambee movement in Kenya. Argues that government grants-in-aid can improve

the project rate in districts of low activity but that the strength of local integration and leadership is the critical factor in the movement.

47-129 WINANS, EDGAR V., and HAUGERUD, ANGELIQUE. "Rural self-help in Kenya: the Harambee movement". Human Organisation, Vol. 36, No. 4, Winter 1977, pp. 334-351.
Examines the extent of correlation between self-help mobilization and various aspects of past development, and ways in which the Harambee movement may be accentuating already existing regional inequalities.

48--Economic geography, natural resources, ecology, wildlife, conservation, and pollution

48-1 ALIBARUHO, GEORGE. "The dynamics of location: a Von Thunen-supply analysis of the changing spatial characteristics of cotton in Uganda". IDS Working P 192, Oct. 1974, 18pp.
Concludes that the pattern of cotton distribution is changing according to the botanic feasibility of growing alternative food crops and according to accessibility of the aminly urban markets for these crops.

48-2 ALLAWAY, JAMES D. Elephants and their interactions with people in the Tana River region of Kenya. Ph.D. dissertation, Cornell University, 1979, 405pp.
DAI, Vol. 40, p. 2452-B.

48-3 BAKER, S.J.K. "A background to the study of drought in East Africa". African Affairs, Vol. 73, No. 291, April 1974, pp. 170-177.
Argues that in view of the unreliability of rainfall, in terms of time as well as space, it is important to penetrate beyond mean annual totals and to make an assessment of variability.

48-4 CAPONE, DONALD L. Wildlife, man and competition for land in Kenya: a geographical analysis. Ph.D. dissertation, Michigan State University, 1972.

48-5 CARLSON, KAREN A. The Kenya wildlife conservation campaign: a descriptive and critical study of intercultural persuasion. Ph.D. dissertation, Northwestern University, 1970.

48-6 CURRY-LINDAHL, KAI. "Comprehensive planning of natural resources: present situation and factors to consider". IDS Disc P 240, Oct. 1976, 28pp.
Uses examples from Kenya and other parts of Eastern Africa

to describe the value of and threats to various renewable natural resources.

48-7 FLEURET, A.K. "Fuel wood use in a peasant community: a Tanzanian case study". J Dev Areas, Vol. 12, No. 3, April 1978, pp. 315-322.

48-8 GAILE, GARY L. "Geomathematical analysis of growth centre patterns: the Nairobi region". IDS Working P 203, Dec. 1974, 12pp.
Finds that a significant amount of regularity exists in the spatial pattern of development around Nairobi.

48-9 HENRY, WESLEY R. Relationships between visitor use and tourist capacity for Kenya's Amboseli national park. Ph.D. dissertation, Colorado State University, 1980, 121pp.
DAI, Vol. 41, p. 2765-A.

48-10 HILLMAN, KES, and MARTIN, ESMOND B. "Will poaching exterminate Kenya's rhinos?". Oryx, Vol. 15, No. 2, Nov. 1979, pp. 131-132.
Describes the desperate situation to which poaching has brought the numbers of black rhinos in East Africa.

48-11 JAHNKE, HANS E. Conservation and utilization of wildlife in Uganda. IFO-Institute for Wirtschaftsforschung, Munich, 1974, 132pp.

48-12 KABAGAMBE, DENNIS M. "Aspects of resource conservation and utilization: the role of charcoal industry in the Kenyan economy". IDS Working P 271, June 1976, 23pp.
Discusses charcoal as a product of limited scarce forest and scrubland to highlight possible future supply constraints of raw-materials and environmental imbalance.

48-13 KENYA, GOVERNMENT OF. Ground water resources of Kenya. Ministry of Water Development, 1978, 85pp.

48-14 KING, K.F.S. "The wasted lands: the programme of work of ICRAF". International Council for Research in Agroforestry, Nairobi, 1978.

48-15 KING, R.B. "Land resources of the Rukwa region". BRALUP Research Paper, University of Dar-es-Salaam, 1977, 24pp.

48-16 LAWS, RICHARD M. Elephants and their habits. Clarendon Press, Oxford, 1975, 376pp.

THE AGRICULTURAL SECTOR

48-17 MARTIN, ESMOND BRADLEY. "The craft, the trade and the elephants". Oryx, Vol. 15, No. 4, Aug. 1980, pp. 363-366.
Points out that from 1965 to 1974 Kenya, Tanzania, and Uganda supplied 99 per cent of India's imported ivory, but since 1974 middlemen in Europe, Dubai, and Hong King have been supplying about 47 per cent of the total.

48-18 ___. "The international trade in rhinoceros products". World Wildlife Fund Yearbook 1979-80, World Wildlife Fund Public Affairs Division, Morges, Switzerland, 1980, pp. 75-81.
Argues that approximately 90 per cent of the rhinoceros population in Kenya, Uganda, and northern Tanzania was killed during the 1970-1980 period. Suggests and discusses reasons for the accelerated killings in the 1970s.

48-19 MASAYA, TICHAENDEPI R. "Spectral analysis of rainfall series in Kenya". IDS Working P 211, March 1975, 28pp.
Looks at rainfall variation and how it affects policy making and farming in Kenya. Finds that rainfall behaviour requires irrigation schemes capable of combating drought for periods of up to four years.

48-20 MENON, P.A. "Urban primacy in Kenya". IDS Working P 282, Aug. 1976, 30pp.
Based on an historical Kenyan case study, describes the series of interrelated and recursive growth processes that led to polarization in primate cites of urban-based economic activities in colonial spatial systems.

48-21 MISIKO, P.M. (ed.). "Soil and water conservation in Kenya". IDS Occ P 27, Feb. 1978, 160pp.
Collection of papers presented at Workshop held in Sept. 1977, sponsored by the Land and Farm Management Division of the Kenya Ministry of Agriculture and the Department of Agricultural Engineering of the University of Nairobi and of Egerton College. Authors and titles are listed below.

1. Braun, H.M.H. and Muchena, F.N. "The Kenya Soil Survey and Soil Conservation".
2. Thomas, D.B. "Some Observations on Soil Conservation in Machakos District, with special reference to Terracing".
3. Wanjama, A.M.W. "Specification, Construction and use of the Metric Line Level".
4. Ogola, J.F. "Soil and Water Conservation on Subdivided Large-Scale Farms in Uasin Gishu".
5. Mwangi, G.G. "Work done by the Soil Conservation Station at Mariakani, Coast province".

6. Fisher, N.M. "Cropping systems for Soil Conservation in Kenya".
7. Wachiira, K.K. "Some promising native legumes for rehabilitating degraded, subhumid Kenya Highland Soils".
8. Othieno, C.O. "An assessment of Soil Erosion on a field of young tea under different soil management practises".
9. Marimi, A.P.M. "The effects of certain Tillage methods and cropping systems for conserving rainfall in a semi-arid area of Eastern Kenya".
10. Ongweny, G.S. "Problems of Soil and Water conservation within the Upper Tana Catchment".
11. Edwards, K.A. "Representative and experimental Basin Programme".
12. Gichuki, J.J. "Natural Resources conservation in Nyanza Province".
13. Mbithi, P.M., and Kayongo-Male, D. "Local environmental perceptions and soil and water conservation activities".

48-22 MSANGI, A.S., and GRIFFIN, J.J. (eds.). International Conference on marine resources development in Eastern Africa. University of Dar-es-Salaam, 1974, 130pp.

A collection of papers presented at the conference and summaries of supplementary comments and discussions.

48-23 MUIRURI, WANJIKU. "The Aberdare ecosystem". Journal of Eastern African Research and Development, Vol. 4, No. 1, 1974, pp. 49-66.

Examines the possibility of applying the concept of ecosystem as an analytical tool in the problem of resource evaluation studies within the forested areas of Kenya".

48-24 ___. "Environmental resource management and quality of life". Regional meeting for Africa on Human Settlement, Finance and Management, Nairobi, Oct. 1978, 12pp.

48-25 MURRAY-RUST, H. "Soil erosion and sedimentation in Kisongo catchment, Arusha region". BRALUP Research Paper No. 17, University of Dar-es-Salaam, June 1971, 70pp.

Looks into soil erosion and sedimentation problems and their economic consequences in parts of Tanzania, particularly Arusha.

48-26 MYERS, NORMAN. The relationship of parks and other protected areas to their environs in Masailand, East Africa. Ph.D. dissertation, University of California, Berkeley, 1973.

48-27 ___. "The ecological-socioeconomic interface of wildlife conservation in emergent Africa: Lakes Nakuru and Naivasha in

THE AGRICULTURAL SECTOR

Kenya". Journal of Environmental Economics and Management, Vol. 1, Aug. 1974, pp. 319-334.

Within the theme of land-use planning the author discusses the problems faced in trying to balance the environmental disruptions which development brings against wildlife interests in Kenya. He analyses the advantages and shortcomings of already existing strategies with a view to formulating better ones.

48-28 ___. "Under the gun". International Wildlife, Vol. 6, Nov.-Dec. 1976, pp. 5-16.

Describes the plight of elephants in East African preserves that are faced with scarcity of space and food. Argues that those elephants that are likely to die due to such hardships should be "harvested" through regulated trade that would benefit the survivors.

48-29 ___. "The seeling of the zebra". International Wildlife, Vol. 8, Jan.-Feb. 1978, pp. 26-31.

Describes zebra poaching in Kenya and the illegal marketing of zebra-hide products.

48-30 OKIDI, C. ODIDI. "The Kenya Draft Articles on exclusive maritime economic zone concepts: analysis and comments". IDS Working P 289, Nov. 1976, 26pp.

The concept of exclusive economic zone has continued to gain wider international support. Countries which have accepted the concept will adopt national legislation to prescribe their own general principles to guide subsequent management of access, exploration, exploitation, and conservation of resources of the zone. Kenya should press for a 200-mile exclusive economic zone, although it will take time before the benefits are realized.

48-31 ___. "Role of environmental law in rural development". Seminar on Law and Rural Development in Eastern Africa, Kisumu, July 1977, pp. 637-663.

Argues that environmental law is very important in facilitating rural development. Such a legal framework must assist in the provision of essential services such as water and health, should ensure balanced use of natural resources, and should ensure that the impact of modernization does not negate development objectives.

48-32 O'LEARY, MICHAEL. "Responses to drought in Kitui district, Kenya". Disasters, Vol. 4, No. 3, 1980, pp. 315-328.

48-33 PARKER, I.S.C., and MARTIN, ESMOND BRADLEY. "Trade in African

rhino horn". ORYX, Vol. 15, No. 2, Nov. 1979, pp. 153-158.
Provides data on the export trade of rhino horn from East Africa between 1926 and 1976. Concludes that the price of rhino horn will continue to rise, thus providing greater incentives to hunt rhinos.

48-34 RODGERS, W.A. "The Stiegler's Gorge dam and environmental values in the Rufiji basin". BRALUP Research Paper No. 27, University of Dar-es-Salaam, 1977, 21pp.

48-35 TANZANIA. Tanzania National Scientific Research Council. Workshop on solar energy for villages of Tanzania, Dar-es-Salaam, Aug. 1977, 167pp.

48-36 WESTLEY, SIDNEY B. (ed.). "Arid lands: economic, social and ecological monitoring". IDS Occ P 22, Sept. 1977, 41pp.
Report of a workshop held at IDS, Nairobi, in June 1976; workshop was organized by P.N. Hopcraft and P. Reining.

48-37 WISNER, BEN. "Man-made famine in Eastern Kenya: the interrelationship of environment and development". University of Sussex Institute of Development Studies Discussion Paper No. 96, Brighton, 1976, 31pp.

48-38 ___. "Construction of a livelihood system: the peasants of Tharaka division, Meru district, Kenya". Economic Geography, Vol. 53, No. 4, Oct. 1977, pp. 353-357.
With a particular case shows the inevitable desertification of the area due to economic oppression.

5--THE INDUSTRIAL AND SERVICE SECTORS

50--Industrial structure and organization

50-1 BARKER, C.E.; BHAGAVAN, M.R.; VON MITCHKE-COLLAND, P.M.; WIELD, D.V.; and COULSON, A.C. "The structure and balance of industrial production in Tanzania". Utafiti, Vol. 2, No. 1, 1977, pp. 79-87.
Analyses Tanzanian industrial production as reflected in the national data. Attempts to see the extent to which the assertion that the dominant relationship in capitalism is, at the centre, between production of capital goods and mass consumer goods, and, at the periphery, between production of goods for export and luxury goods, as reflected in the Tanzanian economy.

50-2 DE VRIES, BAREND A. "Choice of technology and industrial transformation: the case of the United Republic of Tanzania". Industry and Development, No. 5, 1980, pp. 85-106.

THE INDUSTRIAL AND SERVICE SECTORS

50-3 GERSHENBERG, IRVING. "Industrial structure and the performance of firms in economically less developed countries: Uganda". EA USSC Conference, Dec. 1974, Kampala, 41 pp.
Concludes that entrepreneurs in Uganda, unlike their counterparts in the developed countries, were not primarily concerned to maximize returns to equity or assets but to maximize their profit margins.

50-4 KIGGUNDU, S.I. "Some aspects of excess industrial capacity in East Africa". EA USSC Conference, Nairobi, Dec. 1972, 11pp.
Concludes that the present arrangements of plan coordination between the three partner states do not appear to be effective in arresting excess industrial capacity.

50-5 KIM, K.S. "The linkage of basic industries in Tanzania: some policy issues and suggestions". ERB Paper 76.11, University of Dar-es-Salaam, Nov. 1976, 22pp.
Concerned with the possibilities, constraints, and perspectives for future development of an industrial strategy aimed at development of basic industrial activities. Attempts to identify the constraints that may be imposed by the existing structure of the Tanzanian economy. Some possibilities for overcoming the handicaps are also examined.

50-6 MUREITHI, L.P. "Patterns of industrialisation in the countries of the Indian Ocean Region". In Alex Kerr (ed.), Resources and Development of the Indian Ocean Region. University of Western Australia Press, 1981.

50-7 OGENDO, R.B. "Industrial location in the Nairobi area". Geo Journal, Vol. 2, No. 5, 1978, pp. 451-461.
Discusses the pattern of Nairobi industrial areas and the structure and location of the manfacturing and service industries in the Nairobi area. Concludes by discussing industrial location determinants.

50-8 PHILLIPS, DAVID. "Industrialization in Tanzania small-scale production, decentralization and a multi-technology program for industrial development". In K.S. Kim; R.B. Mabele; M.J. Schultheis (eds.), Papers on the political economy of Tanzania. Heinemann, Nairobi, 1979, pp. 78-94.
Considers the industrialization strategy and the requirements for transformation in a Tanzanian context. Analyses the role of small-scale production in industrial transformation as well as the choice of technology in a socialist economy. Initially appeared as ERB Paper 76.5.

50-9 WANG'OMBE, JOSEPH KIBUCHI. Industrial market structure and

development in East Africa. M.A. thesis, University of Nairobi, 1975, 130pp.
Looks at the relationship between performance of industries and market structure. Market structure is represented by the concentration index, barriers to entry, import to domestic sales ratio, and export output ratio. Concludes that certain market phenomena may not be reflected by the variables used.

51--Industrialization and import substitution

51-1 KARANI, LEVIS K. The industrialisation of Kwale district, Kenya. M.A. thesis, University of Nairobi, 1976, 246pp.
Attempts to explore the industrial potential of Kwale district. Argues that in the absence of a strong industrial base, the district has to invest in agricultural-based industries and in other activities oriented toward agriculture.

51-2 KIM, KWAN S. "Industrialization strategies in a developing socialist economy: an evaluation of the Tanzanian case". Developing Economies, Vol. 16, No. 3, Sept. 1978, pp. 254-268.
Analysis of Tanzania's strategy of industrialisation; the strategy aims at self-sustaining development with minimum external dependency. The strategy has tended to fail in some cases like in the engineering industries, leading to unintended import-dependency in the short run.

51-3 KUUYA, P.M. "Import substitution as a strategy of industrial development: the Tanzanian case". ERB Paper 76.10, University of Dar-es-Salaam, 1976, 55pp.

51-4 LANGDON, S.W. "Export oriented industrialisation through the MNC: Kenya". In A. Idris-Soven, et al. (eds.), The world as a company town. Mouton, The Hague, 1978, pp. 295-319.

51-5 MONTEIRO, A.D., and OJOW, F.I. "Industrial strategy for East African Community: retrospect and prospects". Uganda Economic Journal, Vol. 2, No. 2, Dec. 1972, pp. 201-213.
Deals with efforts to increase manufacturing production in the three states and suggests a strategy for rapid industrialization in the region.

51-6 ROEMER, M.; TIDRICK, G.M.; and WILLIAMS, D. "The range of strategic choice in Tanzanian industry". Journal of Development Economics, Vol. 3, No. 3, Sept. 1976, pp. 257-275.
Reports the results of a strategic planning exercise carried out in Tanzania and shows that under actual planning conditions there can be a wide range of potential outcomes

to consider. Summary of this appears in Ekistics, Vol. 43, No. 259, June, 1977, pp. 346-350.

52--Industry studies

52-1 BARCLAY, ALBERT H., Jr. The Mumias sugar project: a study of rural development in western Kenya. Ph.D. dissertation, Columbia University, 1977.

52-2 BEAKBANE, RENAULT. Report on the shoe and leather goods industries in Tanzania. Intermediate Technology Services, 1976.

52-3 BROWN, E.J. "Metal-working in eastern and central Kenya". IDS Disc P 8, June 1970, 16pp.
Discusses metal working among the Bantu of eastern and central Kenya. Also shows the differences that arise from the same craft west of the Rift Valley where tools, techniques, and attitudes toward these trades are quite different.

52-4 CHILD, FRANK C. "Small-scale rural industry in Kenya". African Studies Center New Occasional Papers No. 17, University of California, Los Angeles, ca. 1976.

52-5 CHILD, P.E., and LANGLANDS, B.W. (eds.). Conference on energy in Uganda. Makerere University Department of Geography, Kampala 1976, 135pp.
Deals with Uganda's energy resources and energy problems in a world focus. Discussion of the potential demand and utilization of energy in Uganda.

52-6 COOPER, CHARLES, and KAPLINSKY, RAPHAEL. Second-hand equipment in a developing country: a study of jute-processing in Kenya. ILO, Geneva, 1974, 145pp.
Attempts to provide empirical evidence on second-hand machinery and compares the output performance of second-hand jute equipment with similar types of equipment purchased new. Examines some possibilities for reorganizing second hand markets in the interest of buyers in the developing countries.

52-7 COULSON, ANDREW C. "Tanzania's fertiliser factory". J Mod Afr Studs, Vol. 15, No. 1, March 1977, pp. 119-125.
A brief study of the procedures followed to establish a fertilizer factory in Tanzania and of the problems encountered to construct, install, and operate it.

52-8 CURRY, S. "Prices, exchange rates and the hotel sector in Tanzania 1967-77". ERB Paper, University of Dar-es-Salaam, 1978, 57pp.

52-9 EDELMAN, DAVID J. "The energy crisis and the development prospects of low income countries: case studies of Kenya and Tanzania". International Technical Co-operation Centre Review, Vol. 4, No. 2, Oct. 1975, pp. 29-51.

Shows how the two countries are affected differently because of their divergent development strategies. Stresses that Kenya's strategy is increasingly dependent on energy intensive sectors.

52-10 FERGUSON, A.G. "Spatial variations in oil prices in Kenya: a case of peripheral exploitation". EA USSC Conference, Dar-es-Salaam, 1976, 6pp.

Investigates the spatial effects of the pricing policies of multinational oil companies in Kenya. Alternative pricing and transport policies are suggested.

52-11 GIBBONS, ERIC T. "The characteristics, structure and development of Kenya's food, feedstuffs and beverage industries". Zeitschrift für Ausländische Landwirtschaft (Quarterly Journal of International Agriculture), Vol. 15, No. 2, April-June 1976, pp. 141-160.

Describes and explains these industries and the framework they operate within. The home market, government policies and current and future developments are examined.

52-12 GLENTWORTH, GARTH. "Resource allocation and income distribution in Uganda: the supply extension policies of the Uganda Electricity Board". EA USSC Conference, Nairobi, Dec. 1969.

Examines how the electricity supply network in Uganda expanded, what were the external pressures on supply extension policy, the relationship between the provision of electricity and the patterns of resource allocation and income distribution within Uganda, and whether there is any evidence under the third topic to make the interaction of the first two meaningful in terms of development patterns.

52-13 HERMAN, B. "A case of multinational oligopoly in poor countries: oil refinery investments in East Africa". Journal of Development Economics, Vol. 2, No. 2, June 1975, pp. 121-143.

Argues that the multinational oil refinery investments in Mombasa and Tanga were neither necessary nor efficient.

52-14 HOUSE, WILLIAM J. "Market structure and industry performance: the case of Kenya revisited". Journal of Economic Studies, Vol. 3, No. 2, Nov. 1976, pp. 117-132.

Reaffirms the results of an earlier study ("Market structure and industry performance: the case of Kenya", Oxford Economic Papers, Nov. 1973, pp. 405-419). Finds that between 1963 and 1967 the proportion of employment and the number of firms in competitive markets has declined, and that private firms perform differently from parastatals. See also chapter in Tony Killick (ed.), Papers on the Kenyan economy.

52-15 ___. "Development strategy and the energy balance: an East African study". Development and Change, Vol. 11, No. 1, Jan. 1980, pp. 17-31.
Examines the impact that the energy crisis, especially the oil crisis, has on Kenya's development strategy and on the country's economic growth. Conservation of energy and improvement and expansion of hydro-electricity production as well as discovery of new energy sources, such as solar, wind, and biogas energy, have to be accorded major attention if dependence on oil imports is to be reduced in future.

52-16 ___. Technological choice, employment generation, income distribution and consumer demand: the case of furniture making in Kenya. Working Paper 60, WEP, ILO, Geneva, May 1980.
Gives a description of the various furniture products on the Kenya market as well as the technologies used. It then analyses the consumer behaviour of the low, medium, and high income classes in both rural and urban areas and on this basis estimates the direct employment effect in the furniture industry as a result of changes in the distribution of income.

52-17 HUUHTANEN, H.J.I. Forest industries development planning, Tanzania: appraisal of the present and future demand-supply situation for wood and wood-based products. FAO (Access No. 27561), Rome, 1974, 97pp.

52-18 KHAMALA, C., and CASTELINO, J.B. (eds.). Energy resources in East Africa. Kenya National Academy, Nairobi, 1980, 164pp.
Collection of papers presented at 12th annual Symposium.

52-19 KHAMIS, I.A. "Industrial development in Zanzibar". ERB Paper 75.6, University of Dar-es-Salaam, 1975.

52-20 KOPEC, D.; KOUBA, L.; and MAXFIELD, D. "An application of linear programming to the African copper industry". East African Geographical Review (Makerere), June 1975, pp. 71-87.
Discusses the African copper export flow pattern of 1970 and compares that pattern to a set of more efficient export flows between exporters and importers through the use of linear programming. Inherent in this analysis is an examination of the comparative locational advantages of the mines of those African states that produce and export copper, for example, Uganda.

52-21 LUTTRELL, WILLIAM L. Planning post-capitalist industrialization: an introduction to planning methodology for the economic independence of underdeveloped countries, using data for an iron and steel industry in Tanzania. Ph.D. dissertation, University of Texas, 1980, 599pp.
DAI, Vol. 41, p. 1694-A.

52-22 MANUNDU, M.; HOUSE, W.M.; and SENGA, J.W. "The demand for energy in the monetary economy". IDS Paper, ca. 1981.
Study was initially carried out in late 1978.

52-23 MATHENGE, J.G. The measurement of relative economic efficiency in manufacturing in Kenya. M.A. thesis, University of Nairobi, 1979.

52-24 MIKKELSEN, BRITHA. "Formation of an industrial labour force in Kenya: participation of state and capital in training labour for metal manufacturing industries". IDS Working P 377, Dec. 1980, 20pp.
A discussion of the first stage of a research project dealing with the prospects for metal manufacturing in Kenya. Emphasizes the state's role in industrialization.

52-25 MITSCHKE-COLLANDE, P.V. "Engineering industries and manpower requirements: industrial training and strategy in Tanzania". ERB Paper, University of Dar-es-Salaam, 1977, 42pp.

52-26 ___. "Structure and development of the engineering sector in Tanzania". ERB Paper, University of Dar-es-Salaam, 1977, 35pp.

52-27 MOYINI, YAKOBO Z.G. "Energy and forestry in Uganda: trends and prospects". EAJ Rural Devel, Vol. 10, Nos. 1-2, 1977, pp. 31-66.
Shows that forestry plays a vital role in supplying energy requirements in Uganda and considers the continuation of this role into the future.

52-28 MULLER, J. "Promotion of the manufacture of rural implements in Tanzania". Industrialization and Rural Development (UNIDO), 1978, pp. 76-102.

52-29 MWANGI, K.W. Utilisation of industrial capacity and employment promotion in Kenya's manufacturing sector. M.A. thesis, University of Nairobi, 1980.

52-30 ODADA, J.E.O. "The sugar industry and the economy of the Lake Victoria basin". IDS Seminars on Lake Victoria Development

Authority, Nairobi, 1979.
These seminar papers appear as IDS Occ P 34, edited by C.O. Okidi.

52-31 PHELPS, M.G. "Marketing problems in textiles and garments in Nairobi". IDS (unnumbered paper), July 1970, 75pp.
Concludes from a survey that there appears to be excess capacity in both industries which might be accounted for by competition from abroad, trade licensing, transfer taxes, and the State Trading Corporation in Tanzania.

52-32 RAJARAM, R. "Electrical energy demand forecast for Uganda". Promotion of Science and Technology, Vol. 5, No. 1, Jan.-April 1980, pp. 23-27.
Forecasts the electrical energy demand in Uganda up to the year 2000.

52-33 RAKE, A. "Kenya textiles' problems". African Development, Vol. 10, No. 3, March 1976, pp. 201-202.

52-34 SILVER, M.S. "A regional analysis of industrial production and labour productivity trends in Tanzania, 1965-72". Can J Afr Studs, Vol. 13, No. 3, 1980, pp. 479-485.
Describes real production and labour productivity trends in mainland Tanzania for manufacturing establishments both within and outside Dar-es-Salaam.

52-35 SMITH, L.D. "The biscuit and pasta product industries in Kenya". IDS (unnumbered paper), Oct. 1968, 43pp.
Covers the growth potential and need for protection of these industries. Recommends investigation of the feasibility of replacing imported raw materials with locally produced materials.

52-36 THIURI, PHILIP JOHN. The dairy industry in spatial perspective, with a focus on recommendations for development in Kenya as drawn from the New York state case. Ph.D. dissertation, Syracuse University, 1974, 356pp.
Develops guidelines and an eligibility matrix for use by planners in the development of a nationwide dairy industry. Assumes that analysis of the spatial structure of the existing industry in more developed countries will make possible better recommendations for a plan in the less developed country.

52-37 WANGWE, S.M. "The problem of underutilization of capacity in industry--a case study of the Mara dairy industry". ERB Paper 75.4, June 1975, 37pp.

Argues that of the explanatory variables for excess capacity in the Mara dairy industry, by far the most important is the short supply of milk. The others are transport facilities, maintenance and repair of machines, quality of raw milk, exchange control, and pricing policies.

52-38 ___. "The excess capacity in manufacturing: a case study of selected firms". In K.S. Kim; R.B. Mabele; M.J. Schultheis (eds.), Papers on the political economy of Tanzania. Heinemann, Nairobi, 1979, pp. 111-117.
Attempts to examine the cuases of excess capacity in manufacturing industry of Tanzania based on the results of a survey of manufacturing firms for the period 1973-1975. Initially appeared as ERB Paper 76.2.

52-39 ___. "Factors influencing capacity utilisation in Tanzanian manufacturing". International Labour Review, Vol. 115, No. 1, Jan.-Feb. 1977, pp. 65-77.
Discusses supply and demand factors constraining capacity utilization of a sample of Tanzanian firms. Calls for improvements in the service facilities provided to industry.

52-40 WELLS, E.J., and RADO, E.R. "Constraints and costs in the Kenya building industry". IDS (unnumbered paper), Nov. 1968, 83pp.
Concludes that the rapid rise in tender prices is not an indication of excessively high profits resulting from a shortage of contractors, but is in part a reflection of a general increase in costs and prices throughout the economy.

53--Entrepreneurship; business finance and administration

53-1 ALMY, SUSAN W. The conservative rich man in Meru, Kenya. IDS (unnumbered paper), March 1974, 10pp.
Presents data from a rural area in Kenya to demonstrate that the richer members of society avoid risky innovations until they have been proven safe in the local context by the less wealthy.

53-2 PALMER, J.C. Entrepreneurs and economic development in a small town in Kenya. Ph.D. dissertation, University of London, 1978, 389pp.

53-3 STEELE, DAVID. "Theory of the dual economy and African entrepreneurship in Kenya". J Dev Studs, Vol. 12, No. 1, Oct. 1975, pp. 18-38.
Argues that the dual economy concept incorrectly identifies the key features of a developing economy. Explores the possible existence of a third, transitional sector in Kenya.

THE INDUSTRIAL AND SERVICE SECTORS

53-4 SWAINSON, NICOLA. "The rise of a national bourgeoisie in Kenya". Review of African Political Economy, No. 8, Jan.-April 1977, pp. 39-55.
Using detailed analysis of two case studies, evidence is provided of the growth of an indigenous capitalist class, independent of, and competitive with, foreign firms.

54--Policies toward industry and private business

54-1 CLARK, W. EDMUND. Socialist development and public investment in Tanzania, 1964-73. University of Toronto Press, Toronto, 1978, 319pp.

54-2 EAST AFRICAN DEVELOPMENT BANK. "The East African Development Bank and the industrial development of East Africa". Kampala, 1977, 45pp.

54-3 EDMONDS, GEOFFREY A. "The construction industry in developing countries". International Labour Review, Vol. 118, No. 3, 1979, pp. 355-369.
Summarizes a recent ILO survey in Kenya that provides a picture of typical problems facing indigenous contractors in relation to availability of capital and labour. Suggests policies to stimulate the sector for the sake of employment creation.

54-4 GRUNDMANN, H.E. "What kind of patent law does Tanzania need?" ERB Paper 68.15, University of Dar-es-Salaam, Sept. 1968, 18pp.
Argues that the guiding principle for an East African law on inventions has to be that it should promote the use of technology to the greatest extent possible.

54-5 HARPER, M.C. The development of a cost-effective extension service for small business: a Kenyan experiment. Ph.D. dissertation, University of Nairobi, 1974, 332pp.
Examines the hypothesis that individual extension services are necessary for promoting the development of small business in general and small-scale retailers in particular. Argues that such services can economically be provided by staff with only four years of secondary education, no business experience, and little formal training.

54-6 ___. "An approach to the training of extension workers". World Development, Vol. 3, Nos. 2-3, Feb.-Mar. 1975, pp. 137-139.
Contends that an experiment in Kenya showed that secondary school leavers with no practical experience and a minimum of specialised training can provide an economical individual advisory service for small-scale businessmen.

54-7 KENYA, GOVERNMENT OF. Industrial investment guidelines. Ministry of Commerce and Industry, Nairobi, 1979, 50pp.
Describes the business climate, economic situation, taxation and investment opportunities.

54-8 KONGSTAD, P. "Extension services to rural industries: a partial assessment of rural industrial development programme". Institute for Development Research Project Paper D. 75.1, Nairobi, April 1975, 63pp.
Assesses the Rural Industrial Development Programme as an extension service programme. It is hoped that the findings may lead to a review of the role of extension service as a tool for assisting existing rural workshops and for promoting new industries outside the metropolitan areas.

54-9 KRISTENSEN, HANS. "Rural industrial development programme". Institute for Development Research Paper, Nairobi, April 1974.
An evaluation report for a programme conference held in Kisumu in April 1974 on rural development.

54-10 MWANGI, JAMES WANJOHI. Planning standards for future urban industries, based on the performance of the present Nairobi industrial area. M.A. thesis, University of Nairobi, 1975, 85pp.
Notes that planning standards operating at present have been successful on allocation of plots, but various improvements, notably in transportation, housing, and services for workers, must become a prerequisite for future planning.

54-11 NANJAPPA, K.L. "Tanzania on the march towards development of small-scale industries". Sedme, Vol. 1, No. 3, Dec. 1974, pp. 215-220.

54-12 NGORORANO, A. "Uganda's industry sector--an appraisal of recent growth and the industrial strategy in plan III". Uganda Economic Journal, Vol. 2, No. 2, Dec. 1972, pp. 168-200.
Looks at the impact plan III will have on Uganda's industrial sector and argues that it will give the government monopoly control over certain undertakings of strategic importance to the economy.

54-13 NIXSON, F.I. "Nationalisation as an aid to development: the case of Uganda". Uganda Economic Journal, Vol. 1, No. 1, Dec. 1971, pp. 31-41.
Against the background of the government's acquisition of 60 per cent shareholding in manufacturing and commercial activities, examines economic and political factors underlying

nationalization. Considers problems involved in public ownership.

54-14 TANZANIA. Factors affecting the setting and attainment of targets in selected manufacturing industries. National Institute for Productivity, Dar-es-Salaam, 45pp.

54-15 WACHIRA, CHARLES. Criteria for location of industries in rural settlements: a case study of Kirinyaga district. M.A. thesi University of Nairobi, 1976, 173pp.
Examines spatial effects in a rural settling with the obje of finding out space demands by which rural industrialization efforts could be further assisted. Suggests that a method of ranking industrial activities to correspond with the ranking of infrastructural and land resources similarly, would suit the dispersal of rural industrial development.

54-16 WESCOTT, CLAY G. "Industrial location and public policy: the case of Kenya's textile industry". IDS Working P 288, Nov. 1976, 73pp.
Argues that if the government desires to influence location decisions it should determine the critical locational criteria of potential investors, make the investor aware of potential locations which satisfy these criteria, and apply pressure in bargaining with firms to see that the location is selected.

54-17 ___. "Industrial policy: a case study of incentives for industrial dispersion". In Tony Killick (ed.), Papers on the Kenyan economy. Heinemann, London, 1981.

54-18 WHITWORTH, ALAN. "The case for price control in Tanzania, with particular reference to locally-manufactured products". ERB Paper 78-2, University of Dar-es-Salaam, Feb. 1978, 70pp.
Discusses why prices are probably lower than they would have been in the absence of the national price commission, and discusses the experience with cost-plus pricing in Tanzanian price control in the mid-1970s.

55--Transport and communications

55-1 ASFAW, SHIMELES. The economic evaluation of low traffic roads: the Kenya experience. Kenya Ministry of Works, Government Printer, Nairobi, 1980, 50pp.

55-2 BERECE, EDGAR HERMAN. Promotion of an efficient and effective urban transport system in Tanzania. M.Arch. thesis, Universi of Nairobi, 1976, 157pp.

Suggests that in order to solve successfully urban transportation problems in Dar-es-Salaam, as well as to achieve well-planned urban growth, an efficient and economical means of mass transport needs to be fostered.

55-3 BIRDSALL, STEPHEN S. Transportation and agricultural development in western Kenya: an appraisal to the problem of investment priorities. Ph.D. dissertation, Michigan State University, 1969.

55-4 CHITEJI, FRANK MATTHEW. The development and socio-economic impact of transportation in Tanzania, 1844-present. Ph.D. dissertation, Michigan State University, 1979, 160pp.
DAI, Vol. 40, p. 4177-A.

55-5 CHYBIRE, G.K. Problems in estimating the costs and benefits of a road project. M.A. thesis, University of Nairobi, 1974, 237pp.
Decides that three distinct problems can be identified. One is that of identifying what are the costs and benefits of a road project, the second is evaluating costs by determining resource opportunity cost values and converting these into social values, and the third is the inadequacy of data for project evaluation. The case study was the project of upgrading the murram road linking Nakuru and Thompson's Falls.

55-6 COLEBATCH, H.K. "Government services at district level in Kenya: roads, schools and health services". University of Sussex IDS Discussion Paper No. 38, Brighton, May 1976.
Examines the experience under differing forms of control, that is, from elected councils at district levels to the ministries of central government. Case studies are made of each of the three services. Concludes with a discussion of the policy implications of the analysis.

55-7 DATOO, B.A. Port development in East Africa: spatial patterns from the ninth to the sixteenth centuries. East African Literature Bureau, Nairobi, 1975, 138pp.
Integration of the Coast of Eastern Africa into the Indian Ocean commercial system. Focuses primarily on Kenyan and Tanzanian coasts.

55-8 DUE, JOHN F. "The problems of rail transport in tropical Africa". J Dev Areas, Vol. 13, No. 4, July 1979, pp. 375-393.
Summarizes the development of rail systems in a group of tropical African countries to indicate major trends and the relationship of rail and road transport; also reviews

governmental transport policy. The study covers Kenya, Tanzania, Uganda, Sudan, Zambia, Nigeria, and Ghana.

55-9 FUNNEL, D.C. "Methods of measuring the modality of places of a transportation network, an assessment, based upon studies of the Uganda roads system". EA USSC Conference, Nairobi, Dec. 1969.
Examines methods available that present an index of modality. Examines the usefulness of these methods in their computational difficluty and ease of interpretation.

55-10 HALL, RICHARD S. The great Uhuru railway. Gollancz, London, 1976, 208pp.

55-11 HIDE, H., et al. "The Kenya road transport cost study: research on vehicle operating costs". Overseas Transport and Road Research Laboratory Report 672, Crothorne, Berkshire, 1975, 70pp.
Argues that the availability of accurate, up-to-date information on vehicle operating costs is one of the most important pre-requisites for evaluating total road transportation costs or for estimating future benefits in a feasibility study.

55-12 HODGES, J.W. "The Kenya road transport cost study: research on road deterioration". Overseas Transport and Road Research Laboratory Report, Crothorne, Berkshire, 1975.

55-13 KIRKPATRICK, C.H. "The relevance of road-pricing in developing countries: some results for Tanzania". The Manchester School of Economic and Social Studies, Vol. 49, No. 4, Dec. 1972, pp. 357-374.
Suggests that recommendations on road pricing should not be formulated solely on the basis of allocative efficiency, but should give attention to road user charges as a source of general development finance.

55-14 ___. "Distributional objectives and the optimum level of road user charges in developing countries: some results for Kenya". Manchester School of Economics and Social Studies, Vol. 47, No. 2, June 1979, pp. 139-159.
Considers the interdependency of the investment and pricing decisions in the context of road-user charges, using data for the Kenyan economy in 1969. Also shows how the objectives of interpersonal and intertemporal distribution might be incorporated in the determination of an optimum level of price.

55-15 McKAY, J., et al. "Road feasibility studies in Tanzania". BRALUP Research Paper No. 16, University of Dar-es-Salaam, April 1971, 100pp.
Consists of two papers relating to the preparation of feasibility studies for road improvement projects in Tanzania. The first reviews methods used in the past while the second is a study of the feasibility of improving a number of cotton roads in Geita district.

55-16 McKAY, J. "A guide to basic data on road transport in Tanzania". BRALUP Paper, University of Dar-es-Salaam, 1972, 45pp.
Outlines the sources of available information on road transport in Tanzania. Designed to assist researchers coming to Tanzania for the first time. It complements the review and summary of road feasibility studies already published by the Bureau. Emphasis is placed here on the location, nature, and probable accuracy of data.

55-17 MADUNGHA, J.K. The role of roads in rural and regional development in East Africa: case studies in Kenya and Uganda. M.A. thesis, University of Nairobi, 1975, 151pp.
Argues that for better utilization of roads as development projects, priority should be given to the provision of primary and secondary feeder roads, and that these roads should be followed by the location along them of services, especially rural centres and social facilities.

55-18 MAPUNDA, N.K., and MWAMBI, F.M. "A critical approach to project appraisal: a case study of transportation in Dar-es-Salaam city". ERB Paper 75.5, University of Dar-es-Salaam, 1975.

55-19 MKAMA, J. "Transport planning in Tanzaina: an assessment". BRALUP Research Paper No. 8, University of Dar-es-Salaam, 1969, 62pp.
Examines the history of rail, road, and water transport in Tanzania in light of the objectives for which it was designed and its impact on the country's development. An assessment of the adequacy of the communication network for present needs is also given, and recommendations for future transport policy.

55-20 MURIUKI, J.N. A study of transportation modes into Nairobi and their implications to planning: a case study of the external bus transportation system into Nairobi. M.A. thesis, University of Nairobi, 1976, 101pp.
Presents a picture of the infrastructural institutional and management deficiencies identified as hindering the healthy growth of the country bus transportation sector.

THE INDUSTRIAL AND SERVICE SECTORS

55-21 MWASE, NGILA. "A survey of transport studies in Tanzania". ERB Paper 78.3, University of Dar-es-Salaam, March 1978, 45pp.
Attempts to bring together the key parameters examined in transport studies in Tanzania with a view to possible standardization in method of analysis.

55-22 ____. "The Japanese report on construction of the proposed Arusha-Musoma railway line--an appraisal". Utafiti, Vol. 4, No. 1, 1979, pp. 41-43.
Argues that the report falls short of providing an adequate basis for decisions, and brings out some of the important issues that are omitted in the report.

55-23 NDULU, BENNO JOSEPH. The role of transportation in agricultural production: the case of Tanzania. Ph.D. dissertation, Northwestern University, 1979, 153pp.
DAI, Vol. 40, No. 3579-A.

55-24 OMARI, AYOOB R. Length of journey and the choice of mode of travel to work: a case study of Dar-es-Salaam city. M.A. thesis, University of Nairobi, 1976, 152pp.
The travel characteristics in the city are examined under the headings of journey purpose, peak period traffic volumes, peak period travel demand, and length of journey. It is argued that these factors are useful in understanding traffic generation and distribution, plus factors which contribute to delays for various modes of travel to work. The study found that the choice of mode is more influenced by income than the lengths of journey.

55-25 TANZANIA. "Transportation in Tanzania". Jenga, No. 17, Public Relations Division, NDC, Dar-es-Salaam, 1980.
Tries to show the role of transport planning as related to economic development policy in Tanzania. Contends that economic growth, dispersal of economic activity, development of health, education, housing, and all the road infrastructure depend on the efficiency of national transport planning.

55-26 VOORHEES, ALAN M., and ASSOCIATES. Nairobi urban study: calibration of the transportation model: a report for the Nairobi City Council. Nairobi, n.d. (ca. 1970), 57pp.
A transportation model developed in an attempt to reflect the large changes in travel characteristics occuring, mainly as a result of alterations in the distribution of population, employment and income.

55-27 YU, G.T. "Working on the railroad: China and the Tanzania railway". Asian Survey, Vol. 11, No. 11, 1971.

56--Marketing, Trading, and cooperatives

56-1 ALIBARUHO, GEORGE. "Pricing policy and the disappearing farmer's income in Uganda's cotton industry". Journal of Eastern African Research and Development, Vol. 5, No. 1, 1975, pp. 56-68.
Finds that the existing methodology for analyzing and testing income stabilizing effects of the relevant marketing board policies has been inadequate.

56-2 BYARUHANGA, J.K. "The performance of the horticultural cooperative union of Kenya". Department of Agricultural Economics Paper, University of Nairobi, 1977.
Concludes that the nature of the horticultural marketing system has enabled middlemen to make serious inroads into a restructured system.

56-3 CLIFFE, LIONEL R.; LAWRENCE, P.; LUTTRELL, W.; MIGOT-ADHOLA, S.; and SAUL, JOHN S. (eds.). Rural cooperation in Tanzania. Tanzania Publishing House, Dar-es-Salaam, 1975.
A collection of essays on rural Tanzania intended to describe and explain the nature and the historical background of the changes currently taking place in Tanzania.

56-4 EL NAMAKI, M.S.S. "The future organisation, planning and control over domestic trade in Tanzania". Journal of Eastern African Research and Development, Vol. 6, No. 1, 1976, pp. 61-68.
Sketches some of the fundamental alterations in decision-making, structural organization, and control needed in order to reach the goal of a planned trade sector.

56-5 GATANG'I, SAMUEL K. Members' participation in Kenyan rural cooperative organisation: the case of Kirinyaga district. M.A. thesis, University of Nairobi, 1974, 149pp.
Concludes that the general trend is that inter- and intra-societal coordination and equity in allocations and representations are essential for active participation of members in cooperative development.

56-6 HAY, M.J. "Local trade and ethnicity in western Kenya". African Economic History Review, Vol. 2, No. 1, 1975, pp. 7-12.

56-7 JACKSON, R.T. (ed.). "Essays on rural marketing in West Nile district". Makerere University Department of Geography Occasional Paper No. 47, Kampala, 122pp.
Incorporates the following: R.T. Jackson, "Markets,

market prices and local trade in West Nile"; A.L.B. Mogga, "Ama market"; E.E. Aziga-Guma, "Marketing in Vurra country"; A. Andresile, "The evolution of markets and shops in Aringu and Terego".

56-8 MWANGI, J.N.A. The development of small-scale African retailers in Kenya. M.B.A. thesis, University of Nairobi, 1975, 195pp.
Attempts to identify the major problems inherent in the Africanization of distributive trade in general, and small-scale retail trade in particular, and to assess measures formulated by the government and manufacturers to alleviate these problems.

56-9 MYAKA, T.L. Socialization of wholesale trade in Tanzania. M.B.A. thesis, University of Nairobi, 1976, 270pp.
Attempts to analyse the Tanzania experience during 1967-75 regarding the implications of substituting a publicly controlled organization for a private wholesaler. The analysis is centred on the now defunct State Trading Corporation, the Board of Internal Trade, and producer marketing co-operatives.

56-10 PARSON, JACK. "Planning and the Africanisation of trade and commerce in Uganda". Uganda Economic Journal, Vol. 2, No. 2, Dec. 1972, pp. 154-167.
Highlights the most important features of the commercial sector related to government attempts to shape and control it. Concludes that more serious research needs to be done on trade within Uganda.

56-11 WICKSTROM, BO, and GUSTAFSSON, KARL ERIK (eds.). Increasing marketing efficiency in East Africa. Seminar held at Jadini Beach Hotel, Mombasa, Dec. 1974, 293pp.
A collection of papers on marketing structures, tools for marketing analysis, marketing planning and control, etc.

57--Tourism

57-1 BASSAN, A.S. "Tourism development in Kenya". Standard Bank Review, Dec. 1974, pp. 2-4.

57-2 CURRY, STEVE. "Tourism and underdevelopment; and the Tanzanian case". ERB Paper 77-6, University of Dar-es-Salaam, 1978.

57-3 ___. "Prices, exchange rates, and the hotel sector in Tanzania 1967-77". ERB Paper, University of Dar-es-Salaam, 1978, 43pp.

57-4 ELKAN, WALTER. "Employment in the East African hotel and tourist industries: a survey". IDS Miscellaneous Report,

Nairobi, 1973, 43pp.
Presents findings of a survey of employment in the hotel and tourist industries in Kenya and Tanzania. Discusses the policy implications of the findings for each country and for East Africa as a whole.

57-5 ___. "The relation between tourism and employment in Kenya and Tanzania". J Dev Studs, Vol. 11, No. 2, Jan. 1975, pp. 123-130.
Presents findings of a survey of employment in the hotel and tourist industries of Kenya and Tanzania.

57-6 GESHEKTER, C.L. "International tourism and African underdevelopment". Studies in Third World Societies, Vol. 6, 1978, pp. 57-88.

57-7 HENRY, WESLEY R. "A preliminary report on visitor use in Amboseli national park". IDS Working P 263, March, 1976, 33pp.
Concludes that if the integrity of the park is to be maintained and tourism promoted, research, planning, and management must proceed together to ensure that the resources of the park are not adversely damaged.

57-8 KIMURA, F.K. Tourist hotel. M. Arch. thesis, University of Nairobi, 1975, 150pp.

57-9 MIGOT-ADHOLLA, S.E. "Toward alternative tourism in Kenya". IFDA Dossier, Vol. 19, Sept.-Oct. 1980, pp. 67-78.
Demonstrates the declining importance of tourism as a foreign exchange earner in Kenya.

57-10 MITCHELL, FRANK H. The economic value of tourism in Kenya. Ph.D. dissertation, University of California, Los Angeles, 1972.

57-11 ___. "The economic impact of tourism". The 1970 Dag Hammarskjold/UNECA Seminar on the Development of Tourism in Africa. The Dag Hammarskjold Foundation, Uppsala, May 1971, 35pp.
An evaluation of tourism as a sector in Africa with specific reference to its economic impact in Kenya. Although tourism earns foreign exchange, a proper evaluation of it requires that domestic resources be properly costed. If this is done, the net value of tourism will probably be substantially less than the GNP generated in tourism.

57-12 OUMA, JOSEPH P.B.M. "Evolution of tourism in East Africa

1900-1969". EA USSC Conference, Nairobi, Dec. 1969.
Traces the evolution of the significant aspects of tourism in East Africa, such as organization, policies, development of tourist attractions, and service facilities. Makes some suggestions and proposals on possible lines of future development.

57-13 STEELE, WILLIAM E. "Toward an optimal tourism development plan for Kenya". EAER, Vol. 7, No. 2, Dec. 1975, pp. 27-34.
Outlines a procedure, based on an econometric model, by which planners may evaluate alternatives for achieving the goals they have set for the tourism sector. Examines Kenya's competitive gains or losses in the market for United Kingdom tourists in the period 1969-1972.

58--Public corporations and other parastatals

58-1 AKE, CLAUDE, et al. (eds.). "Measures for improving performance in management of public enterprises in Tanzania". Afr Rev, Vol. 5, No. 2, 1975, pp. 119-234.
An issue of this journal confined to selected papers presented and discussed at a seminar on this topic.

58-2 DOBRSKA, Z. "Criteria for public investment in manufacturing: five Tanzanian case studies". ERB Paper 68.28, University of Dar-es-Salaam, 1968.

58-3 DRESANG, D.L.; and SHARKANSKY, I. "Sequence of change and the political economy of public corporations: Kenya". The Journal of Politics (Gainesville), 1975, pp. 163-186.

58-4 EL-NAMAKI, M.S.S. "The effectiveness and the managerial behaviour of company boards in Tanzania". International Review of Administrative Sciences, Vol. 42, No. 3, July 1976, pp. 241-247.
Surveys the structure of a selected number of public corporations and reviews their composition. Argues that the dominant role of the state and the frantic scramble for resources necessitate a higher quality of management.

58-5 FRIEDMANN, W.G., and GARNER, J.F. (eds.). Government enterprise: a comparative study. Columbia University Press, New York, 1970, 351pp.
Includes A.W. Bradley and J.P.W.B. McAuslan, "Public corporations in East Africa".

58-6 HOPCRAFT, PETER, and OGGUTU, JOSEPH. "Parastatal development agencies and their relationship with the private sector".

IDS Conference on the Role of Public Enterprises in Development in Eastern Africa, University of Nairobi, Nov. 1980, 11pp.
Critically appraises the role of parastatal bodies in Kenya's development. Criticizes them as not fulfilling the objectives stated by the government.

58-7 HYDEN, GORAN. "Public policy-making and public enterprises in Tanzania". Afr Rev, Vol. 5, No. 2, 1975, pp. 141-166.
Examines the general style of public policy-making in Tanzania in relation to the management of public enterprises. Includes a review of planning literature with reference to African experience and an analysis of policy-making in Tanzania.

58-8 KENYA, GOVERNMENT OF. Review of statutory boards (Ndegwa Committee Report). Government Printer, Nairobi, May 1979, 30pp.
Committee chaired by Philip Ndegwa makes recommendations on operations and control procedures of parastatal bodies in Kenya.

58-9 KIMUYU, P.D. A study of some ICDC supported businesses in Kenya. M.A. thesis, University of Nairobi, 1977.

58-10 KLAUS, HANS G. "Parastatals in Kenya: analysis of their condition and methods for an improved performance". IDS Working P 370, June 1979, 17pp.
Describes an approach intended to identify problems of internal performance of public enterprises in the Kenyan context. The approach aims at analysing their role, structure and performance.

58-11 ___. "Organization of the decision process in public enterprises in Kenya: an approach to improve their internal performance". IDS Working P 372, Sept. 1980, 38pp.
Taking into account the specific constraints and structure of public enterprises, points out how knowledge about organization and participation helps improve the decision-making process at various management levels of the organization.

58-12 LOXLEY, J., and SAUL, J.S. "The political economy of parastatals". Eastern Africa Law Review, Vol. 5, Nos. 1-2, 1972, pp. 9-37.
Concerned with the crucial relationships which link the Tanzanian parastatals to their wider social, political, and economic context.

THE INDUSTRIAL AND SERVICE SECTORS

58-13 MWAPACHU, H. BAKARI. "The restructuring of public enterprises for improved performance". Journal of Kivukoni College (Dar-es-Salaam), Vol. 8, No. 1, 1976, 23pp.

58-14 ONGONG'A, M.S. An evaluation of a public enterprise: the pyrethrum board of Kenya. M.A. thesis, University of Nairobi, 1979.

58-15 RWEYEMAMU, A.H. "The predicaments of managers of public enterprises in Tanzania". Afr Rev, Vol. 5, No. 2, 1975, pp. 119-126.

Highlights the development of public corporations and enterprises in Tanzania since the Arusha Declaration and suggests some factors which have tended to inhibit productive operation of these enterprises.

58-16 SEN, A. Legal aspects of public enterprises in India and Tanzania. Ph.D. dissertation, University of London, 1978, 546pp.

58-17 TANZANIA. Analysis of accounts of parastatals, 1966-1975. Bureau of Statistics, Dar-es-Salaam, 1976, 36pp.

58-18 TEMU, P.E. "The economic implications of management agreements in Tanzania parastatals". Eastern Africa Law Review, Vol. 5, Nos. 1-2, 1972, pp. 77-88.

Rejects the suggestion that the cost to Tanzania of management agreements with foreign companies is small.

6--POPULATION, MANPOWER, AND TECHNOLOGIES

60--Demographic characteristics, population growth and development, and population policies

60-1 ADEGBOLA, O. "New estimates of fertility and child mortality in Africa south of the Sahara". Population Studies, Vol. 31, No. 3, Nov. 1977, pp. 467-486.

Argues that there is a high fertility in East Africa extending from the south-eastern Sudan through parts of Uganda and Kenya to Rwanda and Burundi, and parts of Tanzania to Mozambique.

60-2 ANKER, R., and KNOWLES, J. Population, employment, and inequality: Bachue Kenya. Gower Press, Farnborough, ca. 1980.

60-3 ANOBI, N.K. Economics of family size: the case of the developing economies of Kenya and Nigeria. Ph.D. dissertation, City University of New York, 1980, 119pp.

DAI, Vol. 41, p. 1961-A.

Demographic characteristics

60-4 ARYEE, G.A. *Population, manpower, and employment--some issues in six eastern African countries*. International Institute for Labour Studies (No. IEME 3073), Geneva, 1975, 51pp.

60-5 AYIEMBA, ELIAS H.O. "Population change in the Kano-sugar belt region: measurements and problems for regional development". *Journal of Eastern African Research and Development*, Vol. 5, No. 2, 1975.
Suggests basic demographic techniques for analysing population between two base periods. Discusses the importance of population change for regional planning purposes.

60-6 BENNET, C.T. *Persistence amid adversity: the growth and spatial distribution of the Asian population of Kenya, 1902-1963*. Ph.D. dissertation, Syracuse University, 1976.
DAI, Vol. 38, p. 3048-A.

60-7 BONDESTAM, LARS. "Population growth in Kenya". Scandinavian Institute of African Studies Research Report No. 12, Uppsala, 1972, 55pp.
Discusses population growth, the arguments for and against a family planning policy, and evaluates the Kenyan programme.

60-8 BRACKNELL, L. "The estimation of adult mortality in Africa from data on orphanhood". *Population Studies*, Vol. 31, No. 1, March 1977, pp. 107-128.
Tells us that the orphanhood data show that in Kenya the general level of adult mortality is lower than infant mortality.

60-9 CANTRELLE, PIERRE, et al. (eds.). *Population in African Development* (2 vols.). Ordina Editions, Dolhain, Belgium, n.d. (ca. 1975).
Contains a number of papers on East African demographic and related topics.

60-10 COL, JEANNE MARIE. "Food, population and reconstruction in Uganda". U.S.A. African Studies Association meeting, Philadelphia, Oct. 1980.

60-11 COLE, W.E., and SAUNDERS, R.D. "Population growth and employment: Mexico's past and Kenya's future". *African Studies Review*, Vol. 19, No. 1, April 1976, pp. 151-163.
Concludes that a reduction in the rate of population growth is the key to Kenya's efforts to transform its labour force by increasing productivity in the subsistence economy.

60-12 CONDE, J. *The demographic transition as applied to tropical*

POPULATION, MANPOWER

Africa. OECD Development Centre, Paris, 1971, 207pp.
A review of the economic, health, and education conditions that have existed in recent years in African countries south of the Sahara and indicates clearly their current state of underdevelopment.

60-13 DATOO, B.A. "Population density and agricultural systems in the Uluguru mountains, Morogoro District, Tanzania". BRALUP Research Paper No. 26, University of Dar-es-Salaam, Oct. 1973, 72pp.
Examines the relationship between population density and agricultural systems in the Uluguru mountains. Tests the hypothesis that, as the density of population increases, so certain structural attributes of agricultural systems undergo change.

60-14 EPSTEIN, SCARLETT, and JACKSON, DARRELL (eds.). The paradox of poverty. Macmillan, Delhi, 1975, 127pp.
Includes Joseph Ssennyonga, "Cost/benefit versus parental immortality: family size in rural Kenya", and George C. Mkangi, "Land tenure, population growth and economic differentiation: the Ribe tribe of Kenya".

60-15 HENIN, R.A., and EGERO, B. "1967 population census: a demographic analysis". BRALUP Research Paper No. 19, University of Dar-es-Salaam, Oct. 1972, 53pp.
Looks into Tanzania's population statistics under the headings mortality, fertility, age distribution, and population growth. Relates these to economic trends and implications particularly as pertains to labour force provision.

60-16 HENIN, ROUSHDI A. Alternative population projections for Kenya 1969-1989 (with reference to demographic trends in Kenya). Population Studies and Research Institute, University of Nairobi, ca. 1979, 120pp.
Gives an outline of prevailing demographic trends in the country and offers a comparison of two sets of population projections showing some of the implications of these projections to economic planning.

60-17 HERZ, BARBARA KNAPP. Demographic pressure and economic change: the case of Kenyan land reforms. Ph.D. dissertation, Yale University, 1974, 339pp.
Addresses the role of demographic pressure in the recent economic history of Kenya, particularly in its efforts through land reform and agricultural modernization to raise living standards. Assesses and compares those efforts and draws policy conclusions.

60-18 HILL, ALTHEA. "The fertility of the Asian community of East Africa". Population Studies, Vol. 29, No. 3, Nov. 1975, pp. 355-372.

60-19 INTERNATIONAL LABOUR ORGANIZATION. "National seminar on population and development: Tanzania". ILO, Arusha, 1980.
Objectives of the seminar included: to review the planning process in Tanzania, to develop an overview of population and demographic activities in the country, to determine whether population and demographic factors have been integrated into the planning process, and to prepare a draft recommendation to the government for follow-up action and programmes.

60-20 KIBUA, T.N. Kenya's population policy: an economic analysis of population growth control. M.A. thesis, University of Nairobi, 1976.

60-21 KNOWLES, J.C., and ANKER, R. "Economic determinants of demographic behaviour in Kenya". ILO, Geneva, 1975.
Reports on a study of the contribution of economic factors to the determination of demographic behaviour in Kenya. Concludes that only as regards rural-urban migration and age at marriage can economic policy affect markedly the future path of demographic behaviour.

60-22 KOCHER, JAMES E. "Rural development and fertility change: preliminary results from a study in Lushoto and Moshi Districts, Tanzania". Proceedings of the East African Agricultural Economics Conference, Kampala, 1975.
Similar item appeared in Smithsonian Institution Occasional Monograph No. 4, New perspectives on the demographic transition, Washington, D.C., 1976, pp. 53-93.

60-23 ___. A micro-economic analysis of the determinants of human fertility in rural northeastern Tanzania. Ph.D. dissertation, Michigan State University, 1976.
DAI, Vol. 37, p. 7873-A.

60-24 ___. "Tanzania: population projections and primary education, rural health, and water supply goals". HIID Development Discussion Paper No. 17, Harvard University, 1976, 36pp.

60-25 ___. "Socio-economic development and fertility change in rural Africa". Food Research Institute Studies, Vol. 16, No. 2, 1977, pp. 63-75.
Attempts to analyse the determinants of fertility levels in selected areas of northern Tanzania. Reference is made

to other countries like Kenya whose population is predicted to quadruple by the middle of the next century due to current age-distribution and fertility rates.

60-26 ___. Rural development and fertility change in tropical Africa: evidence from Tanzania. African Rural Economy Paper No. 19, Michigan State University, 1979, 95pp.
Analyses the effects of socio-economic development on fertility in rural north-eastern Tanzania. The analysis shows that there are frequently interrelated and multiple lines between a given socio-economic change and its ultimate effect on fertility.

60-27 KRAMER, JOYCE MARIE. Production and reproduction at various levels of participation in the modern world system: an analysis of the effects of urbanization on fertility for twelve communities in Kenya. Ph.D. dissertation, University of North Carolina, 1980, 371pp.
DAI, Vol. 41, p. 1786-A.

60-28 LIVINGSTON, IAN. "Prospects for population limitation in Kenya: statistical evidence from the Vihiga programme". IDS Working P 214, April 1975, 23pp.
Compares the response to the expansion of clinics, and other aspects of the SRDP, in the "intensive effort" area of Vihiga-Hamisi with that in the rest of the district.

60-29 ___. "What do economists really know about population? Or, the benefits of cost-benefit". IDS Disc P 222, 1975.
Centres on the economic development approach to reducing the birth rate and presents the macroeconomic approach to evaluating population control. Also considers the complications raised by the value of children to parents.

60-30 MAINA, J.B.M. Structural transformation, population change and sectoral employment in Kenya: 1964-1976. M.A. thesis, University of Nairobi, 1979.

60-31 MAINA, R.M. The role of law in population control in Kenya. LL.B. thesis, University of Nairobi, 1976, 74pp.
A brief survey of Kenyan laws relating to population. Asserts that there is need to change or amend some of these laws to meet the needs of the society to comply with the givernment's population policies as laid down in the development plans.

60-32 MARO, PAUL S. Population and land resources in northern Tanzania: the dynamics of change, 1920-1970. Ph.D. dissertation, University of Minnesota, 1974.

60-33 MARTIN, WALTER T. "Family planning attitudes and knowledge: a study of African families in Nairobi". IDS (unnumbered paper), June 1970, 44pp.

Finds that the African married couples residing in selected housing estates in Nairobi in 1969 show a certain ambivalence toward the role of women, toward the ideal family size, and toward family planning.

60-34 MATI, J.K.G., and BUIGUTT, K.A. (eds.). Population growth and its relevance to socio-economic development. Kenya National Academy, Nairobi, 1980, 160pp.

Contains twenty-two papers presented at the first annual symposium of the Kenya National Academy for Advancement of Arts and Sciences, held in 1978. A sample of the contents include: S.H. Ominde, "Population change and development"; A. Subbakrishniah, "Implications of physical planning to population growth and resource use in Kenya"; U.N. Economic Commission for Africa, "Population and development planning"; and D.D. Kioko, "Some economic implications of Kenya's population growth".

60-35 MLAMBITI, M.E. "The world population and its implications on the development of the developing nations with particular reference to Uganda". EA USSC Conference, Dar-es-Salaam, Dec. 1973, 14pp.

Centres on the population crisis and its causes, the effects of the population explosion on land resources and food supply. Analyses the pressure of population growth in Uganda in relation to employment and output.

60-36 MØNSTED, METTE. "Conditions for a changing family size in selected rural areas of Kenya". CDR Project Paper, Centre for Development Research, Copenhagen, March 1977.

Uses a cost-benefit approach. Finds that the economic costs of children do influence attitudes toward the desirable number of children among poor families with limited access to land but that factors on the benefits side weaken the correlation between costs and desired family size.

60-37 MØNSTED, METTE, and WALJI, PARVEEN. A demographic analysis of East Africa. Scandinavian Institute of African Studies, Uppsala, 1978, 211pp.

Points at the relevance of demography for social and economic development planning in the East African context. Aimed at making the analysis of demography more relevant within the planning process of the East African countries. Main purpose of the book is to produce a textbook in demography which analyses East African demographic data within a sociological framework.

POPULATION, MANPOWER

60-38 MOORE, J.E. "Rural population carrying capacities of the districts of Tanzania". BRALUP Research Paper No. 18, University of Dar-es-Salaam, July 1971, 47pp.
Gives quantitative data on production by agro-economic zones, relates that to population density in respective areas, with a view to assessing the population carrying capacity for each area.

60-39 MUHINDI, F.M. An economic analysis of fertility behaviour in Kenya: a case study. M.A. thesis, University of Nairobi, 1980.

60-40 NTOZI, J.P.M. "The implications of possible paths of future population on an economy: a case study of the age structure of Kenya". In J.K.G. Mati and K.A. Buigutt (eds.), Population growth and its relevance to socio-economic development. Kenya National Academy, Nairobi, 1980, 11pp.
An attempt to use projection techniques to show the impact of different rates of population growth on the Kenyan economy. Outlines the mathematics of the projection technique, gives results, and then discusses the implications of the resulting age structure on the future economy of Kenya.

60-41 OMINDE, SIMEON H. Land and population in the western districts of Nyanza province. Ph.D. dissertation, Makerere University, 1963.

60-42 ___. The population of Kenya, Tanzania and Uganda. Heinemann, Nairobi, 1975, 124pp.
Presents the population situation in the area, that is, its size, composition, distribution, and cause for that distribution, and prospects. Concludes that a comprehensive policy of socio-economic development must seek to harmonize the rate of population growth with the capacity and prospects for sustained development.

60-43 ___. "Demographic trends in Kenya with special reference to employment". Kenya National Seminar on employment, Mombasa, April 1977, 18pp.
Discusses the nature of the population problem in Kenya in relation to population growth, manpower, and employment.

60-44 OUCHO, JOHN O. "A demographic history of Kenya". Historical Association of Kenya, Aug. 1974, 26pp.
An attempt is made to highlight the country's demographic history within the limitations of available information. Analyses types of enumeration that have been used to collect demographic data, the population dynamics of fertility and

mortality, and their implications for demographic transition, and the complementary phenomena of internal migration and urbanization.

60-45 ____. "Demographic statistics and the Kenya experience". Staff Seminar Paper, Department of History, University of Nairobi, March 1979, 22pp.

Launches a debate on demographic statistics in the experience of colonial and post-colonial Kenya. Considers the evolution as well as the spirit and purpose of demography's emphasis on methodology in collecting, analysing, and disseminating statistics.

60-46 ____. "Population and its implications for resource development in the Lake Victoria Basin". IDS Working P 339, March 1979, 44pp.

Examines the population factor in developing the basin.

60-47 ____. "Socio-economic perspectives of fertility regulation in traditional and modern African societies". Institute of African Studies, University of Nairobi, 1979, 18pp.

60-48 OWITI, GUYA C. The life expectancy and mortality of Kenyans. M.B.A. thesis, University of Nairobi, 1976, 149pp.

An attempt at investigation of the main factors responsible for high mortality rates in Kenya. Calculation of "crude" mortality rates for Kenya using age groupings.

60-49 POPULATION STUDIES AND RESEARCH CENTRE. "Population, development and economic planning". University of Nairobi, ca. 1979, 59pp.

60-50 POWELSON, J.P. "Population growth and unemployment in Africa: with special reference to Kenya". Cultures et Développement, Vol. 7, No. 1, 1975, pp. 85-94.

60-51 SCHULTHEIS, MICHAEL J. Population growth, labour utilization, and regional development in Uganda. Ph.D dissertation, Cornell University, 1976.

60-52 SEMBAJWE, ISRAEL S.L. "An analysis of rural-urban differentials in fertility and child mortality in Tanzania". BRALUP Research Paper No. 28, University of Dar-es-Salaam, April 1974.

The findings indicate that urban fertility is lower than rural fertility and urban child mortality is also below rural child mortality. Argues that lower fertility in urban areas is probably due to the lower levels of child mortality.

POPULATION, MANPOWER

60-53 SMITH, T.E. (ed.). The politics of family planning in the third world. Allen and Unwin, London, 1973, 352pp.
Includes David Radel, "Kenya's population and family planning policy: a challenge to development communication".

60-54 SWARTZ, CAROLINE. "Investigations into several economic and demographic decisions in rural Kenyan households: a research proposal". IDS Working P 301, March 1977, 30pp.
The proposed analysis focuses on income, saving and demographic decisions at the household level, and the interactions between these decisions and the roles children play in the household.

60-55 ___. "Some economic and demographic decisions on smallholdings in Kenya". IDS Working P 314, June 1977, 11pp.
Details revised research plans for investigating smallholder decisions relating to production, labour utilization, and saving, employing data from the Integrated Rural Survey.

60-56 THOMAS, I.D. "Infant mortality in Tanzania". East African Geographical Review, No. 10, April 1972, pp. 5-26.
Makes an analysis on the association of certain environmental conditions and discusses problems encountered in such investigations.

60-57 UCHE, U.U. (ed.). Law and population change in Africa. East African Literature Bureau, Nairobi, 1976, 277pp.
Reports of a workshop on the teaching of population dynamics in African law schools. Includes various topics with respect to East African economies relating to laws in relation to population changes, for example, population implications of rural development in Kenya. Offers policy recommendations and conclusions.

60-58 WHITACRE, ROBERT JAMES. "Population growth in Kenya: policy formulation and implementation". IDS Working P 201, Jan. 1974, 21pp.
The analysis indicates that full internalization of costs and benefits associated with population increases requires a significant expansion and change in the methodology of the family planning programme.

60-59 YEAGER, RODGER. "Demography and development policy in Tanzania". U.S.A. African Studies Association meeting, Philadelphia, Oct. 1980.

61--The labour force and migration

61-1 AMEY, ALAN. "Urban-rural relations in Tanzania: methodology, issues, and preliminary results". ERB Paper 76.12, University of Dar-es-Salaam, 1976, 62pp.

61-2 ASETO, OYUGI. "Migration, urbanization and employment situation in Africa". OAU/ILO Seminar on Population, Employment and Development Planning, Nairobi, Nov. 1977, 38pp.
Presents simple interpretations of the concepts in question, examines the relationship that exists among them, and suggests some policy measures that could be adopted to deal with problems arising from the phenomena analysed.

61-3 AYIEMBA, ELIAS H.O. Intercensal population change: a comparative study of Kano locations and the sugar-belt; 1962-1972. M.A. thesis, University of Nairobi, 1974, 380pp.
Concludes that population changes in the area surveyed reflect pre-eminently the influence of migrations particularly in the sugar-belt. However, actual intercensal population increase in the entire Kano locations could be atrributed to the influence of fertility and mortality rates.

61-4 BARNUM, H.N., and SABOT, R.H. Migration, education and urban surplus labour: the case of Tanzania. OECD Development Centre Employment Series No. 13, Paris, 1976, 115pp.
Examines the factors influencing rural-urban migration in Tanzania and provides an empirical analysis of the relationships among education, migration, and urban surplus labour. Concludes that job probability and rural-urban income and differentials are significant determinants of urban migration; rural residents with more education have higher propensity to migrate independently of income differentials.

61-5 ____. "Education, employment probabilities and rural-urban migration in Tanzania". OIES Bull, Vol. 39, No. 2, May 1977, pp. 109-126.
The analysis supports the hypothesis that expected income has a significant influence on the decision of Tanzania rural residents to migrate to town, that the increase in the economic returns to migration with educational level contributes to the explanation of the higher propensity to migrate among educated residents, and that for a given differential between rural and urban incomes, workers with relatively more education have a higher propensity to migrate than workers with less.

61-6 BIENEFELD, M.A., and SABOT, R.H. National urban mobility,

POPULATION, MANPOWER

employment and income survey of Tanzania, 1971 (4 vols.). Economic Research Bureau, University of Dar-es-Salaam, 1972.

61-7 BIENEFELD, M.A. "Occupational structure and industrial distribution of wage earners". In K.S. Kim, R.B. Mabele, and M.H. Schultheis (eds.), Papers on the political economy of Tanzania. Heinemann, Nairobi, 1979, pp. 245-252.
Discusses the occupational structure of Tanzanian urban wage earners, impact of the Tanzanian education system, and distribution of wage earners.

61-8 BROWNLEE, ROBERT J. An empirical investigation of spatial labor mobility within a developing country: Uganda. Ph.D. dissertation, Syracuse University, 1973.

61-9 BYERLEE, D. "Research on migration in Africa: past, present and future". African Rural Employment Paper No. 2, Michigan State University Department of Agricultural Economics, East Lansing, 1972, 22pp.
This paper aims at a critical review of present knowledge of African rural-urban migration and suggests future directions for improved theory and methodology for economic research on migration. Discusses the characteristics of migrants, determinants and effects of migration, and the implications of migration for economic development.

61-10 CLAYTON, ANTHONY, and SAVAGE, DONALD C. Government and labour in Kenya, 1895-1963. Frank Cass, London, 1975, 481pp.
A chronological treatment of the history of labour-government relationships focusing especially on the impact of the introduction in the colonial period of modern forms of wage-labour on ethnic and socio-economic structures.

61-11 COLLIER, VALERIE C., and REMPEL, HENRY. "The divergence of private from social costs in rural-urban migration: a case study of Nairobi, Kenya". J Dev Studs, Vol. 13, No. 3, April 1977, pp. 199-216.
Considers the determinants of different levels of private and social costs associated with different stocks of urban unemployed and attempts to quantity the major private and social costs of migration. Also appears in Tony Killick (ed.), Papers on the Kenyan economy.

61-12 COLLIER, P. "Migration and unemployment: a dynamic general equilibrium analysis applied to Tanzania". Oxford Economic Papers, Vol. 31, No. 2, July 1979, pp. 205-236.
Presents and tests an analytic model of the Tanzania labour market that conflicts radically with the accepted

"Todaro hypothesis" which predicts that urban jobs creation will increase the size of the urban informal sector. Criticizes also the Harris-Todaro model and concludes that it is an inadequate and untested framework in which to analyse rural-urban labour market interactions. The model is tested on Tanzania data for 1969-1975.

61-13 DAHERTY, N.A. "A stochastic dominance model of rural-urban migration". EA USSC Conference, Dar-es-Salaam, Dec. 1970, 18pp.
The focus is on the decision made by the individual whether or not to migrate, and upon the factors determining that decision. A model of individual decision behaviour is constructed and its working is illustrated under a set of conditions which might represent the economic background to the rural-urban migration problem in Central and East Africa.

61-14 EGERO, BERTIL. "Migration and economic development south of Lake Victoria". BRALUP Research Paper No. 32, University of Dar-es-Salaam, March 1974, 34pp.
Argues that local cash crop farming provided the peasant in colonial times with a means of evading recruitment for plantation work and so where ecological and other conditions permitted, an indigenous commercial agriculture developed with a corresponding decline in labour migration.

61-15 ELKAN, WALTER. "Is a proletariat emerging in Nairobi?". Econ Dev Cult Change, Vol. 24, No. 4, July 1976, pp. 695-706.
Argues that a substantial number in Nairobi depend permanently upon wage employment, and that ties with their villages of origin have become severed. Appeared as IDS Disc P 168 in 1973.

61-16 FIELDS, G.S. "Toward a model of education and labour markets in labour surplus economies". IDS Staff P 88, Nairobi, Nov. 1970.
This model describes the essential relationships between the demand and supply of education and the demand and supply of trained workers.

61-17 FLANAGAN, W.G. The extended family as an agent in urbanization: a survey of men and women working in Dar-es-Salaam. Ph.D. dissertation, University of Connecticut, 1977, 234pp.
DAI, Vol. 39, pp. 1135-A.

61-18 GAPPERT, GARY M. The economics of labor migration in an African society: labor aspects of resettlement in southern Tanzania. Ph.D. dissertation, Syracuse University, 1972.

POPULATION, MANPOWER

61-19 GONDWE, D.K. "Some thoughts on the determinants of rural-urban labour migration". EA USSC Conference, Nairobi, Dec. 1972, 15pp.
Concerned mainly with the causes of rural-urban migration and uses as its spring board Todaro's model (American Economic Review, March 1969). Presents several propositions which may be incorporated in Todaro's model so that the model better fits a country like Malawi.

61-20 GOULD, W.T.S. "Economic aspects of international migration in East Africa". University of Liverpool Department of Geography Paper, 1976, 24pp.

61-21 GREEN, J.M., and COLLIER, P. "Migration from rural areas of developing countries: a socio-economic approach". OIES Bull, Vol. 40, No. 1, Feb. 1978, pp. 23-35.
Discusses explanations offered to account for the spatial distribution of migrants. Examines flow of information dissemination incorporating and extending previous approaches. Applies the model to the case of rural-to-urban migration within Kenya.

61-22 GRILLO, R.D. African railwaymen: solidarity and opposition in an East African labour force. Cambridge University Press, Cambridge, 1973, 215pp.
Finds that there is an increasing significance of "modern" status variables in structuring relations between Africans, and a continuing significance of ethnic ties.

61-23 GULLIVER, P.H. "Labour migration in a rural economy: a study of the Ngoni and Ndendeuli of southern Tanganyika". East African Institute of Social Research, Kampala, 1955, 48pp.
Analyses the nature, causes, and consequences of labour migration among two of the more important labour-providing tribes in Tanganyika.

61-24 GUPTA, DESH. "A suggested model of labour supplies and economic development in some African countries with specific reference to Rhodesia and Kenya". EA USSC Conference, Nairobi, Dec. 1969.
As a modification of the Lewis and Ranis-Fei models, considers a transitional period where the traditional environment tends to act as a restraint on the supply of labour to the exchange economy; this influence is reduced over time.

61-25 HIRST, MICHAEL. "A Markovian analysis of inter-regional migration in Uganda". University of Liverpool Department of Geography Africa Population Mobility Project Working Paper, 1974, 23pp.

61-26 ___. "The distribution of migration in Kampala, Uganda". East African Geographical Review, June 1975, pp. 37-55.
Argues that in the rapidly growing cities of tropical Africa, a clearer theoretical understanding of migrant settlement in urban areas and the subsequent role of intra-urban migration is vital if planners wish to intervene and effectively control and direct urban growth toward some desirable objective or to prevent the excesses of accelerating rural-urban migration and urban growth.

61-27 HOUSE, WILLIAM J., and REMPEL, HENRY. "The determinants of interregional migration in Kenya". World Development, Vol. 8, No. 1, Jan. 1980, pp. 25-36.
Finds that population is attracted to districts with better economic opportunities, as measured by wages and employment rates, and is deterred by distance to those better opportunities. Earlier version appeared as IDS Working P 272 in 1976.

61-28 HUNTINGTON, HILLARD GRISWOLD. An empirical study of ethnic linkages in Kenyan rural-urban migration. Ph.D. dissertation, State University of New York, 1975, 174pp.
Presents an empirical estimate of the response to income inequalities between urban and rural areas by specifying a variable for the ethnic ties between the areas. Ethnicity is perceived as an economic variable that affects the expected gains and costs of the decision to migrate. A shorter paper of same title appears as IDS Disc P 260 in Dec. 1977.

61-29 JOHNSON, G.E. "The structure of rural-urban migration models". EA USSC Conference, Dar-es-Salaam, 1970, 13pp.
Examines some of the theoretical aspects of the economics of rural-urban migration.

61-30 JOHNSON, STEVEN L. "Changing patterns of labor mobilization in western Kenya". U.S.A. African Studies Association meeting, Philadelphia, Oct. 1980.

61-31 KALIFA, J.H.M. Strategy for the resolution of the problem of rural over-population and internal migration in Uganda: a case study of Bugisu district. M.A. thesis, University of Nairobi, 1976, 262pp.
Proposes a strategy which would involve land reform, an agricultural development programme, and the establishment of growth poles aimed at siting towns and upgrading and expanding existing ones.

61-32 KING, KENNETH J. The African artisan: education and the informal sector in Kenya. Heinemann, London, 1977, 226pp.

POPULATION, MANPOWER

Describes and analyses the ways in which skills and technology are acquired and used in Kenya's informal sector. Argues that the real problem for the informal sectors of the East African region is their lack of vertical integration into more skill-intensive modes of production.

61-33 KINNISON, S.M. Urbanization and poverty in Nairobi. Ph.D. dissertation, Howard University, 1977, 262pp.
DAI, Vol. 38, p. 6985-A.

61-34 MASSER, IAN. Inter-regional migration in tropical Africa. Institute of British Geographers, London, 1975, 107pp.

61-35 MATINGU, MARY NDUNGE. Rural to rural migration and employment: a case study in a selected area of Kenya. M.A. thesis, University of Nairobi, 1974, 207pp.
Concludes that people in Machakos district who produce few or no food crops due to landlessness or low productivity of land will aspire to migrate to areas where they can at least produce enough to cater for a family's subsistence needs.

61-36 MIGOT-ADHOLA, SHEM E. Migration and rural differentiation in Kenya. Ph.D. dissertation, University of California, Los Angeles, 1977, 218pp.
Explores the influence of socio-economic differentiation upon rural migration and settlement in Kenya.

61-37 MIKKELSEN, BRITHA. "Skill formation and rural industrial development". IDS Working P 199, Dec. 1974, 23pp.
A progress report of the first findings of field work. It raises for discussion propositions about how "informal" skill formation relates to rural industrial development.

61-38 MIRACLE, MARVIN P. "Interpretation of backward-sloping labour supply curves in Africa". Econ Dev Cult Change, Vol. 24, No. 2, Jan. 1976, pp. 399-406.
Argues that the economic behaviour of African labourers in the pre-World War II period was orthodox, at least in Kenya.

61-39 MOOCK, JOYCE LEWINGER. The migration process and differential economic behaviour in south Maragoli, western Kenya. Ph.D. dissertation, Columbia University, 1976.

61-40 ___. "The content and maintenance of social ties between urban migrants and their home-based support groups: the Maragoli case". African Urban Studies, No. 3, Winter 1978-1979, pp. 15-31.

Discusses the nature of social and economic ties which persist between migrants and their home-based kinsmen and friends. Attempts to demonstrate how the redistribution of migrants' income is affected by changing patterns of social organization. Concludes that town and country people are often the same people engaged simultaneously in dual occupations.

61-41 NAKITARE, ELIUD PAUL. Socio-economic consequences of intra-rural migration. M.Sc. thesis, University of Nairobi, 1974, 208pp.
Argues that intra-rural migration results in increased hectarage per migrant, an increase in the individual shamba ownership status, a greater number of families who employ others, and increased argicultural productivity. On the negative side, haphazard intra-rural migration can cause disruption in agricultural production continuity.

61-42 NDAWULA-KAJUMBA, S. "The unknown workers during employment crisis: the case of sisal workers in Tanzania". EA USSC Conference, Dec. 1972, pp. 233-250.
Demonstrate that the existing literature on the labour force in the sisal industry is incapable of providing a basis for explanations of the problems that sisal workers would face in the event of economic disintegration of the industry.

61-43 OLENJA, C.K. "Patterns and trends of migration in Nairobi up to 1978". Institute of African Studies Paper No. 141, Nairobi, ca. 1979, 13pp.
Deals with migration in Nairobi. Gives the characteristics of the immigrant population, reasons for migration, and discusses the implications of this migration.

61-44 OUCHO, JOHN OYARE. Migration survey in Kisumu town. M.A. thesis, University of Nairobi, 1974, 400pp.
Intended to analyse the migration system of Kisumu on a regional as well as national basis, and to highlight the effects of migratory behaviour on the resource base in and around the town.

61-45 ___. "Population movements in Kenya: a review and analysis". Journal of Eastern African Research and Development, Vol. 9, No. 1, 1979, pp. 78-90.
A socio-economic inquiry into the nature and causes of migration in Kenya. Stresses the necessity of an interdisciplinary inquiry into this problem.

POPULATION, MANPOWER

61-46 OWUOR, SAMSON NYAOKE. Primacy of determinants of rural-urban and reverse urban-rural migration in Kenya. M.A. thesis, University of Nairobi, 1974, 104pp.
Confirms the existence of urban to rural migration and ranks the primary determinants of cross migration in the order of job opportunity, clan contacts, level of education, income differential, and land density.

61-47 PARKIN, DAVID (ed.). Town and country in Central and East Africa. Oxford University Press, London, 1976, 362pp.
Includes David Parkin, "Migration settlement and the politics of unemployment: a Nairobi case study"; Tibamanya Nwene Mushanga, "Notes on migration in Uganda"; and Victor C. Uchendu, "Inter-rural migration and East African rural development".

61-48 POSNER, ROBERT. Agricultural labor market in Kenya. Ph.D. dissertation, University of Michigan, 1971.

61-49 REMPEL, HENRY. Labor migration into urban centres and urban unemployment in Kenya. Ph.D. dissertation, University of Wisconsin, Madison, 1971.

61-50 ___. "Urban in-migration and urban unemployment". IDS Interdisciplinary Urban Seminar, University of Nairobi, Feb. 1974, 17pp.
Deals with the extent of rural-urban migration in Kenya. Defines the potential migrants and why they migrate, and the general implications for employment planning in Kenya.

61-51 ___. The determinants of rural-to-urban labour migration in Kenya. IDS (unnumbered paper), n.d. (ca. May 1974), 43pp.
Shows that young, better educated men are the most likely to migrate, pushed by limited economic opportunities in their home areas and pulled by the presence of relatives and job opportunities in the town or city.

61-52 ___. "An analysis of the information on inter-district migration provided in the 1969 Kenya census". IDS Disc P 244, Jan. 1977, 92pp.
Provides calculations indicating the extent of inter-district migration and the nature of various migration flows based on the 1969 census. Also appears as IDS Working P 142.

61-53 ___. "Labour migration into urban centres and urban unemployment in Kenya". In D. Ghai and M. Godfrey (eds.), Essays on employment in Kenya. Kenya Literature Bureau, Nairobi, 1979, pp. 75-96.

Recognizes the existence of minimum wage levels in urban areas which constrain wages from adjusting downward to full-employment levels. Postulates that the level of urban unemployment serves as the equilibrating mechanism for those economies where the rural-urban labour migration is continuing even though the marginal prodjct of labour in agriculture is positive.

61-54 ___. "The labour market". In Tony Killick (ed.), Papers on the Kenyan economy. Heinemann, London, 1981.

61-55 RICHARDS, AUDREY I. (ed.). Economic development and tribal change: a study of immigrant labour in Buganda. Oxford University Press, London, 1973, 319pp.

Contains the results of a survey on the origins, numbers, and conditions of employment of the immigrant labourers who have been pouring into south Uganda since the early twenties.

61-56 RYAN, T.C.I., and HOUSE, W.J. "A dynamic model of rural-urban migration". Kenyan Economic Association Annual Conference, Nairobi, 1977, 29pp.

61-57 SABOT, R.H. "Education, income distribution, and rates of urban migration in Tanzania". ERB Paper, University of Dar-es-Salaam, 1972, 40pp.

Discusses the problems of urban migration. Educational opportunities are seen as a causal factor in the emergence of urban employment problems.

61-58 ___. Economic development and urban migration: Tanzania 1900-1971. Oxford University Press, Oxford, 1979, 279pp.

Study of rural-urban migration during 1900-1971 with respect to its impact on development. Focuses on labour utilization in the urban areas only, especially urban surplus labour and low labour productivity.

61-59 TODARO, MICHAEL P. "Income expectations, rural-urban migration and employment in Africa". International Labour Review, Vol. 104, No. 5, Nov. 1971, pp. 387-413.

Presents a model to explain the mechanism of rural-urban migration. Examines alternative policies to alleviate the problem of rising unemployment levels in Africa. Cites Kenya in many examples.

61-60 ___. "Migration and economic development: a review of theory, evidence, methodology and research priorities". IDS Occ P 18, April 1976, 105pp.

Discusses the role and importance of migration for

development, urban surplus labour, and problems of international migration. Also examines the economics of internal migration in developing countries, and gives a summary review of quantitative migration studies.

61-61 TUMBO, N.S.K. "Labour in Tanzania". Studies in Political Science, No. 5, Tanzania Publishing House, Dar-es-Salaam, 1977, 89pp.

62--Productivity, incomes, and industrial relations

62-1 ANANABA, WOGU. The trade movement in Africa: promise and performance. St. Martin's Press, New York, 1979, 248pp.
Focuses on the development and organization of trade unions in Africa since 1961 with discussions of events during the periods 1939-1945 and 1945-1960. Surveys the general trade union situation by country in Africa.

62-2 ASETO, O.; ATENG', A.B.; and MIGOT-ADHOLA, E.S. "Factors affecting public sector salaries policy in Kenya". IDS Paper, June 1980, 165pp.
Examines the supply and demand for high and middle level manpower in the local market; outlines the major salary changes since 1963; and makes a quantitative assessment of the progress of salary determimation. Discusses the influence of multinational corporations on public sector salary policy determination in Kenya, and the influence of various other factors.

62-3 BENNELL, PAUL. "The formation of engineering labour markets in Kenya 1918-1979". IDS Working P 379, 1981.
Outlines the basic theoretical and empirical objectives of a study on the historical constitution of engineering labour markets. Focuses on supply and demand for engineers, technicians and artisans within the modern sector.

62-4 BIENEFELD, M.A. "Socialist development and the workers in Tanzania". In R. Sandbrook and R. Cohen (eds.), The development of an African working class. Longman, London, 1975, pp. 231-261.
Discusses the role of Tanzania's labour movement in the drive to development.

62-5 ___. "Trade unions and peripheral capitalism". University of Sussex Institute of Development Studies, Brighton, 1977, 45pp.

62-6 ___. "Trade unions, the labour process and the Tanzanian state"

J Mod Afr Studs, Vol. 17, No. 4, Dec. 1979, pp. 553-593.
Seeks to refute previous historical theories of trade unionism. Documents the rapid expansion of trade unionism as an institutional response to changes occuring in the process of colonial production.

62-7 BOLTON, DIANNE. "Unionization and employer strategy: the Tanganyikan sisal industry, 1958-1964". In P.C.W. Gutkind, R. Cohen, and J. Copans (eds.), African labour history. SAGE, Beverly Hills, London, 1978, pp. 175-204.
Argues that plantation workers acted jointly on common issues even prior to the development of unions. Finds that the government's stance shifted from pro-union to pro-management during the period analysed.

62-8 BROWN, J.L., and MUIR, J.D. "Trade union power and the process of economic development: the Kenyan example". Industrial Relations, Vol. 29, No. 3, 1974.

62-9 ___. "The functioning of the Kenyan industrial court". J Mod Afr Studs, Vol. 14, No. 4, 1976, pp. 700-705.
Describes the operation and effects of the Kenyan Industrial Court. Draws attention to some features that have affected its operation.

62-10 BROWN, K.M. "Direct policies to increase employment: stronger version of Kenya's tripartite agreement". EA USSC Conference, Nairobi, Dec. 1972, 9pp.
Attempts to analyse probable costs and benefits of "direct" inducements particularly as these policies might be applied in a developing country.

62-11 CHESWORTH, D. "Statutory minimum wage fixing in Tanganyika". International Labour Review, Vol. 96, No. 1, July 1967, pp. 43-66.
Examines the effects of a system of statutory minimum wage fixing on workers' earnings, employment, the total wage bill, output, and productivity.

62-12 CHILD, FRANK C. "Employment, technology and growth: the role of the intermediate sector in Kenya". IDS Occ P 19, 1976, 100pp.
Finds that productivity and wages in the intermediate sector compare favourably with the modern sector. Recommends a shift of policies from the development of urban enterprise to simpler, more labour intensive small-scale rural enterprise.

POPULATION, MANPOWER

62-13 COCKAR, S. "Kenya industrial court". In A. Gladstone (ed.), Industrial courts in English-speaking developing countries. International Institute for Labour Studies, Geneva, 1976, pp. 43-56.

62-14 GODFREY, MARTIN. "Education, training, productivity and income: a Kenyan case study". IDS Disc P 253, March 1977, 20pp.
Looks at the effect of education and training on productivity, as indicated by performance on government trade tests of craft skills in engineering, building, woodwork, electrical, and tailoring trades. Concludes that this is a relatively inexpensive way of collecting useful information which would be worthwhile repeating on a regular basis with a large coverage.

62-15 GREGORY, PETER. "An assessment of changes in employment conditions in less developed countries". Econ Dev Cult Change, Vol. 28, No. 4, July 1980.
Attempts to test the validity of the proposition that the quality of employment in LDCs has deteriorated generally.

62-16 GUTKIND, P.C.W.; COHEN, R; and COPANS, J. (eds.). African labour history. SAGE, Beverly Hills, London, 1978, 280pp.
Includes Sharon Stichter, "Trade unionism in Kenya 1947-1952: the militant phase", and Dianne Bolton, "Unionization and employer strategy: the Tanganyikan sisal industry, 1958-1964".

62-17 HENLEY, JOHN S., and HOUSE, WILLIAM J. "The changing fortunes of an aristocracy? Determinants of wages and conditions of employment in Kenya". World Development, Vol. 8, No. 1, Jan. 1978, pp. 83-95.
Examines the functioning of the labour market in the modern sector. Concludes that measures of an "ability to pay" characteristic of industries with limited competition in the product market and realizing above-average labour productivity are the best preeictions of inter-industry wage differences.

62-18 HOPCRAFT, PETER N. "Does education increase farm productivity". IDS Working P 279, Aug. 1976, 4pp.
Does not find much evidence of improved farm productivity that can be directly attributable to the schooling experience

62-19 HOUSE, WILLIAM J., and REMPEL, HENRY. "The impact of unionization on negotiated wages in the manufacturing sector in Kenya". OIES Bull, Vol. 38, No. 2, May 1976.
Argues that unions have exerted power on employers to raise wage rates above the opportunity cost of labour to the modern sector in Kenya.

62-20 ___. "Labour market segmentation in Kenya". EAER, Vol. 8, No. 2, Dec. 1976, pp. 35-54.

Argues that the Kenyan labour market is extensively segmented. Inter-occupational wage differentials were found to be parge. To lessen income differentials there is a need for a more progressive tax structure, a review of government's role as wage leader for unskilled labour, and greater security of and reduction in monopoly power in product markets.

62-21 ___. "The impact of unionization on negotiated wages in the manufacturing sector in Kenya: a reply". OIES Bull, Vol. 39, No. 3, Aug. 1977, pp. 233-235.

A reply to C. Mulvey's note in the same issue of this journal, pp. 229-233.

62-22 ___. "Labour market pressures and wage determination in a less developed country: the case of Kenya". Econ Dev Cult Change, Vol. 27, 1978.

62-23 ILIFFE, J. "A history of the dockworkers of Dar-es-Salaam". Tanzania Notes and Records, 1970.

Article centres on the history of the labour movement based on a history of work, its organization, and group consciousness among the workers. Considers how economic conditions transform the mass of the people of a country into workers.

62-24 ___. "The creation of group consciousness among the dockworkers of Dar-es-Salaam, 1929-50". In R. Sandbrook and R. Cohen (eds.), The development of an African working class. Longman, London, 1975, pp. 49-73.

Centres on the history of labour in Tanzania, and the organization and group consciousness among the workers.

62-25 JACKSON, D. "The disappearance of strikes in Tanzania: income policy and industrial democracy". J Mod Afr Studs, Vol. 17, No. 2, June 1979, pp. 219-251.

The declining trend of strikes in Tanzania as from 1963 has been as a result of a transformation of industrial relations whereby obligations have been imposed on organized labour while at the same time new rights have been created for workers.

62-26 ___. "The role of the Tanzania workers organization". University of Aston Management Centre Working Paper No. 127, Birmingham, 1979, 66pp.

62-27 JEDRUSZEK, JERZY. "Development in employment and productivity in Tanzania 1967-1977". ERB Papers 78.5 and 78.6, University of Dar-es-Salaam, May-June 1978, 92pp.

POPULATION, MANPOWER

62-28 KING, K.J. "Skill acquisition in the informal sector of an African economy: the Kenya case". J Dev Studs, Vol. 11, No. 2, Jan. 1975, pp. 108-122.
Explores the acquisition of a wide variety of skills by low-income Kenya Africans outside the scope of government and voluntary agency programmes.

62-29 KNIGHT, J.B. "Wages in Africa: what should a foreign firm do?". OIES Bull, Vol. 37, No. 2, May 1975, pp. 73-90.
Includes brief sketch of way in which wage increases occurred in Uganda from the 1950s to the 1970s.

62-30 KOMBO, R. The role of unions and employers' organizations in economic development and employment promotion in Kenya. International Institute for Labour Studies (No. IEME 3111), Geneva, n.d.
The paper analyses the structure and functions of labour unions, employer organizations, and the Ministry of Labour. Examines the development and role played by formal and informal bipartite and tripartite bodies, and finally highlights the legal regulations that govern industrial relations.

62-31 LEITNER, KERSTIN. Workers, trade unions and peripheral Capitalism in Kenya after independence. Ph.D. dissertation, Freie Universtität, Berlin, n.d. (ca. 1975), 237pp.
Argues that foreign domination in the industrialization process reduces the possibilities for the national government to control the accumulation process and that the government has little power to influence the development of incomes in various occupations. Shows that unions in Kenya after independence have been channeled by dominant political and economic interests to follow "consumptionist" aims.

62-32 ___. "The situation of agricultural workers in Kenya". Review of African Political Economy, No. 6, May-Aug. 1976, pp. 34-50
Argues that the most numerous and degraded workers in Kenya are the agricultural workers. Concludes that the Kenya Plantation and Agricultural Workers Union has failed to improve the conditions of its members.

62-33 MIHYO, P.B. "The workers revolution in Tanzania". Maji Maji, Vol. 17, 1974, pp. 1-61.

62-34 MSEKWA, PIUS. "Workers' participation in management in Tanzania Afr Rev, Vol. 5, No. 2, 1975, pp. 127-140.
Discusses the concept of workers' participation in its historical context and then examines the application of the principle of participation in independent Tanzania.

62-35 MUIR, J.D., and BROWN, J.L. "Trade union power and the process of economic development: the Kenya example". Relations Industrials, Vol. 29, No. 3, July 1974, pp. 474-494.

62-36 ___. "Labour legislation and industrial disputes: the Kenyan case". British Journal of Industrial Relations, Vol. 13, No. 3, Nov. 1975, pp. 334-345.

62-37 MUKUI, J.T. "A prelude to the implementation of the 1979 tripartite agreement". COTU (Kenya)/ICFTU Seminar on Employment, Nairobi, Feb. 1979, 6pp.
Discusses the likely effect of the tripartite agreement on wages, employment, rural-urban migration, industrial relations, and political costs in terms of contributing more to raising expectations.

62-38 MULVEY, CHARLES. "A note on the impact of unionization on negotiated wages in the manufacturing sector in Kenya". OIES Bull, Vol. 39, No. 3, Aug. 1977, pp. 229-233.
A critique of and reply to House and Remple's article that appeared in this Bulletin in 1976. That article asserted that unions exert power on employers to raise wage rates above the opportunity cost of labour to the modern sector.

62-39 MUREITHI, L.P. "Industrial relations, employment promotion and development". Labour and Society, Vol. 4, No. 1, Jan. 1979, pp. 99-110.

62-40 ___ and MOMANYI, S.N. "The interaction of industrial relations and the political process in Kenya". Nairobi, Aug. 1980, 19pp.
Deals with the origin and development of trade unionism prior to independence in 1963, trade union experience in the post-independence period, and the impact of government intervention on bargaining power.

62-41 NYALALI, F.L. Aspects of industrial conflict: a case study of trade disputes in Tanzania 1967-73. East African Literature Bureau, Kampala, 1975, 219pp.
Discusses the cuases of trade disputes during the period; also describes those trade disputes that occurred.

62-42 ODUOR-OTIENO, B.E. "The emergence of a national wages and incomes policy for Kenya: a survey of experience and prospects". IDS Seminar on Price and Marketing Controls in Kenya, IDS Occ P 32, March 1979, 144pp.
Reviews the necessity and effectiveness of a national wages and incomes policy for Kenya in terms of facilitating economic planning and social progress.

POPULATION, MANPOWER

62-43 OSORO, J.M. "Unity and diversity in labour recruitment and welfare: the tea estates versus other employers of labour 1925-1938". Historical Association of Kenya, Nairobi, 1977, 17pp.
Argues that the dismal and neglected African labourer, as portrayed by the existing literature, is not totally applicable to the Kericho tea estates, where the employers were forced into taking a positive interest in the welfare of their labourers.

62-44 PACK, HOWARD. "Review article: unemployment and income distribution in Kenya". Econ Dev Cult Change, Vol. 26, No. 1, Oct. 1977, 157-168.

62-45 SANDBROOK, RICHARD. Proletarians and African capitalism: the Kenyan case, 1960-72. Cambridge University Press, Cambridge, 1975, 222pp.
Seeks to assess the relationship between organized labour and the national bourgeoisie in Kenya. Uses this study as a test of the views of Fanon on the role of unionized labour.

62-46 SANDBROOK, R., and COHEN, R. (eds.). The development of an African working class. Longman, London, 1975, 330pp.
Includes M.A. Bienefeld, "Socialist development and the workers in Tanzania"; J. Iliffe, "The creation of group consciousness among the dockworkers of Dar-es-Salaam 1929-50"; and S. Stichter, "The formation of a working class in Kenya".

62-47 SILVER, M.S. "Labour productivity trends in Tanzania: manufacturing sector 1965-72". University of Aston Management Centre Working Paper No. 91, Birmingham, 1978, 21pp.

62-48 SINGH, MAKHAN. 1952-56: crucial years of Kenya trade unions. Uzima Press, Nairobi, 1979, 330pp.
Concentrates on workers' problems and their attempts to improve their position through organization, strike action, and other forms of protest. The role and contribution of the new local trade union leaders during the crucial years of the Emergency in Kenya is discussed.

62-49 TANZANIA, GOVERNMENT OF. Wages, incomes, rural development, investment and price policy. Government Printer, Dar-es-Salaam, 1967, 25pp.
States government policy as a response to a report submitted to the government by the International Labour Office earlier in 1967.

62-50 TEFERRI, ASEFA. Incomes policy for East Africa with special reference to Uganda. Ph.D. dissertation, Mighigan State University, 1973.

62-51 UCHENDU, VICTOR. "Traditional work groups in economic development". EA USSC Conference, Dar-es-Salaam, 1970.

62-52 WEEKS, JOHN F. "Wage policy and the colonial legacy: a comparative study". J Mod Afr Studs, Vol. 9, No. 3, Oct. 1971, pp. 361-387.
Analyses the development of wage policy in Nigeria, Kenya, and Uganda. Argues that conditions in Uganda and Kenya were transformed from labour shortage to labour surplus as a result of the colonial wage policy.

63--Employment and unemployment; labour intensity; the choice of techniques; the informal sector

63-1 ALI TAHA, A.R.E. Employment problems in Kenya plantations. International Labour Office, Addis Ababa, July 1975.

63-2 ALLEN, HUGH. "The informal urban industrial sector and growth: some thoughts on a modern mythology". IDS Disc P 259, Sept. 1977, 19pp.

63-3 AYAKO, A.B. Output, labour absorption and firm size: an analysis of Kenya data. M.A. thesis, University of Nairobi, 1979.

63-4 BHALLA, A.S. (ed.). Technology and employment in industry. International Labour Office, Geneva, 1975, 324pp.
Includes C. Cooper, R. Kaplinsky, R. Bell, and W. Satyarakwit, "Choice of techniques for can making in Kenya, Tanzania and Thailand"; C. Cooper and R. Kaplinsky, with the collaboration of R. Turner, "Second-hand equipment in developing countries; jute processing machinery in Kenya"; and F. Stewart, "Manufacture of cement blocks in Kenya".

63-5 ___. "Services and employment in Kenya". In D. Ghai and M. Godfrey (eds.), Essays on employment in Kenya. Kenya Literature Bureau, Nairobi, 1979, pp. 131-154.
Examines the importance of self-employment in Kenya. Shows the distribution of employment by income-groups in Kenyan commerce, banking and services, and presents some empirical estimates of labour-income from self-employment.

63-6 BIENEFELD, M.A. "The self-employed of urban Tanzania". University of Sussex Institute of Development Studies Discussion Paper No. 54, Brighton, May 1974, 96pp.
Suggests that rapid urban growth in Tanzania has neither

POPULATION, MANPOWER

greatly exceeded the wage sector's absorptive capacity nor has this resulted in intense competitive and income depressing pressures on other sectors. Argues that the "non-wage" sectors appear relatively stable and integrated into the urban economy. Also appeared as ERB Paper 75.11, Dar-es-Salaam, and as IDS Disc P 54, May 1974.

63-7 BOSHOFF, W.H., and MINTO, S.D. "Energy and labour bottlenecks and their influence on the choice of improved techniques". Faculty of Agriculture, University of Nairobi, Aug. 1975.

63-8 BROMLEY, R., and GERRY, C. (eds.). Casual work and poverty in third world cities. John Wiley & Sons, Chichester, 1979, 323pp.
Focuses on poverty and its relations with the labour process. Provides a range of approaches which can be taken to the study of poverty-in-employment.

63-9 CARLSEN, J., et al. "Rural employment in Nyanza, Kenya: project-description". Institute of Development Studies, No. A 74.9, Copenhagen, 1974, 19pp.
A study of rural households, population, non-farm activities in rural areas, land-tenure, migration, and agricultural productivity. Aim of the study is to derive some guidelines for policy with regard to rural development strategies and foreign assistance in this field.

63-10 CHANA, TARA, and MORRISON, HUNTER. "Nairobi's informal economic sector". Ekistics, Vol. 40, No. 237, Aug. 1975, pp. 120-230.

63-11 CLAYTON, E.S., and GREENIDGE, CARL. A study of rural unemployment in Kenya. Overseas Development Administration, London, 1974, 130pp.
Includes a case study of the absorption of primary school leavers in Embu district and an applied programming analysis of employment creation. Argues that a methodology of cardinally ranking projects according to their income and employment generation is superior to existing investment criteria.

63-12 CRAWFORD, E., and THORBECKE, E. "Employment, income distribution, poverty alleviation and basic needs in Kenya". Report of an ILO Consulting Mission, Cornell University, Ithaca, New York, 1979.

63-13 DALE, MARY. "Sisal on hand-looms in Kenya". Appropriate Technology, Vol. 1, No. 4, 1974-1975, pp. 15-16.
Argues that the introduction of hand weaving on looms which could be adapted to end products of infinite variety

at Eastleigh Community Centre, Nairobi, would increase employment opportunities for school-leaving girls and destitute women in the poorest quarter of Nairobi.

63-14 DAVID, MARTIN, and HOPCRAFT, PETER. "Labour intensive road construction and SRDP". IDS Disc P 229, Jan. 1976, 28pp.
Factors relevant to the success of rural works projects are discussed in relation to labour-intensive roads projects included in Kenya's Special Rural Development Programme.

63-15 DE VEEN, J.J. The rural access roads programme: appropriate technology in Kenya. ILO, Paris, 1980, 167pp.
Describes the Rural Access Roads Programme in Kenya which attempted to implement labour-based methods efficiently on a large scale. Discusses the development of the administrative, organizational and training systems of the programme, describes the technical and financial involvement of the various aid agencies, and the research carried out in the initial stages.

63-16 EDGREN, G. Wages and employment creation objectives and instruments for wages and income policy in Kenya. International Institute for Labour Studies (No. IEME 4125), Geneva, 1973, 19pp.

63-17 ___. Employment exchange in a labour surplus economy (Kenya). International Institute for Labour Studies (No. IEME 3080), Geneva, 1975, 17pp.

63-18 ELKAN, WALTER. "Urban unemployment in Kenya and Uganda". Manpower and Unemployment Research in Africa, Vol. 3, No. 2, Nov. 1970, pp. 1-5.
Examines why there is a slow increase in new jobs and whether a rise in urban employment opportunities would reduce urban unemployment.

63-19 ___. "Enumerated employment and the regional distribution of income in Kenya". Manpower and unemployment Research in Africa, Vol. 8, No. 1, April 1975, pp. 21-25.
Compares urban with rural incomes and examines the distribution of employment and earnings by province.

63-20 EVANS, B. EMMIT, JR. "Secondary education, unemployment and crime in Kenya". J Mod Afr Studs, Vol. 13, No. 1, March 1975, pp. 55-66.
Seeks to identify the occupational and educational aspirations and expectations of secondary-school students in Kenya during 1972. Findings reveal that social stability of Kenya

is threatened in that social strains and pressures from a rising incidence of crime will intensify as more secondary school leavers swell the ranks of the unemployed.

63-21 FARAGO, G. "Employment promotion in Nairobi's informal sector". Ministry of Labour Employment Promotion Division, Nairobi, July 1978, 24pp.

63-22 GAKURU, O.N. "Employment creation in light of the new report on the national committee on educational objectives and policies". IDS Working P 349, Jan. 1979, 14pp.
Evaluates the potential contribution the 1976 Report is likely to make in creating employment.

63-23 GHAI, DHARAM, and GODFREY, MARTIN (eds.). Essays on employment in Kenya. East Africa Literature Bureau, Nairobi, 1979, 181pp.
Concerned with the question of technology and employment. Also discusses the roles of technology and education in employment creation. Shows relationship between urban unemployment, rural-urban migration, and education.

63-24 GILLETTE, A.L. Beyond the non-formal fashion: towards educational revolution in Tanzania. University of Massachusetts Center for International Education, Amherst, 1977, 321pp.
Offers an evaluation of Tanzania's efforts to restructure its educational system in order to reflect and reinforce its social philosophy of "Ujamaa" and "self-reliance". Concludes that although the programmes of formal and non-formal education do seem to be converging in aims, methods, and scope, they still are considerably removed from a final merger into a unified, cohesive system.

63-25 HAKE, ANDREW. African metropolis: Nairobi's self-help city. St. Martin's Press, New York, 1977, 284pp.
The thesis of the book is that Nairobi is a "two-faced city" presenting a modern front to the world, with a growing number of its people living in the "back-yard". The people of the "back yard" represent an immense potential for creative development which will determine the future shape of the city, and contribute enormously to the country's well-being. The "self-help city" provides income and a measure of status for hundreds of thousands who would otherwise be in even greater deprivation in over-populated rural areas.

63-26 HARPER, M. "Appropriate consultancy for small business: a Kenyan experiment". Appropriate Technology, Vol. 2, No. 1, May 1975.

Argues that a consultant's most important task is to identify problems; subsequent recommendations for improvements are often virtually self-evident once the problems have been correctly defined and explained to the clients.

63-27 HARPER, MALCOLM. "Sugar and maize meal: cases in inappropriate technology from Kenya". J Mod Afr Studs, Vol. 13, No. 3, Sept. 1975, pp. 501-509.
Examines the agricultural, industrial, and nutritional implications of jaggery and sugar, and plain and sifted maize meal as to the choice of appropriate agricultural and industrial technology. Also appears as IDS Working P 170, June 1974.

63-28 HENNING, PETER H. "The popular sector: a framework for the analysis of urban employment problems in Kenya". IDS Working P 140, Jan. 1974, 17pp.
Defines the popular sector so that it is possible to use three existing models devised for studying the future prospects of less developed countries to analyse that sector in Kenya.

63-29 ___. "Data needs for analysing the urban employment problem in Kenya: a survey proposal". IDS Working P 195, Oct. 1974, 39pp.
The proposed survey is designed to collect information about the types of goods and services produced by the informal sector which are consumed by households with different socio-economic characteristics.

63-30 and HOUSE, W.J. "The problem of slow employment growth in the manufacturing sector of less developed economies: some observations from the Kenyan experience". EA USSC Conference, Kampala, 1974, 18pp.
Offers an alternative to the existing explanations for the slow growth of employment in the manufacturing sector of Kenya.

63-31 HOUSE, WILLIAM J.; KABAGAMBE, DENNIS; and GREEN, TERRY. "The potential for income and employment generation in Kenya's urban informal sector: a proposed survey". IDS Working P 310, April 1977, 31pp.
Emphasizes the search for more information on the operation of the sector's enterprises, particularly their constraints on expansion, so that policies of encouragement can be formulated from a more complete data base.

63-32 HOUSE, WILLIAM J. "Technology and employment in Kenya's informal sector". In C.P.M. Khamala (ed.), Science and

POPULATION, MANPOWER

technology for development. Kenya National Academy, Nairobi, 1980, pp. 107-114.
Surveys from an economist's viewpoint, the characteristics of past choices of technology, their resulting impact on the overall structure of the economy, and the response of large numbers of Kenyans to such a structure.

63-33 ___. "Nairobi's informal sector: a reservoir of dynamic entrepreneurs or a residual pool of surplus labour?". IDS Working P 347, Dec. 1978, 40pp.
Presents a summary of the evolution of dualistic urban labour market models over the last 25 years and suggests an alternative urban dualism which may be relevant to an understanding of the Nairobi informal sector. See also chapter in Tony Killick (ed.), Papers on the Kenyan economy.

63-34 ILCHMAN, WARREN F., and UPHOFF, NORMAN T. "Beyond the economics of labour-intensive development". In Tony Killick (ed.), Papers on the Kenyan economy. Heinemann, London, 1981.

63-35 INTERNATIONAL LABOUR OFFICE. Employment, status and conditions of non-national workers in Africa. Geneva, 1973, 88pp.
Reviews the scope and characteristics of the migration of Africans between African countries; deals with measures and practical policies regarding the employment of African non-nationals and discusses their conditions of employment, work, and life. It also deals with social security and the special position of refugees. Kenya, Uganda, and Tanzania are among the countries discussed.

63-36 KAPLINSKY, RAPHAEL. "Choice of technology in the Kenyan food processing sector, with particular reference to the situation and orientation of technical change: a project outline". IDS Working P 202, Dec. 1974, 19pp.
Areas of policy concern in the project are (a) economic considerations, (b) nutritional considerations, (c) orientation of technical change, and (d) the growth of an African industrial class. The methodology of the research is described and a number of hypotheses are stated.

63-37 KAPLINSKY, RAPHAEL M., and HOFFMANN, K. "Technical change and some British multinationals in Kenya: some global considerations". IDS Working P 250, Nov. 1975, 34pp.
Considers the effect of global operations on generation and acquisition of new technology by subsidiaries of six multinational firms operating in Kenya. Finds that the Kenyan subsidiary operates autonomously from the parent and is isolated from the implications of changes in the global market.

63-38 KAPLINSKY, RAPHAEL M. "Inappropriate products and techniques in UDCs: the case of breakfast foods in Kenya". IDS Working P 335, April 1978, 9pp.
Demonstrates how the choice of product often determines the choice of technology.

63-39 ___. "Inappropriate products and techniques: breakfast food in Kenya". Review of African Political Economy, No. 14, Jan.-April 1979, pp. 90-96.
Attempts to demonstrate that income inequality, consumption demonstration effects, and advertising lead to demand structures that facilitate introduction of inappropriate products and hence techniques of production.

63-40 KENYA, GOVERNMENT OF. The national industrial training scheme for the training of craft apprentices. Government Printer, Nairobi, 1973.

63-41 ___. Report of the select committee on unemployment (Mwicigi). Government Printer, Nairobi, 1970.
Argues that unemployment in Kenya is mainly caused by agricultural policies and practices that have made it difficult for the farmer to be gainfully employed on the land, high income differentials between rural and urban areas, and widespread use of capital intensive technology.

63-42 KING, KENNETH J. "Kenya's educated unemployed: a preliminary report". Manpower and Unemployment Research in Africa, Vol. 7, No. 2, Nov. 1974, pp. 45-63.
Analyses the school-leavers' conditions as regards future employment, tactics, and conditions.

63-43 ___. "Indo-African skill transfer in an East African economy". African Affairs, Vol. 74, No. 294, Jan. 1975, pp. 65-71.
Argues that the Indian processes of apprenticeship have produced a large and dynamic sector of African craft workers in Kenya.

63-44 ___ (ed.). Jobless in Kenya. TransAfrica Publishers, Nairobi, 1975, 91pp.
Records a series of discussions between the editor and six job-seeking Form IV leavers between July and Sept. 1972. It shows how the "job crisis" is perceived by those who are its victims. Also appears as Bureau of Educational Research Monograph No. 1, 1976.

63-45 ___. "Improvisation and machine-making: Kenya". Appropriate Technology, Vol. 2, No. 4, Feb. 1976.

POPULATION, MANPOWER

Argues that those who are provided with loans by the government for agriculture prefer expensive imported machinery rather than to use some of the funds for research in local technology.

63-46 KINYANJUI, KABIRU. "Opportunities for school leavers outside the major towns of Kenya". Rural Africana, No. 25, Fall 1974, pp. 81-90.
Discusses results from the "tracer project" set up in 1970 to trace where school leavers go after finishing school.

63-47 LIVINGSTONE, IAN. "Employment creation by decree: Kenya's third attempt". University of East Anglia Development Studies Discussion Paper No. 71, Norwich, July 1980.
Suggests that the third tripartite agreement between government, employers, and unions will make no difference to employment in the long run but that an apparently more active policy by the Ministry of Labour is likely to have a more permanent effect.

63-48 MAGOBEKO, L. "The 'fundis' of Tanzania: an attempt at improvement". African Environment, Vol. 2, Nos. 1-2, 1976, pp. 150-158.
Discusses small-scale repairmen/handymen.

63-49 MASAKHALIA, Y.F.O. "A note on employment and selected issues in the development of the manufacturing sector". National Seminar on Employment, Mombasa, April 1977.
Highlights relevant industrial development strategies and employment projections.

63-50 MIKKELSEN, BRITHA. "Conditions for industrial training and rural industrial development in Kakamega district, Western province, Kenya". IDS Working P 223, n.d. (ca. June 1975), 24pp.
Presents preliminary results of research which investigated the process of skill formation within rural small-scale industry. Concludes that workshop training in Kakamega at present is unsystematic and limited in scope.

63-51 MUREITHI, LEOPOLD P. "Effectively increasing employment: an agenda for business". IDS Working P 152, March 1974, 12pp.
Concludes that business can play a vital role in combating the problem of unemployment by, for example, sacrificing their privileged fiscal position and by implementing measures to augument their work forces.

63-52 ___. "Factor intensity in Kenya's industrial sector: an

input-ratio analysis". IDS Working P 184, Aug. 1974, 12pp.
Concludes that small-scale firms are less skill intensive and less capital intensive than their larger counterparts.

63-53 ___. "Optimization with a technological constraint". EA USSC Conference, Kampala, Dec. 1974, 13pp.
Examines the implications and consequences of entrepreneurial technological preference within the framework of a traditional constrained optimization model.

63-54 ___. Employment, technology and industrialization in Kenya: a study in development strategy. Ph.D. dissertation, Claremont Graduate School, 1974, 198pp.
Studies the issue of employment from the point of view of factor combination. Factor substitution and factor intensity are investigated, and data are considered both for the whole economy and the manufacturing sector.

63-55 ___. "Scope and salient features of rural employment in Kenya". Kidima, Vol. 5, No. 2, Sept.-Dec. 1979, pp. 14-20.

63-56 MUTAI, C. "Jobless in Nairobi". Ufahamu, Vol. 9, No. 2, 1979, pp. 119-125.
Describes the conditions of the unemployed in Nairobi. Argues that most people come to Nairobi with a hope of getting a white collar clerical job only to find that such jobs are nearly non-existent. So they lower their sights and search for manual work.

63-57 NATIONAL CHRISTIAN COUNCIL OF KENYA. After school what? Further education, training and employment of primary school leavers. Ministry of Health, Nairobi, 1966, 108pp.
Recommends that family planning is essential and that capital formation for job creation should be achieved through personal sacrifice, intelligent saving, and a realistic national incomes policy.

63-58 ONYANGO, J.A. The employment problem in Kenya: trend, causes, and policy implications. M.A. thesis, University of Nairobi, 1978.

63-59 PACK, HOWARD. "The substitution of labour for capital in Kenyan manufacturing". Economic Journal, Vol. 86, No. 341, March 1976, pp. 45-58.
A study of current production methods in selected manufacturing plants. Found considerable variation in feasible efficient production methods, particularly in peripheral operations but that rapid gains in labour productivity were likely to reduce employment requirements in the medium term.

POPULATION, MANPOWER

63-60 PATEL, L.R. "Economic problems and policies in the labour market, Tanganyika". EA USSC Conference, Dec. 1972, 50pp.
Examines the structure of employment and unemployment, and the national wages and income policy. Seeks possible reasons as to why the problem of unemployment has not become as severe as elsewhere in Africa.

63-61 PHILLIPS, DAVID A. "Choice of technology and industrial transformation: the case of the United Republic of Tanzania". Industry and Development, No. 5, 1980, pp. 85-106.

63-62 REMPEL, HENRY. The determinants and implications of urban unemployment in Kenya: 1964-1968. IDS (Unnumbered paper), n.d. (ca. Dec. 1969), 25pp.
Attempts to specify and quantitatively estimate the underlying determinants of rural-to-urban migratory behaviour. Secondary objectives are to test hypotheses regarding temporary versus permanent migration and the process of selecting employees from a given stock of urban unemployed.

63-63 ___. "The informal sector". IDS Interdisciplinary Urban Seminar, University of Nairobi, March 1974, 8pp.
Demarcates the boundary between sources of income in the formal and the informal sectors, both legitimate and illegitimate. Gives reasons as to why one should analyse the sectors in relation to each other.

63-64 REMPEL, HENRY, and HOUSE, WILLIAM J. The Kenya employment Problem. Oxford University Press, Nairobi, 1978, 194pp.
Analysis of the modern sector labour market. Focuses on the responsiveness of the wage structure to changes in labour supply; the employment effect of changes in the wage structure; and the feedback effects on labour productivity brought about by changes in wages and employment.

63-65 RODGERS, G.B. Urban employment in the 1980s: Kenya and the Philippines. Population and Employment Working Paper No. 63, ILO, Geneva, 1978, 12pp.

63-66 RWEYEMAMU, R.A. "Income and employment effects of coffee production and marketing in Tanzania". Food Research Institute, Stanford University, Nov. 1972.

63-67 SABOT, R.H. "The meaning and measurement of urban surplus labour". Oxford Economic Papers, Vol. 29, No. 3, Nov. 1977, pp. 389-411.
Attempts to clarify the definition of urban surplus labour and to measure its magnitude, using Tanzanian data. Finds a

total surplus in Tanzanian towns equal to about 20 per cent of the urban labour force, made up in roughly equal proportions of open unemployed and employed surplus labour.

63-68 ___. The social costs of urban surplus labour. OECD, Paris, 1977, 103pp.
An assessment of the costs of urban unemployment in Tanzania. Discussion of the effect of demographic and educational characteristics of the unemployed on access to transfers, levels of productivity, and length of time without work. Concludes that the resource costs of urban surplus labour do not appear to be very high in Tanzania and that 10 per cent is the best single estimate of the level of open unemployment.

63-69 ___. "Open unemployment and the employed compound of surplus labour". In K.S. Kim, R.B. Mabele, and M.J. Schultheis (eds.), Papers on the political economy of Tanzania. Heinemann, Nairobi, 1979, pp. 261-271.
Defines and analyses unemployed in terms of sex and dependency status, age and migrant status, and defines the surplus labour found among the urban unemployed.

63-70 SCHMIDT, H., and SWOBODA, REINHOLD. Labour requirement availability and economics of mechanisation. Ministry of Agriculture, Nairobi. 1979, 184pp.
The study was carried out (in Kisii district) mainly to assist agricultural extension officers in the field, and includes a summary of labour requirements in well-managed, mechanized farms. Meant to help improve the understanding of complex labour problems in highly diversified small-farm operations.

63-71 SENGA, WILLIAM M. Wage and foreign investment effects on employment in the East African industrial sector: special reference to Kenya, 1954-1968. Ph.D. dissertation, Claremont Graduate School, 1971.

63-72 STEELE, DAVID. Wages, employment, output and consumption in Kenya. IDS (unnumbered paper), n.d. (ca. May 1970), 6pp.
Concludes from a set of regressions that output, however weak, is still the most powerful stimulant to employment. Appended to this study are comments by L.D. Smith and M.G. Phelps.

63-73 STEWART, FRANCES (ed.). Employment, income distribution and development. F. Cass, London, 1975, 186pp.
Includes K. King, "Skill acquisition in the informal sector of an African economy: the Kenya case", and Walter

POPULATION, MANPOWER

Elkan, "The relation between tourism and employment in Kenya and Tanzania".

63-74 ___. Technology and underdevelopment. Macmillan, London, 1977.
Includes Kenyan case studies of maize grinding and cement block manufacture.

63-75 ___. "Employment and the choice of technique: two case studies in Kenya". In D. Ghai and M. Godfrey (eds.), Essays on employment in Kenya. Kenya Literature Bureau, Nairobi. 1979, pp. 47-74.
The case studies are intended to shed some empirical light on the relation between the level and growth of employment with choice of technique.

63-76 ___. "The tripartite agreements in Kenya". In D. Ghai and M. Godfrey (eds.), Essays on employment in Kenya. Kenya Literature Bureau, Nairobi, 1979, 155-181.
Concerned with the 1970 agreement and its consequences; a comparison with the 1964 agreement is made.

63-77 STEWART, I.G. (ed.). Economic development and structural change. Edinburgh U.P., 1969, 193pp.
Includes J.B.K. Hunter, "The development of the labour market in Kenya".

63-78 TSCHANNERL, G. "Employment and population in Tanzania". Maji Maji, No. 23, 1975, pp. 9-17.

63-79 WALLACE, TINA. "Working in rural Buganda: a study of the occupational activities of young people in rural villages". EA USSC Conference, Nairobi, Dec. 1972, 48pp.
Defines the central concepts of formal and informal employment, and experience in one village in rural Buganda during a two-year period.

63-80 WEEKS, JOHN. "Imbalance between the centre and periphery and the 'employment crisis' in Kenya". In I. Oxaal, T. Barnett, and D. Booth (eds.), Beyond the sociology of development. Routledge and Kegan Paul, London and Boston, 1975, pp. 86-104.
Attempts to explain the roots of the employment problem in Kenya by analysing the distribution of income. Concludes that there exists gross income inequality in Kenya. Identifies the mechanisms which in a dynamic context channel the flow of wealth into a few areas and hands.

63-81 ___. "Employment growth in Kenya manufacturing: another look at labour absorption". In D. Ghai and M. Godfrey (eds.),

Essays on employment in Kenya. Kenya Literature Bureau, Nairobi, 1979, pp. 7-20.
Scrutinizes the employment and income distribution implications of the absolute and relative growth of the large-scale manufacturing sector.

63-82 WEEKS, S.G. "Where are all the jobs? The informal sector in Bugisu, Uganda". Afr Rev, Vol. 3, No. 1, 1972, pp. 245-284.
Concerned with how young people in a village cluster in South Bugisu, Uganda, move in the world of work. Describes and interprets the range of informal occupational activities that are open to and utilized by these rural youth. Also examines how these occupational activities relate to the various factors that influence movement into and between jobs (age, sex, status, education, family background, location of jobs, patterns of assistance).

63-83 WESTLEY, SIDNEY B. (ed.). "The informal sector in Kenya". IDS Occ P 25, Jan. 1978, 195pp.
Collection of papers presented at IDS Workshop held in Nov. 1976. Authors and titles are listed below.

1. Westley, Sidney B. and Kabagambe, Dennis. "Introduction to the Workshop Papers".
2. Muench, H. Louis. "A Final Demand Approach to the Informal Sector and Implications for Public Policies".
3. House, J. William. "The Urban Informal Sector: Its Potential for Generating Income and Employment Opportunities in Keyna".
4. Killick, Tony. "The Informal Sector and Development Strategy in Kenya".
5. Kabwegyere, B.T. "Institutional Bottle-Necks and the Growth of the Informal Section in Kenya".
6. Harvie, H.C. "Some Basic Ideas on the Informal Sector in Kenya".
7. Okoth-Ogendo, O. "Data Collection on the Urban 'Informal' Sector".
8. Marchant, T. "Data Collection Methodology Used in the Rural Areas".
9. Kaplinsky, R. "Appropor ate Technology and Political Economy: A Case Study of the Bread Industry in Kenya".
10. Mukui, T.J. "Anatomy of the Urban Informal Sector: A Study of Food Kiosks and Shoeblacks in Nairobi".
11. Muller, S.M. "Chawama, A good Place in Lusaka: A Description of an Informal Settlement".
12. Hoek-Smit, C. Marja. "Institutional Constraints in the Development of Informal Housing Areas".
13. Muench, Carolyn. "Planning for Informal Sector Enterprises".

POPULATION, MANPOWER

14. Lee, Michael. "Constraints on the Expansion of the Informal Manufacturing Sector--Some Thoughts".

63-84 WILLIAMS, DAVID. "National planning and the choice of technology: the case of textiles in Tanzania". In K.S. Kim, R.B. Mabele, and M.J. Schultheis (eds.), Papers on the political economy of Tanzania. Heinemann, Nairobi, 1979, pp. 41-46.
Evaluates bureaucratic choice of techniques and its impact on policy. Initially appeared as ERB Paper 75.12.

63-85 WINTERFORD, DAVID B. Creative development: the policital economy of the urban informal sector in Kenya. Ph.D. dissertation, University of British Columbia, 1979.
DAI, Vol. 40, p. 5995-A.

63-86 WUYTS, M.E. "The choice of techniques: some critical questions". ERB Paper 74.3, University of Dar-es-Salaam, 1974, 52pp.
Investigates the theoretical underpinning of some of the methods of choosing techniques and discusses the usefulness of the methods as a solution for the development problem.

64--Manpower and educational planning; Africanization

64-1 ANDERSON, LASCELLES F. High level manpower and development alternatives for the Tanzanian economy. Ph.D. dissertation, New School for Social Research, 1972.

64-2 ___. "Manpower and economic planning: a linear programming model for Tanzania". Social and Economic Studies, Vol. 24, No. 1, March 1975, pp. 15-45.
Argues that full Tanzanianization of the labour force in skilled categories may not be a justifiable policy goal and that, as growth rates increase and as foreign aid becomes more difficult to acquire, the skill constraint becomes even more critical if certain patterns of consumption have to be maintained.

64-3 BROOKE-SMITH, R. "The politics of high level manpower supply in Tanzania". Comparative Education, Vol. 14, No. 2, June 1978, pp. 143-151.

64-4 CLAYTON, E.S. "Programming rural employment opportunities in Kenya". International Labour Review, Vol. 112, Nos. 2-3, Aug.-Sept. 1975, pp. 149-161.
Provides estimates of the employment potential of alternative policies for the intensification of the smallholding sector in Nyeri, Kenya. Also appears in Tony Killick (ed.), Papers on the Kenyan economy.

64-5 COURT, DAVID. "East African higher education from the community standpoint". Higher Education, Vol. 6, Feb. 1977, pp. 45-66.

64-6 CURRIE, JANICE. Secondary school selection and occupational placement in Uganda. Ph.D. dissertation, University of Chicago, 1975.

64-7 DINWIDDY, BRUCE. Promoting African enterprise. Croom Helm and Overseas Development Institute, London, 1974, 124pp.
The study is focused on the instruments used for helping small-scale African businessmen to establish and run their own enterprises. Discusses the feeling of African governments as regards foreign control of economic activity in their countries.

64-8 FORD, R.J.C. "The village polytechnic programme in Kenya". International Labour Review, Vol. 111, No. 4, April 1975, pp. 307-320.
Argues that the basic problem in the implementation of the programme has been to develop a training system that really is geared to local work opportunities and avoids the usual mistakes of institutionalized learning.

64-9 GECAU, J.K. "Personnel training and development in East African industries". International Institute for Labour Studies East African Seminar on Labour Problems in Economic Development, Nairobi, April 1967.
Gives the distinction between development and training, discusses some basic conditions which are necessary for successful training, then looks at management development with respect to the British-American Tobacco Company experience.

64-10 GREAVES, M.J. The social and educational backgrounds and career paths of African business managers in Kenya. Ph.D. dissertation, Edinburgh University, 1978.

64-11 INTERNATIONAL INSTITUTE FOR EDUCATIONAL PLANNING. Manpower aspects of educational planning. UNESCO, Paris, 1968, 265pp.
Includes C. Hunter, "Manpower and educational needs in the traditional sector with special reference to East Africa", and Robert L. Thomas, "Implementing a manpower programme in a developing country" (Tanzania).

64-12 KELLER, EDMOND J., Jr. Education, manpower, and national development: secondary schooling and socialization in Kenya. Ph.D. dissertation, University of Wisconsin, Madison, 1974.

64-13 KHAMIS, ISHAW A. Labour economics and manpower planning in

POPULATION, MANPOWER

Tanzania. Kenya Literature Bureau, Nairobi, 1978, 141pp.
Discusses the economics of labour in Tanzanian getting. Discusses topics such as the labour market, wage structure and wage policies in Tanzania, manpower planning, the national educational plan, etc.

64-14 KING, KENNETH. "The politics of training and Africanisation in Nairobi's industrial area: a perspective from Kenya's tenth year of independence". Centre of African Educational Studies. Edinburgh University, June 1973, 20pp.
Critically looks at the role played by foreign companies in training African local manpower in Kenya. Concludes that their role has been minimal in the first ten years of political independence.

64-15 KINYANJUI, KABIRU; MIGOT-ADHOLA, S.E.; and ANAMINYI, PETER. "Notes on the evolution of overseas training policy in Kenya". IDS Working P 361, Feb. 1980, 27pp.
Examines the factors which have influenced the emergence of overseas education and training policy. Concludes that the impact of overseas training on development cannot be isolated from an evaluation of local instiutions of higher education.

64-16 MAMDANI, MAHMOOD. "Class struggles in Uganda". Review of African Policital Economy, No. 4, Nov. 1975, pp. 26-61.
Focuses on the conflict between the Asian commercial bourgeoisie and the African petit-bourgeoisie and the growing fragmentation of the latter since independence.

64-17 MKANDAWIRE, P.T. Development planning and wage employment: a review of practice and issues in six Eastern African countries. International Institute for Labour Studies (No. IEME 3075), Geneva, 1975, 50pp.

64-18 MUTUNGI, O.K. Business organizations and the "Africanization" of commerce and industry in Kenya. J.S.D. thesis, Yale Law School, 1974, 299pp.
Examines the reasons and forces which led the Kenya government to pursue an "Africanization" policy of the country's business, measures taken to carry out that objective, repercussions arising from such measures, and business organizations' propriety in the execution of that policy.

64-19 MWANIKI, N. "Public policy and political development: the implementation of the Africanization policy through ICDC's small industrial loans scheme, 1961-1973". IDS Working P 295, Jan. 1977, 45pp.

Pays particular attention to the incidence of default among ICDC loan recipients as an obstacle to policy implementation and identifies contradictions inherent in the process of Africanization.

64-20 OCHIENG, E.O. "High level manpower planning in Uganda". The Uganda Economic Journal, Vol. 2, No. 2, Dec. 1972, pp. 225-246.
Finds that the quality of paper plans is low and that manpower plans have not been properly implemented.

64-21 ___. "Towards effective high level manpower planning in Uganda". EA USSC Conference, Kampala, 1974, 15pp.
Concludes that the educational system has so far succeeded in producing more secondary school leavers than the economy needs but has failed to produce manpower with the right skills, in correct numbers and at the correct time; therefore the economy has still to depend on expatriates and technical assistance personnel.

64-22 SHEFFIELD, J.R. "The challenges and the role of non-formal education in Eastern Africa". Education in Eastern Africa, Vol. 4, No. 2, 1974, pp. 185-197.
Considers how non-formal education can link with formal education in useful ways and help to solve the problems of unemployment and urban migration.

64-23 STABLER, ERNEST. "Kenya and Tanzania: strategies and realities in education and development". African Affairs, Vol. 78, No. 310, Jan. 1979, pp. 33-56.
Analyses how the educational systems in the two countries have responded to the social, political and economic changes in the post-independence era.

64-24 "Tanzania: the manpower muddle". Jenga, No. 17, 1980. Dar-es-Salaam, 1980.
The theme is that the production of manpower plan goes hand in hand with practical action in the training field. Relates the objectives and problems of manpower planning and tries to examine the accomplishments, or lack of it, of this practice in the world and Tanzania in particular.

64-25 TANZANIA, GOVERNMENT OF. Annual manpower report to the President, 1972. Manpower Planning Division, Ministry of Economic Affairs and Development Planning, Dar-es-Salaam, Dec. 1972, 173pp.
Projects demand and supply for high and middle level skills up to 1990. Looks at the need to establish faculties

of Engineering and Veterinary Science at the University of Dar-es-Salaam.

64-26 TEMU, P.E. "The employment of foreign consultants in Tanzania: its value and limitations". Afr Rev, Vol. 3, No. 1, 1973, pp. 69-84.

64-27 TWADDLE, MICHAEL (ed.). Expulsion of a minority: essays on Ugandan Asians. Athlone Press, London, 1975, 240pp.
Includes M.A. Tribe, "Economic aspects of the expulsion of Asians from Uganda".

64-28 VINNAI, VOLKER. "The Africanization of commerce in Kenya". Vierteljahresberichte, Vol. 55, March 1974, pp. 15-34.

64-29 WACIRAH, H.K.M. "The private sector in Kenya--some observations". Journal of the Kenya Institute of Administration, Jan. 1976, pp. 16-24.
Concerned with Kenyanization in both public and private sectors.

64-30 WIESE, ROY F. "Manpower planning and the provision of training". IDS Working P 222, June 1975, 16pp.
Considers the importance of labour market data as inputs into the planning of industrial training. Data and survey activities of the Kenya government are considered and suggestions made for possible improvements through reorganization and interagency cooperation.

64-31 ___. "The structure of industrial training in Kenya and the role of the Directorate of Industrial Training". IDS Disc P 248, Feb. 1977, 48pp.
Argues that it is not only skills which should be marketable but the ability to learn skills, so that if institutional training can provide this ability it may be of direct value to the firm in reducing the time cost of providing job training. Earlier version appeared as IDS Working P 237 in Aug. 1975.

65--Science and technology, research, and transfer of technology

65-1 CHAGULA, W.K. "The utilization of science and technology for development". East African Academy, Nairobi, 1977, 35pp.

65-2 KHAMALA, C.P.M. (ed.). Science and technology for development: Proceedings of the first seminar of the Kenya National Academy, March 1978. Kenya National Academy for Advancement of Arts and Sciences, Nairobi, 1980, 215pp.

Compilation of twenty-seven papers presented at this seminar.

65-3 KHIMULU, P.J. Technology transfer aspects of transnational corporations' direct investment in the industrialization of Kenya. D.B.A. dissertation, United States International University, 1980, 173pp.
DAI, Vol. 41, p. 1685-A.

65-4 KIMUYU, P.K., and MAITHA, J. "Technological development and patents: the less developed countries' case". In C.P.M. Khamala (ed.), Science and technology for development, Kenya National Academy, 1980.
Paper presented at the March 1978 seminar.

65-5 KUUYA, P.M. "Transfer of technology: an overview of the Tanzania case". Africa Development, Vol. 2, No. 2, April-June 1977, pp. 47-69.
Concludes that technological transfers from development countries can only be useful if they are used in the promotion of objectives that serve the majority of people and that without Tanzania's own effort the transfers cannot lead to the reduction of dependence. Also appeared as ERB Paper 77.3, Dar-es-Salaam.

65-6 LANGDON, STEVEN. "Technology transfer by multinational corporations in Africa: effects on the economy". Africa Development, Vol. 2, No. 2, April-June 1977, pp. 95-112.
Drawing heavily on evidence from Kenya, argues that MNC technology transfer to Africa can generate social benefits in the shape of spread effects of technological know-how among Africans, that its financial cost is high, and that it generates social costs such as frustrating indigenous entrepreneurship.

65-7 LEMUNGE, M. "Science and technology for the building and construction industry". Utafiti, Vol. 4, No. 1, 1979, pp. 27-39.
Looks into the problems of science and technology in the construction industry in Tanzania. Discusses the question of research in the development of building materials, and points out the inadequate system of disseminating research findings to users, particularly in rural areas.

65-8 MITSCHKE-COLLANDE, P.V. "Research for indigenous technology in Tanzania". Symposium on the new international economic order, University of Dar-es-Salaam, April 1978, 14pp.

65-9 MSANGI, A.S., and CHAGULA, W.K. "Development of research

sciences and technology in Tanzania". Utafiti, Vol. 4, No. 1, 1979, pp. 15-25.
Analyses some of the problems of developing science and technology in Tanzania. Argues that useful and applicable results of scientific research and technological development should be applied to solve development problems.

65-10 MUREITHI, L.P. "Choice of technology and the promotion of technological capability in Kenya". In C.P.M. Khamala (ed.), Science and technology for development. Kenya National Academy, 1980, pp. 16-36.
Explores Kenya's experience in fostering technological capability and the prospect of enhancing the country's stance in this sphere. Particular attention is paid to the machinery industry and technical manpower development.

65-11 RAJAN, NIZAR. "Arrangements for the transfer of operative technology to developing countries: case study of Kenya". IDS (unnumbered paper) n.d. (ca. May 1974), 25pp.
Presents the terms of reference and an analytical framework for analysing the nature of the process of transfer of technology from industrially advanced nations to Kenya. The analysis envisaged is limited to the Kenyan manufacturing sector.

65-12 TODARO, MICHAEL P. "Some thoughts on the transfer of technology from developed to less developed nations". EA USSC Conference, Nairobi, 1969.
Attempts to analyse the nature and mechanism of technological transfer from the MDCs to LDCs in view of whether it is for the benefit of the LDCs with their diametrically opposite resource configurations.

65-13 TURYAHIKAYO-RUGYEMA, B. "The problems of technological transfer in Uganda: a case study". Uganda Journal, Vol. 39, 1980, pp. 27-33.
Attempts to define what is meant by technology and its transfer, and elaborates upon the need for modern technology in Uganda and the problems involved in the transfer.

65-14 WANGWE, S. "Transfer of technology: issues and policies". Utafiti, Vol. 4, No. 1, 1979, pp. 3-12.
Reviews the major issues of transfer of technology. Then proceeds to discuss some issues and policies that may be necessary to build up a strong technological base in developing countries with emphasis on the role of the engineering sector. Argues that the problems of transfer of technology are largely a result of the wide technological gap that exists between underdeveloped and advanced countries.

7--SOCIAL ECONOMICS

70--Economics of education

70-1 BARKAN, JOEL D. An African dilemma: university students, development and politics in Ghana, Tanzania and Uganda. Oxford University Press, New York, 1976, 259pp.
Argues that because of their fundamental desire for material security and their propensity to assume technocratic roles to realize this goal, students pose dilemmas for the societies in which they live.

70-2 BENNAARS, G. "The Namutamba project: organizational decision-making in education". EA USSC Conference, Kampala, 1974, 19pp.
Concludes that the social scientist's expertise will be recognized by policy makers if he reciprocates and is willing to recognize the expertise of others, including that of the politically-oriented policy makers.

70-3 BIGALA, J.C.B. "Educational research in East Africa". Education in Eastern Africa, Vol. 5, No. 2, 1975, pp. 123-130.
Research into methods of improving educational selection in secondary schools in East Africa. Looks at the appropriateness of the subjects studies to manpower requirements. Analyses mobility within the teaching profession and the extent of teacher wastage.

70-4 BIGSTEN, ARNE, and COLLIER, PAUL. "Education innovation and income in rural Kenya". IDS Working P 369, Nairobi, 1980, 14pp.
Analyses the relationship between education and smallholder income. Shows that education has a strong and significant effect on incomes from regular employment, such incomes in turn have a strong and significant impact upon smallholder innovation, which has a strong and significant impact upon farm income.

70-5 CAMERON, J. "Education, individuality and community: education for self reliance in Tanzania". British Journal of Education Studies, Vol. 28, No. 2, 1980, pp. 100-111.

70-6 CASHMORE, G.M. Primary school leavers: a study of 197 leavers in one area of western Uganda. M.A. thesis, Nottingham, 1968, 93pp.

70-7 CHAU, T.N., and CAILLODS, FRANCOISE. Educational policy and its financial implications in Tanzania. International

SOCIAL ECONOMICS

Institute for Educational Planning Country Case Studies No. 4, UNESCO Press, 1975.

70-8 COLLIER, P., and BIGSTEN, A. "A model of educational expansion and labour market adjustments applied to Kenya". OIES Bull, ca. 1981.

70-9 COURT, DAVID. "Village Polytechnique leavers: the Maseno story". Rural Africana, No. 25, Fall 1974, pp. 91-100.
It is evident from the study of the Maseno Village Polytechnique that the majority of the polytechnic leavers secured jobs. However, the chances of a male leaver getting a job are higher than those of a female leaver.

70-10 ___. "The education system as a response to inequality in Tanzania and Kenya". J Mod Afr Studs, Vol. 14, No. 4, Dec. 1976, pp. 661-690.
Contrasts the condition of formal education in Kenya and Tanzania. Argues that the striking differences stem from different ideological responses to problems posed by conditions of inequality.

70-11 ___. "Scholarships and university development in Kenya and Tanzania". Higher Education, Vol. 8, 1979, pp. 535-552.
Examines the impact of the Rockefeller Foundation Scholarship programme to train university staff in Kenya and Tanzania.

70-12 ___. "The idea of social science in East Africa: an aspect of the development of higher education". Minerva, Vol. 17, No. 2, 1979, pp. 392-427.
Argues that the development of social science in Kenya and Tanzania has been inhibited by the assumption that it should always be relevant to policy-making.

70-13 ___. "The development ideal in higher education: experience of Kenya and Tanzania". Higher Education, Vol. 9, 1980, pp. 657-680.
The experience of the 1970s suggests that universities are not the most appropriate institutions to provide practical leadership in non-pedagogic development projects or policy-making. However, the universities did build up a significant indigenous teaching and research capacity during that time.

70-14 CURRIE, J., and VAN L. MAAS, J. "Uganda's 1971 secondary school leavers: who were they and what are they doing one year later". EA USSC Conference, Nairobi, 1972.

70-15 CURRIE, JANICE. "Has the die been cast? A study of Ugandan secondary school recruitment patterns before and after independence". Rural Africana, No. 25, Fall 1974, pp. 47-64.
Argues that educational facilities in Uganda were concentrated in the Ganda region around Lake Victoria as a result of the colonial administrative policy. The skewed distribution of educational facilities has led to skewed açcess to job opportunities.

70-16 ELKAN, WALTER. "Out-of school education and training for primary-school leavers in rural Kenya: a proposal". International Labour Review, Vol. 104, No. 3, 1971, pp. 205-216.
Discusses the lack of provision for "topping up" and extending what has been learned at primary school and argues that it is a waste of scarce resources to give people a primary education unless what has been taught is retained. Recommends youth centres as places for further training. (See also Manpower and Unemployment Research in Africa, Vol. 4, No. 1, 1971, pp. 17-28).

70-17 EVANS, E.B. Kenyan secondary school students: a view toward the future. Ph.D. dissertation, University of California, Berkeley, 1974.

70-18 FAO and UNIVERSITY OF NAIROBI DEPARTMENT OF SOCIOLOGY. Mbooni integrated rural educational project: summary of findings and recommendations, Mbooni community survey, November 1974 to January, 1975. FAO (Access No. 32537), Rome, 1975, 45pp.

70-19 FIELDS, GARY S. "Private returns to investment in higher levels of education in Kenya". University of Michigan Center for Research on Economic Development Discussion Paper No. 19, Ann Arbor, 1972, 16pp.
A treatment of education as a profitable personal investment. Considers the effect of some recent developments on private rates of return to higher levels of schooling.

70-20 ___. "Higher education and income distribution in a less developed country". Oxford Economic Papers, Vol. 27, No. 2, July 1975, pp. 245-259.
Finds that Kenya's higher education system is inequitable inter-generationally, since it favours the chindren of the well-to-do, whether measured by income class or various indices of socio-economic status.

70-21 ___. "The private demand for education in relation to labour market conditions in less developed countries". In D. Ghai

SOCIAL ECONOMICS

and M. Godfrey (eds.), Essays on employment in Kenya. Kenya Literature Bureau, Nairobi, 1979, pp. 107-130.
Constructs a model of the demand for education in relation to labour market conditions in less developed countries. Demonstrates that under various labour market situations the sustained private demand for education is quite rational and can be explained by the net private benefits which the educated individual receives in the labour market.

70-22 FISSENA, TEGENE. "Finance of education in Ethiopia, Kenya and Tanzania". Addis Ababa University Department of Economics, Addis Ababa, 1977, 37pp.

70-23 GAKURU, O.N. "Pre-primary education and access to educational opportunities in Nairobi". IDS Working P 321, Sept. 1977, 24pp.
Studies the structural links between pre-primary and primary education in Nairobi.

70-24 GEOFFREY, E.M., and MUTISO, G.C.M. Politics, economics, and technical training: a Kenyan case study. Kenyan Literature Bureau, Nairobi, 1979, 201pp.
A multidisciplinary approach to cover Kenya's development of the Harambee movement and training in technical areas. Gives a case study of Kiambu Institute of Science and Technology.

70-25 GORHAM, A.B. "Developments in primary education in Kajiado district 1963-1975". IDS Working P 297, Jan. 1977, 44pp.
Traces the expansion of first-level educational facilities in Kajiado distruct since independence.

70-26 HALPENNY, P. "Economic determinants and educational policies: the irrelevance of experts". EA USSC Conference, Kampala, 1974, 29pp.
Suggests that educational policies have been determined by the system of economic relationships in Uganda. Concludes that these relationships have not changed greatly in the past 70 years.

70-27 HARTWELL, A.S. "Non-formal education in Uganda: a survey of government out-of-school education programmes". EA USSC Conference, Dar-es-Salaam, 1973.

70-28 HEIJNEN, J.D. "Primary education and proposed agricultural experiment in Mwanza district". BRALUP Research Paper No. 6, University of Dar-es-Salaam, Aug. 1969, 27pp.
A study of the influence of primary school education on

agricultural practices. After comparing non-educated farmers and Standard VII farmers in Mwanza district, it is shown that there was little difference in farming knowledge and techniques between the two groups. A plan is suggested in which students would improve their farming knowledge in the classroom and apply it by working in the fields together with the non-school-going youths.

70-29 HEYNEMAN, STEPHEN P. "Relationship between the primary school community and academic achievement in Uganda". J Dev Areas, Vol. 11, No. 2, Jan. 1977, pp. 245-259.
Argues that contrary to the belief that economic development of the community would be positively associated with a school's academic performance, in a Ugandan sample the two sets of variables are negatively correlated.

70-30 HINKLE, RODNEY J. Educational problems and policies in post-independence Tanzania. Ed.D. dissertation, Columbia University, 1970.

70-31 HINZEN, H., and HUNDSDORFER, V.H. (eds.). The Tanzanian experience: education for liberation and development. UNESCO Institute for Education, Hamburg; Evans, London, 1979, 266pp.
Attempts to elucidate the concept of lifelong education in the Tanzanian context, that is, how education should liberate and develop not only the individual but the whole nation.

70-32 HIRTI, K. "School education and underdevelopment in Tanzania". Maji Maji, No. 12, 1973, pp. 1-22.

70-33 HOPCRAFT, PETER NORMAN. Human resources and technical skills in agricultural development: an economic evaluation of educative investments in Kenya's small farm sector. Ph.D. dissertation, Stanford University, 1974, 248pp.
Examines the production relations of the farm and tests the extent to which educative variables can be shown to affect economic performance. Argues that applied educative services to farmers have been relatively neglected while the development of formal schooling has, from the economic point of view, been grossly overemphasized. His results are briefly summarized in IDS Working P 279 (1976).

70-34 HYDEN, GORAN. "Co-operative education and co-operative development: the Tanzanian experience". Agricultural Administration, Vol. 1, No. 1, Jan. 1974, pp. 35-50.

SOCIAL ECONOMICS

70-35 ISHUMI, ABEL G. Education and development in theory and practice. East African Literature Bureau, Nairobi, 1976, 107pp.

70-36 ISHUMI, A.G., and MMARI, G.R.V. (eds.). The educational process: theory and practice with a focus on Tanzania and other countries. Department of Education, University of Dar-es-Salaam, 1978, 374pp.

70-37 KAAYK, J. Education estrangement and adjustment: a study among pupils and school leavers in Bukumbi, a rural community in Tanzania. Mouton, The Hague, 1976.

Looks at the contribution of primary education to rural development in Tanzania and compares the expectations of pupils at school about their future with the day-to-day experiences of school leavers who find themselves obliged to fit into their local communities.

70-38 KELLER, EDMOND J., Jr. Education, manpower and development: the impact of educational policy in Kenya. Kenya Literature Bureau, Nairobi, 1980, 251pp.

Assesses the impact of Kenya's secondary education policy over the first decade of independence. Concerned with policy outcomes (individual and societal) and provided insights into other aspects of the development policy process.

70-39 KING, K.J. "Productive labour and the school system: contradictions in the training of artisans in Kenya". Comparative Education, Vol. 10, No. 3, Oct. 1974, pp. 181-191.

Concludes that the Kenyan institutional context, whether classified as formal or non-formal, appears inherently unable to prepare people for skilled self-employment.

70-40 ___. "Education and ethnicity in the Rift Valley: Masaai, Kipsigis and Kikuyu in the school system". Education in Eastern Africa, Vol. 5, No. 2, 1975, pp. 197-217.

Focuses on the educational impact of population movement into old white reserves upon the schools of two districts in the Rift Valley, Narok and Kajiado.

70-41 KINYANJUI, KABIRU. "Secondary school strikes: the art of blaming the victim". IDS Disc P 243, Nov. 1976, 33pp.

Discusses the causes of secondary school strikes which took place throughout Kenya in 1974. Four case studies are presented as a basis for discussion of the nature of secondary school strikes. Finally, some changes are recommended in the educational system which should foster a better climate for learning in Kenyan schools.

70-42 ___. "Education for rural development in Kenya: a critical note". IDS Disc P 264, Jan. 1979, 18pp.
Emphasizes the subordinate role that education plays in the process of employment creation and national development, and attributes this to the structure of the political economy rather than the educational system *per se*.

70-43 ___. The political economy of educational inequality: a study of the roots of education inequality in colonial and post-colonial Kenya. Ph.D. dissertation, Harvard University, 1979, 350pp.
DAI, Vol. 40, p. 6021-A.

70-44 KIPKORIR, B.E. The Alliance High School and the origins of the Kenya African elite 1926-1962. Ph.D. dissertation, Cambridge University, 1969.

70-45 KUHANGA, NICHOLAS. "Education and self-reliance in Tanzania: a national perspective". Development Dialogue, No. 2, 1978, pp. 37-50.
Examines the strategy used in Tanzania in providing an education that leads to self reliance.

70-46 LEMA, A.A. "Alternative in education; Tanzania: education for self-reliance". Vienna Institute for Development Occasional Paper 74/5, Vienna, Austria, 45pp.
Presents a picture of the new and radical educational policies which Tanzania has adopted and compares these to Kenya's more traditional attitude toward education.

70-47 LINNE, OLGA. "An evaluation of Kenya Science Teachers College, Phase II 1970-72". Scandinavian Institute of African Studies Research Report No. 15, Uppsala.
Attempts to determine whether the college, sponsored by the Swedish International Development Authority, is meeting the objectives set for it by the Kenya Government.

70-48 LOCKHART, LAWRENCE. "The economics of nine years' education for all". In Tony Killick (ed.), Papers on the Kenyan economy. Heinemann, London, 1981.

70-49 MALIYAMKONO, T.L. (ed.). The impact of overseas training on development. East Africa Publications, Arusha, 1979.

70-50 ___. Educational reform for development: a review of the Tanzanian approach. World Bank, Washington, D.C., 1976.

70-51 MBILINYI, M.J. "Attitudes, expectations and the decision to

SOCIAL ECONOMICS

educate in rural Tanzania". BRALUP Research Paper No. 3.1, University of Dar-es-Salaam, Nov. 1973.

70-52 ___. "The problem of unequal access to primary education in Tanzania". Rural Africana, No. 25, Fall 1974, pp. 5-28.
Summarizes the works done by K. Kinyanjui, D. Court, and himself on access to education in East Africa. From their works it is evident that access to formal and informal education at all levels depended on the sex of the individual, family background, the traditional social stratification among the peasants and traders, and the area from which the individual comes.

70-53 ___. "Peasants' education in Tanzania". Afr Rev, Vol. 6, No. 2, 1976, pp. 167-253.
Analyses Tanzania's educational reforms in relation to the specific historical and material conditions in Tanzania. Explores education policy and practice, historical origin of the reform, sources of contradictions in education practice and policy, and implications of the reforms for peasants.

70-54 MLEKWA, V.M. "Policy and practice in adult education: a district case study". Utafiti, Vol. 1, No. 2, 1976, pp. 149-166.
Evaluates the extent to which adult education policy has been implemented in Tanzania since the Adult Education year (1970), with focus on one district.

70-55 MORRISON, DAVID R. Education and political development: the Tanzanian case. Ph.D. dissertation, Sussex, 1970, 632pp.
Explores the relationship between national politics and formal education in mainland Tanzania. It is a study of educational policies that affect the structure of political conflict and authority, and the development of political capacity.

70-56 ___. Education and politics in Africa--the Tanzanian case. C. Hurst and Co., London, 1976, 352pp.
The study explores the circular relationship between formal education and politics in mainland Tanzania. Examines the politics of education in relation to social structure, occupational integration, and political socialization.

70-57 MSEKWA, P., and MALIYAMKONO, T.L. The experiments in educational policy formation in Tanzania before and after Arusha. University of Dar-es-Salaam, 1977, 80pp.

70-58 MUKRAS, M.S. Kenya: the provincial distribution of secondary education services, 1964-1972. Ph.D. dissertation, University

of Toronto, 1976.
DAI, Vol. 39, p. 4382-A.

70-59 ___. "Comparative regional availability of secondary school educational opportunities in Kenya". Kenyan Economic Association Annual Conference, Nairobi, 1977, 26pp.
Finds that the regional distribution of various secondary school educational facilities is inequitable, and the distribution shows no changes in the direction of greater equality.

70-60 MUSYOKI, RACHEL N. "Non-formal education and the levels of living: a study of factors affecting the quality of life for rural families in Mbooni: a research proposal". IDS Working P 318, July 1977, 18pp.
The enquiry is intended to make an empirical examination of how non-formal education is related to and affects levels of living of rural families, and what the concomitant factors in such a relationship are.

70-61 MUTISO, G.C.M. Kenya: technical education and change. IDS (unnumbered paper), 1970, 23pp.
Argues that if Kenya is to break from a technocratic society and to create a techno-consuming society it has to begin by drastically expanding the lower level of technological training.

70-62 MWAKALASI, A.L. "Education and population change in Tanzania". In J. Kocher (ed.), Social and economic development and population change in Tanzania. BRALUP Research Paper No. 36, University of Dar-es-Salaam, 1975, pp. 43-48.

70-63 NDWIGA, P.N. The decision to invest in university education in Kenya: an economic appraisal. M.A. thesis, University of Nairobi, 1978.

70-64 NGURU, GODFREY M. A study of educational expenditures in Kenya 1963-1975. Ph.D. dissertation, University of Tennessee, 1977.

70-65 NKINYANGI, JOHN A. "Socio-economic determinants of repetition and early school withdrawal at the primary level and their implications for educational planning in Kenya". IDS Working P 325, Sept. 1977, 53pp.
Argues that a socio-economic disadvantage is the equivalent of an educational disadvantage which may in turn be productive of poor school performance, repetition, disinterest, and school withdrawal. Suggests a methodology for a study to test the hypothesis that the phenomena of repetition and dropping out are positively and consistently related to pupil socio-economic background.

SOCIAL ECONOMICS

70-66 NKONOKI, SIMON R. "A case study on the implementation of education for self reliance". Education in Eastern Africa, Vol. 6, No. 1, 1976, pp. 77-84.
Attention is drawn to Kigoma secondary school in Tanzania which has had some success in changing students' attitudes towards working with hands so that labour is eventually dignified.

70-67 NSEKELA, A.J. "The university's changing role in a developing country: the Tanzanian case". J of Admin Overseas, Vol. 17, No. 2, April 1978, pp. 134-143.
Concludes that the university as a national institution must not ignore its responsible involvement in the solving of the problems of its environment.

70-68 NSIBAMBI, A.R. "The politics of education in Uganda". Uganda Journal, Vol. 38, 1976, pp. 58-82.
Seeks to examine the reasons why the central government decided to take over the administration of schools in 1964 and the factors which complicated the realization of its declared policy.

70-69 OLEMBO, JOTHAM O. Financing primary school facilities in Kenya. Ed.D. dissertation, Ball State University, 1974.

70-70 OLSON, J.B. "Secondary schools and elites in Kenya: a comparative study of students in 1961 and 1968". Comparative Education Review, Vol. 16, No. 2, Dec. 1972, pp. 44-53.
Concludes that, even if Kenya has not been able to obliterate the educational inequities of the colonial period, she has been able to carry the generally egalitarian character of that system into the early years of independence.

70-71 OMARI, I.M. "Educational expansion and the pattern of occupational choices of university students in Tanzania". Education in Eastern Africa, Vol. 5, No. 2, 1975, pp. 177-195.
Reviews developments in primary, secondary, and teacher training education in Tanzania and analyses degree choices of university education students.

70-72 OMINDE, S.H. "The Harambee movement in educational development". IDS Occ P 4, 1974, 28pp.

70-73 PATTERSON, DOUGLAS B. "Education, employment and income: incipient economic stratification in land-scarce Bunyore". IDS Working P 371, Aug. 1980, 22pp.
A case study presenting data describing one village in East Bunyore; the central focus is the problem of land

scarcity among Kenyan agriculturists. Indicates a strong reliance on non-farm income for households in the sample area; considers the role of kinship and social networks in securing wage employment; and contends that the people place a high value on education as a means of obtaining a good job.

70-74 RUKARE, E.H.; BENNAARS, G.A.; and MUWONGE, S.W. "The Namutamba project: an innovative Uganda experimental project on education for rural development". Government Printer, Kampala, 1974, 62pp.

An evaluation of the outcome of the Namutamba project which was initiated by UNESCO in 1968 as an experimental, integrated project on education for rural development. The aim was to measure the role of organizational decision-making in education.

70-75 SAMOFF, J. "Education in Tanzania: class formation and reproduction". J Mod Afr Studs, Vol. 17, No. 1, March 1979, pp. 47-69.

Argues that in Tanzania the major route to power and wealth is via the educational system, but access to this is far from equitably distributed across regions, age group, social strata, religions, and ethnic clusters. This leads to the perpetuation of particular patterns of social stratification and class differentiation.

70-76 SHEFFIELD, JAMES R. "Basic education for the rural poor: the Tanzanian case". J Dev Areas, Vol. 14, No. 1, Oct. 1979, pp. 99-110.

Argues in favour of technical education as a means of providing employment to school leavers in the rural areas.

70-77 SIDHU, S.S. "The productive value of education and agricultural development". EA USSC Conference, Kampala, 1974, 19pp.

70-78 SIFUNA, D.N. "Observations on some aspects of non-formal education in Kenya". Education in Eastern Africa, Vol. 5, No. 1, 1975, pp. 95-102.

Argues that non-formal education programmes are divorced from rural economic realities and frequently result in a waste of scarce resources.

70-79 SINCLAIR, M. "Brigades in Botswana and village polytechnics in Kenya". Annual Meeting of Canadian Association of African Studies, Toronto, Feb. 1975.

70-80 SSEKAMWA, J.C. "Sources and influences on educational policies in Uganda 1925-1960". EA USSC Conference, Kampala, 1974, 30pp.

SOCIAL ECONOMICS

Concludes that at times the Uganda Protectorate government introduced policies and executed them in such a way that they could not produce the desired results and had adverse implications for the development of education itself and on the society.

70-81 SWAI, B. "The political economy of Tanzanian primary school leavers: a theoretical consideration". Taamuli, Vol. 8, No. 1, 1978, pp. 38-49.
Seeks to show that the education reforms introduced in Tanzania after the Arusha Declaration were intended to solve a specific economic crisis; thus the emphasis on agricultural education.

70-82 SWARTZ, CAROLINE. Human capital, labour force participation, and the extended family in urban Kenya. Ph.D. dissertation, Duke University, 1979, 173pp.
DAI, Vol. 40, 5518-A.

70-83 TANZANIA INSTITUTE OF EDUCATION. "Brief report of secondary education project on economic achievements of education for self reliance in Tanzania secondary schools". Institute of Education, Dar-es-Salaam, 1977.

70-84 TARIMO, ELEUTHER. "Health and self-reliance: the experience of Tanzania". Development Dialogue, No. 1, 1978, pp. 35-40.
Examines the efforts made in Tanzania in provision of medical facilities and education for self-reliance.

70-85 TER WEELE, ALEXANDER HENDRIK. Equity in financing education in East Africa: the cases of Ethiopia, Kenya and Tanzania. Ed. D. dissertation, Harvard University, 1975, 531pp.
Analyzes the inequities of education distribution, such as across regions and social groups, and the inequities of transfer which occur when the financial burdens and the benefits of education are incident upon different groups of persons.

70-86 WALLACE, C.C. "Family background and education: structural factors influencing educational opportunities in Buganda". Makerere University Department of Sociology Working Paper No. 122, Kampala, 1972.

70-87 ___. "Relationship between education and occupation of early school leavers in Uganda". Research Abstracts, Vol. 1, No. 3, 1973, pp. 59-64.

70-88 ___. Youth in rural Buganda: a study of their education and employment. Ph.D. dissertation, Makerere University, 1973.

70-89 WALLACE, TINA. "Educational opportunities and the role of family background factors in rural Buganda". Rural Africana, No. 25, Fall 1974, pp. 29-46.
Analyses social stratification on the basis of occupations in Uganda in 1962. Found that the achievement of status by son or daughter depends on the status of the father or mother in the past and present.

70-90 WASS, PETER. "Developing research skills in professional staff: a study of adult education training in Kenya". Convergence, Vol. 9, No. 1, 1976, pp. 63-72.

70-91 WEEKS, S.G. "Blight or blessing? Fact and fantasy on school leavers in Uganda: a position paper for policy makers". Manpower and Unemployment Research in Africa, Vol. 5, No. 1, April 1972, pp. 38-48.
Discusses the position of school leavers in society and considers some of the approaches that have been used or recommended to solve the problem of unemployed school leavers.

70-92 WHITACRE, R.J. "Educational enrollment: optimal pricing policy". IDS Working P 248, Oct. 1975, 7pp.
Suggests that the efficiency of the University of Nairobi, as measured by enrollment of qualified students, may be significantly increased by a change in admission policy.

71--Health, nutrition, housing, water, social policy, and basic needs

71-1 ADALA, P.A. An economic study of the urban housing market in Nairobi. M.A. thesis, University of Nairobi, 1978.

71-2 ALGER, BERNARD C. Rural health services in Kenya since 1946: implications of a development perspective. Ph.D. dissertation, University of Iowa, 1973.

71-3 AMUNGA, WILLIAM E.O. A study of the housing policy in Kibera, with specific reference to low income communities. M.A. thesis, University of Nairobi, 1976, 198pp.
Concludes that new housing schemes in Kibera are not meeting the housing needs of low-income communities although they are contributing to the housing stock in the city. Recommends that since most low-income households lack capital, the policy guiding housing development in their area should aim at producing reasonably cheap accommodation, or at preserving existing housing with the view of improving or gradually replacing it as funds become available.

71-4 ANNERSTEN, LENHART. "Water and environment in Tanzania".

SOCIAL ECONOMICS

African Environment Special Report 1, International African Institute, London, 1975, pp. 55-61.
Argues that hydrological research and development is a pre-requisite for solving social and economic problems in Tanzania.

71-5 BIENEFELD, M.; GODFREY, M.; and LAMB, G. "Basic needs in Eastern Africa: a preliminary survey of Kenya, Tanzania and Somalia". University of Sussex Institute for Development Studies Brighton, 1977.

71-6 BYRNE, TONY. The church and the development dilemma. Gaba Publications, Eldoret, Kenya, 1977, 46pp.
Discusses the positive relationship between the church and development.

71-7 COLEBATCH, H. "Institutional forms and the access to services: a Kenyan case". University of Sussex Institute of Development Studies Discussion Paper No. 30, Oct. 1973.
Examines how institutional structure affects access to primary education, minor roads, and health services, and in particular with the question of local authorities versus central ministries as providers of these local services. Concludes that what is important is not the provider of the service, but what the relationship is with the higher reaches of the service structure, and how this affects their relationship with their clients.

71-8 DAVIES, MICHAEL A. "Krioporos--a cooperative search for improved health service in Kenya". Kidma, Vol. 3, No. 1, 1976, pp. 4-8.

71-9 DUNLOP, DAVID W. The economics of Uganda's health service system: implications for health and economic planning. Ph.D. dissertation, Michigan State University, 1973.

71-10 EYGELAAR, J. "Housing for low-income workers". University of Nairobi Housing Research and Development Unit, 1977, 22pp.
Outlines some of the problems facing low-income workers, and attempts to explain why houses within the financial reach of these low-income workers are not built in sufficiently large numbers in Kenya. Some solutions to the obstacles are suggested.

71-11 FAO. Planning for better family living manual series No. 5: Improving family life in Kenya. FAO, Nairobi, 1977, 179pp.

71-12 FELDMAN, ROBERT H.L. "A social psychological approach to

nutrition education utilizing ethnographic and experimental methods". IDS Working Paper No. 376, Nairobi, Nov. 1980, 15pp.
Attempts to determine the communicators which are most effective in producing nutritionally advantageous changes in knowledge and beliefs.

71-13 GHAI, D.; THORBECKE, E.; and GODFREY, M. Alleviating poverty and meeting basic needs in Kenya. ILO, Geneva, 1980.

71-14 GISH, OSCAR. Planning the health sector: the Tanzanian experience. Croom Helm, London, 1975, 209pp.
Illustrates the development of socialist thinking and doctrine in Tanzania in the context of the country's changing pattern of health service development.

71-15 GOLDSON, J. "Water, a constraint to increased milk production on the small-holder farm". National Agricultural Research Station, Njoro, Kenya, 1976, 44pp.
Describes the present water situation of farms and evaluates this information in the context of small-holder dairying enterprise. An attempt is also made to give some recommendations to the farmer on how th make the best use of limited water supplies for dairy cattle.

71-16 GOTTLIEB, MANUEL. "The problem of goiter in Tanzania: a programme for prevention by salt iodization and a programme for improved salt marketing in Tanzania". ERB Paper 73.6, University of Dar-es-Salaam, 1973, 42pp.
Considers means for the prevention of goiter and thyroid desease by means of salt iodization and to this end the author presents information on the state of the salt industry and the economic consequences of iodization.

71-17 ___. "Health survey of selected households, rural and urban, mainland Tanzania, six districts, summer 1972". ERB Paper 74.1, University of Dar-es-Salaam, May 1974, 47pp.
The object of the survey was to collect information regarding health care attitudes, experience, and financing from a small sample of Tanzanian households. The financial information collected needed to be considered in the context of experiences and values related to health care provided by different health sectors of Tanzania.

71-18 ___. "The health care sector in Tanzania". In K.S. Kim, R.B. Mabele, and M.J. Schultheis (eds.), Papers on the political economy of Tanzania. Heinemann, Nairobi, 1979, pp. 288-294.
Describes the way health care is now provided in Tanzania.

Scrutinizes the budget of the central government health services to ascertain the existence of financial pressure on the satisfaction of health care needs. Initially appeared, unedited, as ERB Paper 73.7.

71-19 HALL, B.D. Mtu ni afya: Tanzania's health campaign. Clearing House on Development Communication, Washington, D.C., 1978, 74pp.

71-20 HARTWIG, CHARLES W. Health policies and national development in Kenya. Ph.D. dissertation, University of Kentucky, 1975.

71-21 HOORWEG, J.C. Evaluation of nutrition education in Africa. Mouton, The Hague, 1979, 158pp.

71-22 HUGHES, G.A. "Low-income housing: a Kenyan case study". In I.M.D. Little and M. Scott (eds.), Using Shadow Prices. Heinemann, London, 1976, pp. 43-87.
Discusses the application of the Little-Mirrlees method of social cost-benefit analysis to evaluate the viability of the Dandora housing project in Nairobi for submission for a World Bank loan.

71-23 HUTCHINSON, ALAN. "Health by radio in Tanzania". African Development, Vol. 8, No. 4, April 1974, pp. 15-16.

71-24 JAKOBSEN, ODDVAR. "Economic and geographical factors influencing child malnutrition: a study from the southern highlands, Tanzania". BRALUP Research Paper No. 52, University of Dar-es-Salaam, 1978, 105pp.

71-25 JORGENSEN, N. "Housing finance for low income groups: with special reference to developing countries". University of Nairobi Housing Research and Development Unit, 1977, 240pp.
Deals with the problem of mobilizing and allocating resources in a mixed economy in order to meet the increasing need for housing.

71-26 KAMUKALA, GODFREY L. Towards a housing policy for Bukoba town. M.A. thesis, University of Nairobi, 1976, 167pp.
Argues that Bukoba town, Tanzania, experiences an acute housing shortage despite its low population and in-migration, that limited resources devoted to new housing construction contribute to the deficit, that there is misuse and non-use of local building materials, and that commuters prefer better rural housing to urban house construction.

71-27 KAYONGO-MALE, D. "Urban squatters in Nairobi and policies

geared to improving on their condition". East African Urban Legal Studies Workshop, University of Nairobi, April 1976.
Details the essence of two approaches--grassroots development and directed planning--which seem to underlie much of the implementation of urban planning in Nairobi and elsewhere.

71-28 KENYA, CENTRAL BUREAU OF STATISTICS. Child nutrition in rural Kenya. Government Printer, Nairobi, 1979?, 134pp.
Covers a survey on nutribion in Central, Western, and Nyanza provinces. Relates malnutrition to farm size and different types of crops grown in the relevant areas.

71-29 ___. Report of the child nutrition survey 1978/79. Government Printer, Nairobi, 1979, 55pp.
The report contains the preliminary findings of a survey of the nutritional status of the young children carried out in late 1978 and early 1979. Reports a small overall improvement in nutritional status between 1977 and 1979.

71-30 KAIMBA, JOHNSTONE M. Planning for housing in Machakos: a case study of old Machakos town. M.Arch. thesis, University of Nairobi, 1979, 111pp.
Suggests that by taking part in housing schemes both the public authorities and individuals will gain useful experience to provide more houses for low-income people.

71-31 KREYSLER, J. "'Uhuru na maji': health, water supply and self reliance in Mayo village". BRALUP Research Paper No. 3, University of Dar-es-Salaam, n.d. (prior to 1973), 15pp.
Examines experimental projects set up with a view to raising health and nutritional levels among children in Tanzania.

71-32 MATENDE, M.A. Planning for housing the economically weak section of the urban population. M.Arch. thesis, University of Nairobi, 1977, 112pp.
States that due to shortage of houses in Nairobi, the policy of providing serviced plots aims at increasing the total low-cost housing stock for both ownership and rental purposes.

71-33 MAYALLA, MASOTA G. Planning for low income housing in Arusha town, Tanzania. M.A. thesis, University of Nairobi, 1976, 130pp.
Attempts to assess the extent to which low income housing in Arusha has met the needs of low income people, to analyse the extent to which the government and other agencies have encouraged and stimulated peoples' efforts in solving their

SOCIAL ECONOMICS

housing problems, to discover what factors have hindered the realization of goals focused on the needs of low income people, and to suggest corrective measures aimed at achieving the goals.

71-34 MUJWAHUZI, MARK M. Self-help in the development of improved rural water supply: Tanzania experience and potential. Ph.D. dissertation, Clark University, 1976.

71-35 MULLER, M.S. "Housing co-operative societies in Kenya: performance and potential". University of Nairobi Housing Research and Development Unit, 1978, 37pp.
Policy issues and institutions of both the low-cost housing and the co-operative movement field are briefly discussed and the characteristic features and performance of the existing housing co-operatives are analysed. Suggests that more attention be given to the formation of building groups among low-income urban workers and to the creation of a non-profit housing development agency.

71-36 MWANIKA, T. "Planned youth organizations in Uganda: prospects for rural development". Rural Africana, No. 30, Spring 1976, pp. 87-97.
Describes two major planned youth programmes established in Uganda and provides a critical analysis of their organization, membership, objectives, activities, and underlying philosophy.

71-37 NOORMOHAMED, SIDIK O. Economic consequences of rent control in Kenya: a case study of Eastleigh, Nairobi. M.A. thesis, University of Nairobi, 1975.

71-38 NSEKALA, AMON J. The development of health services and society in mainland Tanzania: a historical overview. East African Literature Bureau, Nairobi, 1976, 124pp.

71-39 OCULI, OKELLO. Colonial capitalism and malnutrition: Nigeria, Kenya and Jamaica. Ph.D. dissertation, University of Wisconsin, Madison, 1977, 215pp.
DAI, Vol. 38, No. 6, p. 3706-A.
Argues that the logic of social and economic change under colonial capitalism in Nigeria, Kenya, and Jamaica was such that the nutritional status of the colonized people was jeopardized and the ability of those economies to be self-sufficient in food production was undermined.

71-40 ONDONGO, JOHN, and LEA, JOHN P. "Home ownership and rural-urban links in Uganda". J Mod Afr Studs, Vol. 15, No. 1,

March 1977, pp. 57-73.
Develops an hypothesis that interest and investment in rural house building by urban migrants in Uganda tends to decline with increasing length of residence in the town. Finds that a diffusion of housing funds from regular urban savings may diminish considerably in the future.

71-41 OKIDI, C.O., and OKOTH-OGENDO, H.W.O. (eds.). "Reflections on law and development". IDS Occ P 29, 1978.
Collection of papers presented at Seminar on Law and Development, University of Nairobi, July 1976. Authors and titles are listed below.

1. Seidman, A.W. and Seidman, R.B. "On the Theory of Law and Development".
2. Gutto, S.B.O. "Law and development: a theoretical analysis".
3. Seidman, A.W. and Seidman, R.B. "General perspectives on law and development administration".
4. Oyugi, W.O. "Law and the administration of development: with examples from Kenya".
5. Seidman, A.W. "The law of development administration: perspectives on experience".
6. Mutunga, Willy. "Commercial law and development in Kenya".
7. Obaso, J.H. "The need for flexibility in the law as an administration tool in development".
8. Seidman, A.W. and Siedman, R.B. "I--Why do people disobey law? The problem of high level bribery".
9. Kenya Department of Land Adjudication. "II--Reforms in the field of land adjudication and consolidation".

71-42 OKOTH-OGENDO, H.W.O., and SCHÖNHERR, SIEGFRIED. "Discussion of a food and nutrition policy for Kenya". IDS Working P 241, Sept. 1975, 9pp.
Discusses basic policies for improving the nutritional status of those likely to be affected by malnutrition, namely, mothers and pre-school children of low income groups.

71-43 RITCHIE, KENNETH G. "The identification and analysis of nutritional problems in rural areas: an approach for voluntary agencies". IDS Working P 265, June 1976, 29pp.
Looks at the case for using nutritional status as an indicator of problems, and suggests that at present in East Africa removal of malnutrition should be the paramount objective of voluntary agencies.

71-44 SORKIN, A.L. Health economics in developing countries. Lexington Books, Toronto, 1976, 200pp.

SOCIAL ECONOMICS

Reviews in successive chapters the subjects of nutrition, the impact of health on economic development, population growth, health planning, expenditure and funancing of health services, health centres and hospitals, and health manpower.

71-45 STREN, RICHARD E. Urban inequality and housing policy in Tanzania: the problem of squatting. University of California, Institute of International Studies, Berkeley, 1975, 24pp.
The author argues that urban and rural areas are drifting apart, helpless in seeking an anchorage which will sustain either. He concludes that today two diametrically opposed forces concentrate their interest on squatters: the World Bank, and the "radical" social scientist or planner and some politicians.

71-46 ___. Housing the urban poor in Africa: policy, politics, and bureaucracy in Mombasa. University of California Institute of International Studies, Berkeley, 1978, 330pp.
Contains historical discussion of land tenure, physical planning, and rent controls in Mombasa. Discusses the urban squatter problem in Mombasa, and includes one chapter on housing in Nairobi.

71-47 THOMAS, I.D., and MASCARENHAS, A.C. "Health facilities and population in Tanzania, Part One". BRALUP Research Paper No. 21.1, University of Dar-es-Salaam, 1973, 34pp.
Documents the need for more rural health clinics.

71-48 TSCHANNERL, GERHARD (ed.). "Water supply" (Conference proceedings, April 1971). BRALUP Research Paper No. 20, University of Dar-es-Salaam, Aug. 1971, 265pp.
This paper looks into the problems of rural water supply in Tanzania and Kenya.

71-49 ___. "The cost of rural water supply construction in Tanzania". BRALUP Research Paper No. 30, University of Dar-es-Salaam, Jan. 1974, 36pp.
Concludes that the cost curves for the various components of water supply schemes are of a similar shape: the unit cost is high for small capacities, diminishing with rising capacity, at first rapidly and then more slowly until unit cost becomes nearly constant.

71-50 ___. "Rural water supply in Tanzania: is 'politics' or 'technique' in command?". Afr Rev, Vol. 6, No. 2, 1976, pp. 108-166.
Analyses the process of implementation of the rural water-supply programme on the Tanzanian mainland. Empirical

evidence is drawn from selected case studies. Paper of same title also appeared as EA USSC Conference Paper, Dar-es-Salaam, 1973.

71-51 TURSHEN, M. The political economy of health with a case study of Tanzania. University of Sussex, Brighton, 1975, 394pp.

71-52 VAN DER HOEVEN, R. Meeting basic needs in a socialist framework: the example of Tanzania. WEP, ILO, Geneva, 1979.

71-53 VAN STEENBERGEN, W.M. "Nutrition and the Akamba child". Medical Research Centre, Nairobi, 1977, 74pp.
A survey on nutrition to assess the food and breast milk intake of children under three. The objective was to obtain quantitative data on food consumption of pre-school children and to determine the quality of breast milk.

71-54 WARNER, DENNIS (ed.). "Rural water supply in East Africa". BRALUP Research Paper No. 11, University of Dar-es-Salaam, May 1970, 189pp.
Looks into different aspects of water supply with a view to integrating professional and technical know-how in water supply planning for rural East Africa.

71-55 ____. "Design criteria for water supply systems in East Africa". BRALUP Research Paper No. 27, University of Dar-es-Salaam, Sept. 1973, 40pp.
Gives comparative water supply policies and respective recommendations for Kenya, Uganda, and Tanzania.

71-56 ____. Evaluation of the development of rural water supply projects in East African villages. Ph.D. dissertation, Stanford University, 1974.

71-57 WERLIN, H.H. "Nairobi's politics of housing". Afr Rev, Vol. 3, No. 4, 1973, pp. 611-629.

71-58 WESONGA, WEKESA MOSES. "Application of alternative patterns of development to human settlements planning and management in Africa". United Nations Habitat and Human Settlements, Foundation Regional Meeting on Human Settlements, Finance and Management, Nairobi, Oct. 1978, 14pp.

71-59 WESTLEY, S.B.; JOHNSON, F.B.; and DAVID, M. (eds.). "Summary report of a workshop on a food and nutrition strategy for Kenya". IDS Occ P 14, May 1975, 40pp.
Gives views on the formulation and implementation of a national food and nutrition strategy, determination of

SOCIAL ECONOMICS

priorities among food and nutrition policies, and analyses Kenya's existing nutrition programmes and organizational arrangements.

71-60 WESTLEY, SIDNEY B. (ed.). "Nutrition planning and policy for African countries". IDS Occ P 21, Aug. 1976, 116pp.

Collection of summaries of presentations during an IDS seminar in June 1976. Staff members and topics are listed below.

1. Latham, Michael. "Nutritional problems of Africa and some ordering of their importance".
2. ___. "Underlying causes of malnutrition and diagnosis of the nutrition situation".
3. Robinson, K.L. "Food policies designed to improve nutrition".
4. Sanjur, Diva. "Nutrition and socio-cultural factors".
5. ___. "Nutrition education: implications for nutrition planning and policy making".
6. Morgan, Bryan T. "Some nutritional factors in agricultural development planning".
7. ___. "The need for trained nutrition personnel in the formulation of nutrition plans and in their implementation".
8. Schuftan, Claudio. "Nutrition and the development process".
9. Adams, Robert L. "Organisational behaviour: an outline".
10. Pines, James. "The planning process".
11. Nesheim, M.C. "Human protein requirements".
12. ___. "Efficiency of animal production".
13. Slater, Charles C. "A framework and a strategy for nutritional improvements in underdeveloped societies".
14. Maletnlema. "Solving the nutrition problem in Tanzania".
15. McDowell, J. "Realism and self-reliance in food production".

71-61 YUDKIN, JOHN S. "The economics of pharmaceutical supply in Tanzania". International Journal of Health Services, Vol. 10, No. 3, 1980, pp. 455-478.

Examines patterns of purchasing, distribution, and utilization of pharmaceuticals in Tanzania. Argues that the market has been largely developed by the drug companies, using techniques that would be neither acceptable nor legal in developed countries.

72--Regional and urban planning and policies

72-1 AMEY, A.B. Rural-nonrural relations in Tanzania 1965-74. Ph.D. dissertation, University of East Anglia, 1978, 354pp.

72-2 BECKER, ROGER. "Problems of urbanization in Africa: administrative implications". African Administrative Studies, Vol. 12, July 1974, pp. 145-150.

72-3 BELSHAW, D.G.R. An outline of procedures for district development planning in Kenya. IDS (unnumbered paper), July 1972, 27pp.

72-4 BERRY, L., et al. "Some aspects of regional planning in Tanzania". BRALUP Research Paper No. 14, University of Dar-es-Salaam, Feb. 1971, 44pp.
Examines the types of planning which exist at various spatial levels in Tanzania and suggests that the main gap in the present system is the regional and district levels. Also takes a closer look at district level planning.

72-5 BRIAN, ALAN R.L. The political economy of urbanization in Tanzania. Ph.D. dissertation, University of British Columbia, 1979.
DAI, Vol. 40, p. 6010-A.

72-6 DELP, PETER. "Dsitrict planning in Kenya". In Tony Killick (ed), Papers on the Kenyan economy. Heinemann, London, 1981.

72-7 ETHERTON, DAVID (ed.). "Mathare Valley: a case study of uncontrolled settlement in Nairobi". Housing Research and Development Unit, University of Nairobi, 1970, 96pp.
Describes two surveys of Mathare Valley in 1969 and 1970, in an effort to bring into focus the problem of uncontrolled settlement which is one of the most crucial aspects of Nairobi's future development.

72-8 GAILE, GARY L. "Notes on the concept of spread". IDS Disc P 219, Feb. 1975, 29pp.
The concept of spread is widely used in regional planning and is integral to the strategy of growth centres. The concept is restated here by specifying the processes which are elemental to spread and delineating factors which influence the extent of core-periphery spatial relationships.

72-9 ___. "Analysis of growth centre patterns: the Nairobi region". East African Geographical Review (Makerere), June 1975, pp. 57-70.

The analysis tests modified versions of the first two of Moseley's hypotheses as they relate to the growth centre concept.

72-10 ___. "Processes affecting the spatial pattern of rural-urban development in Kenya". African Studies Review, Vol. 19, Dec. 1976, pp. 1-16.
Argues that Kenya's development plans are based on the optimistic assumption that development generated in the urban centre will spread to the hinterlands.

72-11 HARRIS, JOHN R. "Urban and industrial deconcentration in Kenya: an analytical framework". IDS Staff P 34, May 1969, 16pp.
Presents an analytical multi-region linear programming model to facilitate discussion about the costs that would be incurred from forcing industrial and urban growth into a less concentrated pattern than has been emerging spontaneously in Kenya. Suggests data requirements to empirically implement the model.

72-12 INSTITUTE FOR DEVELOPMENT STUDIES. "A manual for rural planning". Nairobi, June 1974, 70pp.
The manual was prepared by IDS on behalf of the Ministry of Finance and Planning. It discusses district planning, the data necessary for planning for specific sectors, how to use the planning machinery, and plan implementation.

72-13 ILCHMAN, W.F., et al. (eds.). Policy sciences and population. Lexington Books, Lexington, Mass., 1975.
Includes C.G. Wescott, "Growth centres and primacy in Kenya", which examines the cost-effectiveness of urban planning as a means of inducing a higher proportion of urban migrants to remain in intermediate rather than primary cities.

72-14 KABAGAMBE, D.M. The role of small-scale industries in developing urban economies: a case study of Kisumu semi-urban areas. M.A. thesis, University of Nairobi, 1975, 171pp.
Examines and evaluates existing planning standards, prohibitive regulations, and government efforts, and their effects on small-scale industrial promotion.

72-15 KAMWERU, D.N.D. The role of service centres in rural development. M.A. thesis, University of Nairobi, 1977, 101pp.
Finds that the proliferation of centres and over-duplication of businesses resulted in their decline.

72-16 KANYEIHAMBA, G.W., and McAUSLAN, J.P.W.B. (eds.). Urban legal problems in Eastern Africa. Scandinavian Institute of

African Studies, Uppsala; International Centre for Law in Development, New York, 1978, 298pp.

72-17 KARUGA, J.G. "Thresholds in the transformation of an economy: some preliminary thoughts on the structure of the Nairobi/Kiambu peri-urban zone". In IDS Occ P 4, 1971.

72-18 KIKAIRE, J.H.W. "Industrial location in rural area case study in Bugweri country". EA USSC Conference, Kampala, 1974, 11pp.
Concludes that the three entrepreneurs that decide on location are usually the corporate capitalists, the private capitalists, and the state administrators. The decision is taken according to the demand for products and accessibility, as well as transport.

72-19 LANGLANDS, B.W. (ed.). Geographical studies on rural markets in East Africa from Makerere, Makerere University Department of Geography Occasional Paper No. 63, Kampala, 1975.
Examines the evalution, role, and structure of some rural markets in Kenya and Uganda. These markets tend to locate at communication nodes of maximum accessibility such as road-junctions and river crossings.

72-20 LAUBSTEIN, K.H. The failure of physical planning in post-colonial Kenya. Ph.D. dissertation, University of Toronto, 1978.
DAI, Vol. 39, p. 4488.

72-21 ___. The organization and administration of physical planning in Kenya. IDS (unnumbered paper), n.d. (ca. Aug. 1974), 28pp.
Tentatively concludes that there is growing acceptance of the need for physical planning, very little understanding of the basic principles involved, and virtually no effective methods of administrating it.

72-22 LUHRING, J. "Regional entities, growth centres and decentralized industries in African development planning--reflections on the cases of Ghana and Tanzania". African Administrative Studies, Vol. 12, July 1974, pp. 169-180.

72-23 MCKIM, WAYNE LLOYD. The role of interaction in spatial economic development planning: a case study from Kenya. Ph.D. dissertation, Northwestern University, 1974, 221pp.
Examines the process of planning for economic development, with emphasis on the role of spatial interactions in gaining a clearer understanding of the spatial organization of an area, in delimiting planning regions, and in identifying underserved areas.

SOCIAL ECONOMICS

72-24 MAHIGA, A.P. National development strategies and regional integration in East Africa. Ph.D. dissertation, University of Toronto, 1975.

72-25 MARO, P.S., and MLAY, W.F. "Decentralization and the organization of space in Tanzania". Africa, Vol. 49, No. 3, 1979.

72-26 MUWONGE, J.W. "Functions and characteristics of trading centres in Uganda". East African Geographical Review, No. 11, June 1973, pp. 52-64.
Appraises the functions and other characteristics of trading centres in some parts of southern Uganda as they existed during 1971-1972.

72-27 NAIROBI URBAN STUDY GROUP. Nairobi: metropolitan growth strategy. City Council of Nairobi, Nairobi, 1973.

72-28 NKARI, P.M.M. Planning for Meru town, Kenya: a case study of land use conflicts in urban development. M.Arch. thesis, University of Nairobi, 1977, 129pp.
Urges that industrial investment be given priority.

72-29 NORCLIFFE, G.B. "Towards a locational policy for manufacturing industry in Kenya". Ministry of Finance and Planning, Nairobi, 1977.

72-30 OBUDHO, ROBERT A. "Urbanization and regional planning in western Kenya". U.S.A. African Studies Association meeting, Philadelphia, 1972, 43pp.
Reckons that planning at the grassroot level using the periodic market approach is the only way urban regional planners can re-orient the towns from parasitic to generative roles and help lessen the gap between hinterland and town.

72-31 ___. Development of urbanization in Kenya: a special analysis and implications for regional development strategy. Ph.D. dissertation, Rutgers University, 1974, 346pp.
Analyses the problem of dualism within the urban system. Uses Kenya as a case study in order to study the evolution, problems and prospects of dualism of development.

72-32 ___. "Urbanization and development planning in Kenya: a historical appreciation". African Urban Notes, Series B, Vol. 1, No. 3, 1975, pp. 1-56.
Traces the evolution of urbanization in Kenya through time and space. Concludes that the main concern should be with the growth-centre concept.

72-33 OBUDHO, R.A., and WALLER, P.P. Periodic markets, urbanization and regional planning: a case study from western Kenya. Greenwood Press, Westport, Connecticut, 1976.

72-34 OGENDO, R.B. "Industrial role of the main Kenyan towns". EA USSC Conference, Nairobi, Dec. 1969.

Examines 13 industrial towns of Kenya with respect to qualitative location aspects, quantitative location aspects, location factors that favour urban industrial concentration, and the structural aspects of the urban-located industries.

72-35 OKIDI, C.O. (ed.). "Natural resources and the development of Lake Victoria basin of Kenya". IDS Occ P 34, July 1979, 608pp.

Collection of papers presented at a series of workshops between March and July 1979 at IDS, Nairobi. Authors and titles are listed below.

1. Oucho, John O. "Population and its implications for resource development in the Lake Victoria Basin".
2. Ominde, S.H. "Education Needs and services in the Lake Victoria Basin".
3. Aseto, Oyugi. "Employment opportunities in the Lake Victoria Basin".
4. Ongweny, G.S. "Water resources of the Lake Victoria Drainage Basin".
5. Meadows, B.S. "The quality of water of the Lake Victoria Basin and its protection".
6. Okidi, C.O. "International Law and the Lake Victoria and Nile Basins".
7. Owayo, C.Y.O., and Nyambok, I.O. "Mineral resources of the Lake Victoria Basin".
8. Odenyo, V.A.O. and D'Costa, V. "Soils of the Lake Victoria Basin".
9. Mwagiru, W. "The Lake Victoria Basin: Ecological Land Productivity as a Critical Policy issue".
10. Ogot, J.O. "Argonomic Land use strategies for the Lake Victoria Basin".
11. Odada, J.E.O. "The role of the Sugar Industry in Kenyan Economy: A case study of the Lake Victoria Basin".
12. Obara, D.A. "Cotton production and marketing in the Lake Victoria Basin of Kenya".
13. Okoth-Ogendo, H.W.O. "The state and the individual in land use policy: a case study of Lake Victoria Basin authority".
14. Ogendo, R.B. "Resource-Base for Integrated Industrialization and Development in the Lake Victoria Basin".
15. Odero, N. "Fish species, distribution and abundance in Lake Victoria".

SOCIAL ECONOMICS

16. Kongere, P.C. "Production and socio-economic aspects of the fisheries in Lake Victoria, Kenya".
17. Owino, E. "Wildlife and forestry in the Lake Victoria Basin".
18. Aseto, Oyugi. "Applications of the concept of comprehensive and integrated regional planning to the development of Lake Victoria Basin".
19. Oyugi, W.O. "A recommended institutional framework for the Lake Victoria Basin authority".
20. Wambura, W.P.O. "Roads and communication system in the Lake Victoria Basin".

72-36 OKOTH-OGENDO, H.W.O. "The urbanization process in Kenya: research priorities". Workshop on Urban Law in East Africa, Nairobi, April 1976, 9pp.

Attempts to bring out the character of the process of urbanisation in Kenya, the problems it has created, and the interaction between them.

72-37 RICHARDSON, HARRY W. "Growth centres, rural development and national urban policy: a defense". International Regional Science Review, Vol. 3, No. 2, 1978, 133-152

Using a case study of Kenya as illustration, argues that growth centres as an instrument of spatial policy may still be valuable if harmonized with local economic and social conditions. Such centres must be integrated with rural development policies by promoting agro-processing industries rather than capital-intensive manufacturing, by functioning as an alternative destination for rural migrants, and by strengthening the service hierarchies in rural regions.

72-38 SHAYO, P.R.E. "Tanzania: moving the capital". Plan East Africa, Vol. 5, No. 1, Nov.-Dec. 1974.

Observes that from planning and development points of view, moving the capital would not only facilitate administration, but would among other advantages reduce congestion of activity in Dar-es-Salaam, act as a growth pole, and stimulate development in the surrounding areas which have so far remained relatively backward.

72-39 STREN, RICHARD. "Urban policy and performance in Kenya and Tanzania". J Mod Afr Studs, Vol. 13, No. 2, June 1975, pp. 267-294.

Compares the formulation and implementation of key urban policies in both countries from independence until the end of 1973. Land allocation, housing and planning are singled out for discussion. Finds that these needs of lower-income groups have been more constrained by bureaucratic problems of implementation. Similar paper appears as IDS Disc P 232 in Jan. 1976.

72-40 TAYLOR, D.R.F. "Spatial aspects of Kenya's rural development strategy". In B.S. Hoyle (ed.), Spatial aspects of development. Wiley, London, 1974.

72-41 TIBENDA, A.K.B. An appraisal of resource and land use maximization for integrated regional development in the western Rift Valley of Uganda: a case study of Busongora county. M.A. thesis, University of Nairobi, 1976, 151pp.
Concerned with the distribution of the utilization of resources in Busongora county, the resultant land uses, and how best the spatial structure can be organized to allow for maximum benefits to acrue to investors.

72-42 WACHTEL, ANDY. "Changing attitudes towards urban redevelopment in Kenya: the Old Bondeni redevelopment schemes". IDS Disc P 242, Nov. 1976, 35pp.
Discusses various plans suggested over the years, and the reactions and expectations these aroused in the community.

72-43 WESCOTT, CLAY GOODLOE. The political economy of industrial location in Kenya. Ph.D. dissertation, Boston University, 1980, 354pp.
DAI, Vol. 40, p. 6454-A.

73--Women's studies

73-1 ABBOTT, SUSAN. "Women's importance for Kenyan rural development". Community Development Journal, Vol. 10, No. 1, Oct. 1975, pp. 179-182.

73-2 BRYCESON, DEBORAH FAHY. "The proletarianisation of women in Tanzania". Review of African Political Economy, No. 17, Jan.-April 1980, pp. 4-27.
Argues that Tanzania peasant women have voluntarily become more proletarianized as urban workers since the late 1950s.

73-3 BRYCESON, DEBORAH F., and MBILINYI, M. "The changing role of Tanzania women in production". Jipemoyo, Vol. 2, 1980, pp. 85-116.

73-4 BUTTERFIELD, CYNTHIA. "Women and the modern wage sector: a study of female participation in commercial banks and finance companies in Nairobi". IDS Disc P 256, May 1977, 28pp.
Attempts to empirically assess the participation of women

in Kenya's modern wage sector, focusing on these two industries in Nairobi.

73-5 ELKAN, W. "The employment of women in Uganda". Inter-African Labour Institute Bulletin, Vol. 4, No. 4, July 1957, pp. 8-23.
The paper is primarily concerned with consideration of the demand and supply of women workers in the present Uganda labour force. This is contrasted with 18th century England.

73-6 FORTMANN, LOUISE. "Women and Tanzania agricultural development". In K.S. Kim, R.B. Mabele, and M.J. Schultheis (eds.), Papers on the political economy of Tanzania. Heinemann, Nairobi, 1979, pp. 278-287.
Examines the current role and status of women in both food and cash crop production, and identifies the factors that affect their participation in agricultural development. Critically evaluates the degree of women's access to resources such as land, labour and information. Originally appeared as ERB Paper 77.4.

73-7 GUPTA, A. "Illusion of progress: women of Kenya". In V. Phadnis and A. Malani (eds.), Women of the world. Vikas, New Delhi, 1978, pp. 244-259.

73-8 GUTTO, SHADRACK B.O. "The legal status of women in Kenya: paternalism and inequality". Fletcher Forum, Vol. 1, Fall 1976, pp. 62-82.
Describes the present legal status of women in Kenya and examines the extent to which this system permits, condones, and reinforces discrimination against women.

73-9 KNOTTS, MARY ANN. The social and economic factors associated with the rural-urban migration of Kenyan women. Ph.D. dissertation, Johns Hopkins University, 1977, 316pp.
DAI, Vol. 41, p. 795-A.

73-10 MBILINYI, MARJORIE J. "Women: producers and reproducers in peasant production". ERB Paper 77.3, University of Dar-es-Salaam, 1977, 39pp.

73-11 MICKELWAIT, D.R., et al. Women in rural development: a survey of the roles of women in Ghana, Lesotho, Kenya, Nigeria. Westview Press, Boulder, Colorado, 1976, 223pp.
Includes a report on current and potential roles of rural Kenyan women with special emphasis on the role of women in agriculture.

73-12 MOOCK, P.R. "The efficiency of women as farm managers: Kenya".

American Journal of Agricultural Economics, Vol. 58, No. 5, Dec. 1976, pp. 831-835.

Investigates possible differences between male and female farm managers in the possession of, and means of acquiring, technical information relevant to agricultural production of maize in Vihiga. Finds that the impact of schooling on output is greater for women than for men, and that women seem not to benefit, as the men do, from extension contact.

73-13 NELSON, M.C.N. Dependence and independence: female household heads in Mathare Valley. Ph.D. dissertation, University of London, 1978, 426pp.

73-14 NELSON, NICI. "Mobilizing village women: practical considerations in the organization and management of integrated rural development programmes which involve women". In Nici Nelson (ed.), African women in the development process. Frank Cass, London, ca. 1980.

73-15 OBBO, CHRISTINE. "The myth of female submission: economic activities of Luo women in Namuwongo-Wabigalo, Kampala". EA USSC Conference, Dec. 1972, 16pp.

Shows that Luo women are also participants in the system of urban self-employment that is aimed at providing them with an independent source of income.

73-16 ___. "Town migration is not for women": African women's struggle for economic independence. Zed Press, London, 1980, 240pp.

73-17 OBOLER, REGINA SMITH. "The economic rights of Nandi women". IDS Working P 328, Nov. 1977, 18pp.

Outlines women's traditional economic rights, for example, ownership of chickens, vegetables, etc. and the changes they are undergoing in the modern setting. It is felt that a stable equilibrium will be re-established involving a redefinition of wives' economic rights.

73-18 PALA, A.O., et al. (eds.). "The women's group programme in the SRDP". IDS Occ P 13, 1975, 105pp.

Collection of papers. Authors and titles are listed below.

1. Pala, A.O.; Reynolds, J.E.; and Wallis, M.A.H. "The women's group programme in the S.R.D.P.".
2. Reynolds, J.E. "The case studies: Kapenguria".
3. Browne, D.L. and Pala, A.O. "Case study: Kwale".
4. Wallis, M.A.H. "Case study: Mbere".
5. Pala, A.O. "Case study: Migori/Kuria".

SOCIAL ECONOMICS

6. Browne, D.L. "Case study: Tetu".
7. Reynolds, J.E. "Case study: Vihiga/Hamisi".

73-19 PALA, ACHOLA O. "A preliminary survey of the avenues for and constraints on women in the development process in Kenya". IDS Disc P 218, University of Nairobi, June 1975, 33pp.
Reviews the social conditions of women in Kenya with specific reference to the position of women in the rural areas. It also presents information on factors which facilitate the participation of women in the national economy and others which act as constraints on their full involvement in Kenya.

73-20 ___. "The role of African women in rural development: research priorities". Journal of Eastern African Research and Development, Vol. 5, No. 2, 1975, pp. 137-161.
Considers the salient concepts and goals of rural change, the means which have been employed to realize these goals, and the operating constraints. Stresses the need to promote complementarity of men and women in society. Calls for greater women's involvement in rural development.

73-21 ___. "The women's group programme in Migori/Kuria". IDS Working P 234, Aug. 1975, 10pp.
Argues that in spite of the women's programme being part of the Special Rural Development Programme, respondents showed limited knowledge of SRDP. Concludes that this is due to alienation between government ministries and group members.

73-22 ___. "African women in rural development: research trends and priorities". American Council on Education Overseas Liaison Committee Paper No. 12, Washington D.C., 1976, 35pp.

73-23 ___. "Women's access to land and their role in agriculture and decision making on the farm: experiences of the Dholuo in Kenya". IDS Disc P 263, April 1978, 22pp.
Examines the productive role of women in regard to changing patterns in access to land, land use, and subsistence agriculture.

73-24 PALMER, I. "The role of women in agrarian reform and rural development". Land Reform, No. 1, 1979, pp. 57-70.

73-25 REYNOLDS, D.R. "An appraisal of rural women in Tanzania". USAID, Nairobi, 1975, 46pp.

73-26 REYNOLDS, J.E. "The women's group programme in Vihiga/Hamisi".

IDS Working P 236, Aug. 1975, 16pp.
Concludes that the programme has been retarded in its development due to problems with former staff in the Department of Social Services.

73-27 ROSS, MARC H., and THADANI, VEENA. "Participation, sex, and social class: some unexpected results from an African city". Comparative Politics, Vol. 12, April 1980, pp. 323-334.
From data on Nairobi, concludes that sex is a more important basis for political differentiation among the upper-middle than the working class.

73-28 SHIELDS, N. Women in the urban labor markets of Africa: the case of Tanzania. World Bank Staff Working Paper No. 380, Washington, D.C., World Bank, 1980, 136pp.
Based on results of the 1971 Tanzanian National Urban Mobility, Employment and Income Survey, this study attempts to ascertain the characteristics of women in the modern sector urban labor market and to compare the labor market performance of men and women in the urban economy. Concludes that the urban women's low economic status in the labor force is primarily a result of cumulative discrimination over time in both the provision of and the demand for educational services. This has the effect of limiting the supply of women in the urban labor force and making the female labor supply curve less elastic than that of men.

73-29 SMOCK, AUDREY CHAPMAN. "Women's education and roles in Kenya". IDS Working P 316, July 1977, 90pp.
Examines women's opportunities for education and the impact of varying levels of education on three dimensions of women's roles: family decision-making, labour force participation, and fertility. See also chapter in Tony Killick (ed.), Papers on the Kenyan economy.

73-30 STAUDT, KATHLEEN A. "The effects of government agricultural policy on women farmers: preliminary findings from Idakho location, Kakamega district". IDS Working P 225, July 1975, 30pp.
Shows that women usually have less access to technical, informational, and financial inputs, but despite this disadvantage, they adopt new crops and husbandry practises in a manner similar to other farm managers.

73-31 ___. Agricultural policy, political power, and women farmers in western Kenya. Ph.D. dissertation, University of Wisconsin, Madison, 1976.

SOCIAL ECONOMICS

73-32 ___. "Inequities in the delivery of services to a female farm clientele: some implications for policy". IDS Disc P 247, Jan. 1977, 21pp.
Found that women farm managers experience a persistent and pervasive bias against them in the delivery of government agricultural services. This bias increases in intensity as the value of the service increases. Argues that women farmers cannot maintain their productivity in the face of lower administrative support over time.

73-33 ___. "Administrative resources, political patrons, and redressing sex inequalities: a case from western Kenya". J Dev Areas, Vol. 12, No. 4, July 1978, pp. 399-414.
Examines the western Kenya case aimed at illustrating pervasive discrimination. Argues that agricultural policy implementation contains structural sex and class inequalities; productive small holdings are still managed by women even though they do not benefit from administrative resources.

73-34 ___. "The Umoja Federation: women's cooptation into a local power structure". Western Political Quarterly, Vol. 33, No. 2, 1980, pp. 278-290.

73-35 STICHTER, SHARON. "Women and the labour force in Kenya 1895-1964". Rural Africana, No. 29, Winter 1976, pp. 45-68.
Shows how the participation of women in wage labour force grew after 1945 in Kenya. The rate of growth of participation was more rapid prior to 1960 than thereafter. Women have remained concentrated in the lowest-paid and least skilled occupations. Appeared also as IDS Disc P 258, Sept. 1977.

73-36 STROBEL, MARGARET ANN. Muslim women in Mombasa, Kenya, 1890-1973. Ph.D. dissertation, University of California, Los Angeles, 1975.
Combines an historical approach with an analysis of contemporary ritual as an avenue to investigate the evolution of women's social and political organizations.

73-37 SWEDISH INTERNATIONAL DEVELOPMENT AUTHORITY. Women in developing countries: case studies of six countries. Stockholm, 1974, 98pp.

73-38 ___. "Rural women in Kenya and Tanzania". Development Digest, Vol. 13, No. 3, July 1975, pp. 53-60.
Assesses the changing roles of women from traditional agriculture to modern methods of farming.

73-39 THADANI, VEENA N. The forgotten factor in social change: the case of women in Nairobi, Kenya. Ph.D. dissertation, Bryn Mawr, 1976.

73-40 ___. "Women in Nairobi: the paradox of urban progress". African Urban Studies, Vol. 3, Winter 1978-79, pp. 67-83.
Deals with the rural roles of women and men, the structure of the family in the rural areas, and the impact of urban life on marriage customs.

73-41 WACHTEL, E. "Minding her own business: economic enterprises of women in Nakuru, Part I". IDS Working P 189, Sept. 1974, 17pp.
Attempts to assess the extent to which women share problems common to the general run of Kenyan small businesses or whether their problems differ in kind or degree as businesswomen (see also 73-42).

73-42 ___ and WACHTEL, A. "Groups and cooperatives: economic enterprises of women in Nakuru, Part 2". IDS Working P 190, Sept. 1974, 23pp.
Complementary to the study of individual business ventures run by Nakuru women in part I (see item 73-41), this paper focuses on groups and co-operatives formed by women in an attempt to collectively advance themselves.

73-43 ___. "Women's co-operative enterprise in Nakuru". IDS Disc P 250, March 1977, 18pp.
A wide range of women's groups are discussed which were active in Nakuru in 1974. Five formally registered associations, whose explicit purpose was co-operative economic activity, are discussed in great detail. Finally, some of the basic attitudes and patterns of behaviour which seem to underlie many of the activities of these groups are described as well as the economic and political environment in which they operate.

73-44 WALLIS, M.A.H.; REYNOLDS, J.E.; and PALA, A.O. "The women's group programmes in the SRDP". IDS Working P 230, Aug. 1975, 29pp.
Discusses the justification for having a development programme focused on rural women, reviews its contribution, and identifies areas of weakness.

73-45 WALLIS, M.A.H. "The women's group programme in Mbere". IDS Working P 233, Aug. 1975, 9pp.
Argues that many farms in Mbere have insufficient labour to be run fully and therefore women do not have much time for "extra-farm" activities.

8--ECONOMIC STATISTICS

80--General and macro-economic statistical publications

80-1 DAHL, H.E. Some notes on the construction of a Kenyan input-output table for 1966. IDS (unnumbered paper), n.d. (ca. Sept. 1972), 7pp.
Discusses the methods of constructing the input-output table, the type of table to be constructed, and the uses to which it may be put.

80-2 GRANBERG, PER. "A numerical study of the Kenyan 1971 input/output table". C. Michelsen Institute, Bergen, Norway, 1977, 51pp.

80-3 HARVEY, JOAN M. (ed.). Statistics Africa: sources for social, economic and market research (2nd ed.). ABCD Research Publications, Detroit, 1978, 374pp.

80-4 KENYA, CENTRAL BUREAU OF STATISTICS. Sources and methods used for the national accounts of Kenya. Nairobi, 1977, 192pp.
Describes the methods used in collecting national data for different sectors. Applies sectoral accounting which is later aggregated for the nation as a whole.

80-5 KRAVIS, I.B.; KENESSEY, Z.; HESTON, A.; and SUMMERS, R. A system of international comparisons of gross product and purchasing power. Johns Hopkins Press, Baltimore, 1975, 294pp.
Provides a wealth of detailed information on ten selected countries of which Kenya is one.

80-6 TANZANIA, GOVERNMENT OF. 1978 population census preliminary report. Bureau of Statistics, Dar-es-Salaam, 1978, 182pp.
A 1978 population census report. Census was conducted in Aug. 1978. Showed a total population of 17,048,329 for mainland Tanzania and 479,235 in Zanzibar and Pemba.

81--Micro-economic statistical publications

81-1 ANKER, RICHARD, and KNOWLES, JAMES C. "An empirical analysis of mortality differentials in Kenya at the macro and micro levels". Econ Dev Cult Change, Vol. 29, No. 1, Oct. 1980, pp. 165-186.
Analyses mortality differentials in Kenya in an effort to obtain a better understanding of the factors affecting mortality. Concludes that mortality rates in Kenya are related to economic as well as to social and environmental factors.

81-2 BELSHAW, D.G.R. "Crop production data in Uganda". Overseas Development Group, University of East Anglia, Norwich, 1975, 68pp.

81-3 DEBEBE, B. Estimation of the social price of investment and the shadow wage rate of unskilled labour for the Kenyan economy. M.A. thesis, University of Nairobi, 1977.

81-4 EAST AFRICAN STATISTICAL DEPARTMENT. East African statistics of energy and power, 1966-1973. East African Community Common Market and Economic Secretariat, Nairobi, 1976, 119pp.

81-5 ___. Economic and Statistical Review. Dar es Salaam, Kampala, Nairobi.

Those issues shortly before the East African Community broke up were No. 55, June 1975; No. 56, Sept. 1975; No. 57, Dec. 1975; No. 58, March 1976.

81-6 HALL, C. "Mombasa labour force survey". Provincial Planning Office, Mombasa, 1969.

81-7 KENYA, CENTRAL BUREAU OF STATISTICS. "Towards a social perspective: a statistical appraisal". K Stat Dig, Vol. 13, No. 3, Sept. 1975, pp. 5-9.

Introduces a proposed list of social indicators for Kenya. Discusses the availability and utility of data for each item on the list.

81-8 ___. "The national integrated sample survey programme: sample design". K Stat Dig, Vol. 14, No. 3, Sept. 1976, pp. 4-8.

Summarizes the process of developing a sample design as a focal point for a programme of field surveys to collect information on socio-economic trends between 1976 and 1981.

81-9 ___. "The household and the holding in Kenya". K Stat Dig, Vol. 14, No. 4, Dec. 1976, pp. 5-7.

Adopts a definition of the household for future use in all surveys involving households. Discusses the concept of a holding.

81-10 ___. Integrated rural survey, 1974-75. Nairobi, March 1977, 172pp.

This is a series of sample surveys providing data on socio-economic trends.

81-11 ___. "The new trade indices". K Stat Dig, Vol. 15, No. 2, June 1977, pp. 1-11.

Introduces a new series of price and quantum indices for Kenya's imports and exports.

ECONOMIC STATISTICS

81-12 KMIETOWICZ, Z.W., and RWAMASAKA, H.M.K. "An index of industrial production for Uganda, 1963-1971". EAER, Vol. 8, No. 2, Dec. 1976, pp. 75-89.
Describes construction of an index of industrial production based on annual surveys, and briefly compares it with the official quarterly index.

81-13 MANUNDU, M., and MAITHA, J.K. "Production techniques, factor proportions and elasticities of substitution". In T. Killick (ed.), Papers on the Kenyan economy. Heinemann, Nairobi, 1981.

81-14 NEWBERY, D.M.G. "The social value of private investment in Kenya". In I.M.D. Little and M. Scott (eds.), Using shadow prices. Heinemann, London, 1976, pp. 154-204.
A social cost-benefit analysis of private investment in Kenya. Argues that the social cost of transferring £1 from the public sector to the private sector is very low, because the private sector is very successful at generating social profits.

81-15 OLUM, G.H. "Collection of consumer price data in rural and urban areas of Kenya". IDS Seminar on Price and Marketing Controls in Kenya, University of Nairobi, March 1979, 7pp.
An account of the methodology of price collection in Kenya with particular emphasis on practical problems arising therefrom and possible solutions.

81-16 OMINDE, S.H. "Some problems of census mapping in Kenya, 1969". EA USSC Conference, Nairobi, Dec. 1969.
Analyses specific features of the Kenya census mapping programme in 1969. Comments on the significance of the geographical base or framework for the census. Gives some maps of the census enumeration areas.

81-17 ONYONKA, ZACHARY. "Public and semi-public housing stock in 22 municipalities". Ministry of Housing and Social Services, Nairobi, 1977.

81-18 PADFIELD, H., and EAST, RICHARD. "Nairobi household survey". Oregon State University, Feb. 1973, 82pp.
Tabulations of the occupational and social-economic data of low income households within the medium and high density areas of Nairobi.

81-19 RASHIDI, I.M. "Tax revenues". Bank of Tanzania Research and Statistics Department, Dar-es-Salaam, 1978, 22pp.

81-20 SINGLETON, CAREY B. Basic agricultural resources of Kenya. U.S. Department of Agriculture Economic Research Service, Washington, D.C., 1974, 78pp.

81-21 TANZANIA, MINISTRY OF AGRICULTURE. Bulletin of food crop production statistics 1963/64-1977/78. Dar-es-Salaam, April 1979, 39pp.
Collection of statistical tables.

81-22 UNITED NATIONS. Social and demographic statistics, 1980 world population and housing census programme. U.N. (Document E/CN.3/481), New York, 1976, 12pp.
Draws largely on experience of Kenya Central Bureau of Statistics to review role of cartography in population and other censuses and surveys.

81-23 UNITED STATES BUREAU OF THE CENSUS. Country demographic profiles: Kenya. U.S. Government Printing Office, Washington, D.C., 1978, 17pp.

81-24 WOOD, L.J. "Temporary variations in levels of activity at three Kenyan markets". Cultures et Développement, Vol. 9, No. 2, 1977, pp. 355-364.

Subject Index

Numbers refer to individual entries. The letters K, T, and U indicate the country to which the entry refers; absence of a letter implies that the entry refers to more than one of the countries, or to East Africa as a whole.

Author Index

Author Index

Author Index

Author Index

Author Index